OF THE SOMETHING MORE

Praise for *Of the Something More*:

"As his pastor, friend and fellow servant in Jesus Christ, I have known Glen since 1974. Glen brings a sharp mind to every endeavor. *Of The Something More* is the result of many years of study, experience, debate and witness for God. Academically, Glen brings a great diversity of understanding: from science, modern philosophic thinking, theology, and human psychology. In life experience, Glen has been a successful geophysicist, businessman and inventor. He has worked with people from around the world. He has known the highs of business success and lows of financial downturn. Above all, Glen has a passion for God and the truth of His Word. *Of The Something More* brings together Glen's academic knowledge and practical life experience with his skills as a teacher and debater to make a book that will make you think hard before you write yourself off as just a chance random evolutionary accident."

—REV. DAVID FAIRBROTHER
Pastor of Emmanuel Fellowship Baptist Church, Vernon, B.C.
Former President of the Fellowship of Evangelical Baptist
Churches in B.C. and the Yukon

of
the
Something
MORE

Glen E. White

Essence
PUBLISHING

Belleville, Ontario, Canada

OF THE SOMETHING MORE
Copyright © 2002, Glen E. White

All Scripture quotations, unless otherwise specified, are from *The Holy Bible, New International Version*. Copyright © 1973, 1978, 1984 International Bible Society. Used by permission of Zondervan Publishing House. All rights reserved.

Editing thanks to Editor Mavis Andrews, former editor of *Focus on Women* magazine, and to Wayne Wilson and Robert Smith for ideas and chart design.

National Library of Canada Cataloguing in Publication

White, Glen, 1941-
        Of the something more / Glen White.

Includes bibliographical references.
ISBN 1-55306-494-1

1. Tribulation (Christian eschatology) 2. Second Advent. I. Title.

BT877.W49 2002   236'.9   C2002-905712-4

To order additional copies, please contact:

Kargen Books
P.O. Box 1754
Vernon, BC V1T 8C3
Fax: 250-545-7770
1877 4 THE MORE
www.kargenbooks.com

Essence Publishing is a Christian Book Publisher dedicated to furthering the work of Christ through the written word. For more information, contact:
44 Moira Street West, Belleville, Ontario, Canada K8P 1S3.
Phone: 1-800-238-6376 • Fax: (613) 962-3055.
E-mail: info@essencegroup.com • Internet: www.essencegroup.com

AMAZING LOVE
How Can it Be?

The bubbles seem to float upwards through water clear as glass, yet my wide-open eyes can clearly see the tree roots in the swollen stream. I have a vague memory of a voice that seemed to say, "Take hold of the roots." The way the story goes, from my mother's viewpoint, is that she, in a great panic, finds her three-year-old toddler son stumbling up the woodland trail from the flooding creek, sobbing because he is soaking wet. Now in my boyhood years, having swum in many a fresh-water stream with my eyes wide open, I can recognize the significance of this event. That little boy should have drowned—just one more of life's casualties. But what about the voice, the clear understanding to grab the roots?

Is there something more, something much more, such that our lives have an infinite worth in the cosmos?

To all those who ask why?

Table of Contents

From the Office of an Ambassador
for King Jesus Christ 9

   1. Are We of the Something More?. 13

   2. Who Are We? 25

   3. The Adversary. 49

   4. The Lion of Judah. 75

   5. Twisted Arts and Science 97

   6. Man: Alive 127

   7. Divine Romance 155

   8. Freedom 181

   9. The Whole Heaven 213

  10. Signs of the Times. 251

  11. Sound the Shofar. 291

Figure 1, Diagram: Our Relationship to God 191
Figure 2, Chart of BC *and* AD *Periods*. 272
Index 309

From the Office of an Ambassador for King Jesus Christ

Dear Citizens of Earth,

arth is an occupied planet in league with the Legions of Doom—evil angelic forces in rebellion against God, creator of all there is. Earth is totally anthropomorphic (man-centered). It is a spiritual battleground where the Legions of Doom strive to maintain the allegiance of humanity. Moreover, battles of the supernatural will explode upon Earth, concluding the great divergent war of the cosmos. World view philosophies questioning the very meaning of our existence are affected by this extraterrestrial rebellion.

Secular evolutionary humanism, the prevailing philosophy of our 21st century, is founded on synthesis, meaning there is no absolute moral right or wrong. The evolutionary concept of an impersonal beginning, with time-plus-chance yielding sentient creatures such as mankind, leaves no reference point for concepts such as morals. Nor from this philosophical perspective is there any future for mankind other than as disseminators of DNA into the cosmos. The terms "evolutionary psychology" and "evolutionary sociology" become only platitudes to cover man's despair: meaningless meaningless, utterly meaningless.[1] The Bible teaches that the God-man, Jesus Christ, is the focus all of history wherein His death and resurrection gives meaning and purpose to our lives if we accept His provision of grace (unmerited favor), admit our rebellion and let Him change our lives from autonomous self-taking beings to celestial individuals with God having control of our lives. With this, the whole man—the spiritual and the physical— becomes a new dynamic being as shown by Jesus Christ at His resurrection. Christianity is then logical and rational, and faith is an extension of the seen to the unseen.

> **AGES OF AGES**
>
> The term is taken from Ephesians 3:21: *"Unto him be glory in the Church of Christ Jesus throughout all ages, world without end."*[3]

Man, made in the image of God, has a powerful, magnificent reason to exist.

God is working in our space-time world to bring individual wills to Him and redeem them from eternal confinement of Hell prepared for Satan and his Legions of Doom. God promises, in His Word: *"For God so loved the world that he gave his one and only Son, that whoever believes in him shall not perish but have eternal life"* (John 3:16). John 1:12 says: *"Yet to all who received him, to those who believed in his name, he gave the right to become children of God."*

God is working in our lives: for the believer, to increase his trust and faith; for the unbeliever, to bring him or her to accept His gift of eternal life in the ages of ages to come. It is this action of God in our daily lives which we want to explore, so we will have encouragement in a world of meaningless despair and know that "God is good and His love endures forever."[2]

NOTES:

[1] Ecclesiastes 1:2

[2] Psalm 107:1

[3] Bible, King James Version, New York, Oxford University Press, 1945.

Are We of the Something More?

ach of us struggles with the question of the purpose and meaning for our lives in an atmosphere of uncertainty and despair that permeates the media and our culture. Life is not easy, and when we least expect it, we get kicked, knocked down and stomped on. Children mess up; a husband or wife betrays; love dies; a plane is blown up; a car crashes; we miss our chance in life; loved ones are killed… on and on wails the drama of despair.

This book is not being written in a field of fresh clover while warm idyllic breezes blow. Unforeseen circumstances have made my life difficult professionally and financially, so we have a base for communication—from the bottom, so to speak. Encouragement is needed in this realm of despair. Whatever the circumstances, we need to discover that God

> **COMMUNICATION**
>
> The basis for communication requires a firm reference point. The Bible is God's complete revelation to mankind; thus, the Holy Scriptures are our reference point for this book.

is a loving God, working in each of our lives for His purpose and glory. And just what is His purpose and glory, you might ask?

His purpose and glory is for His will to be done on Earth as it is in Heaven.[1] His desire is for creation not destruction, for love, hope, joy, peace, loving kindness, justice, mercy, purpose and meaning for our being.

Lucifer, the fallen angel known as Satan, occupies planet Earth as his home. Under his direction, his army, the Legions of Doom, has established an ethereal city in the aerial spaces around this planet;[2] a web of spiritual darkness permeates our cultures. The Bible tells us: *"for our struggle is not against flesh and blood, but against the rulers, against the authorities, against the powers of this dark world and against the spiritual forces of evil in the heavenly realms."*[3] Satan, as usurper-ruler of mankind, seeks to destroy our lives in this great divergent war of the cosmos. Spiritual darkness leads to hopelessness and despair which saturate our philosophy, music, art, science and religion. Let me reiterate: this book is a book of encouragement; my hope is that you come away from reading it with a "yes, I can make it, I can run the race,[4] I see a purpose for my life. And, yes, I will succeed for I know that God is working all this out for His purpose."[5]

Consider the possibility—even though this may be a new way of looking at what is happening in the world—that there is a tremendous war going on around us in the hidden world of ethereal beings, commonly known as angels, as they strive to affect our thought patterns and, consequently, our decisions. This war of psychological persuasion is startlingly evident around us if we take time to see and analyze the paradigm shift (pattern of things) of cosmic consciousness unfolding daily. Satan does not want the sons of man to be reborn spiritually as children of God, for he knows they will be the new rulers of the cosmos.

One might say, "I do not believe in spirit beings, Satan, or anything of this sort." Based on the philosophy of evolution, mankind has set up elaborate electronic surveillance systems searching space in an attempt to locate evidence of other technologically advanced civilizations. No evidence of any alien technology has ever been detected.[6] The assumption that all life forms and alien technologies are like us is a premise based on the concept of local evolution of all biological species. Yet, based on slightly more advanced technology, aliens could have had colonies within a radius of 200 light years within a period of 10,000 years. Could unseen ethereal forces have already invaded our planet from another dimension?

The Philosophy of Cosmic and Local Evolution

In recent years, the theory of evolution has come under critical attack from many PhD-level secular and Christian scientists who claim the biological cell structure of life is so complex, time-plus-chance macroevolution is virtually impossible.[7] Although many in our society continue to believe the highly artistic pictures of monkey to man, there has been a dramatic shift of thought. Our biological systems have been seeded by panspermia, meaning organic matter initiating

Cosmos

The term "cosmos" includes the universe as a systematic space-time whole and interdimensional spirit reality. Evolutionary theory is that our universe resulted from a "Big Bang" of energy from a "singularity" some 16 billion years ago, and eventually our solar system and Earth came into being. Somehow, inorganic atoms of hydrogen, oxygen, carbon, nitrogen and sulphur combined as living organic matter. This living matter evolved by random chance over billions of years to yield form, context and innate programming of the complex biological life forms inhabiting Earth. This is local evolution. Alien evolution, if there is such a thing, may not be the same.

life came from space, or we were created by unknown aliens. This only moves the problem of evolution to some other planet-enhanced solar system (which in itself is proving to be the exception rather than the rule). If it has taken the lifetime of our solar system to evolve life, how could life evolve faster elsewhere?

The underlying premise of evolution is non-accountability to God, creator of all. Assuming that we were biologically engineered by a more advanced species only makes matters worse because our race would then be controlled by intelligence with unknown intentions. No descriptive document or monument has been found attesting to this questionable class of founders. Only Jehovah, the monotheistic God of Jews and Christians, has left a supernaturally inspired document outlining the history of creation, His purpose and intentions.

SPECIAL CREATION

Creationists have always considered the possibility that there could be other civilizations created by a loving God. However, none of these civilizations, if they exist, were redeemed by God as was man—His special creation.

THE MARTIAN THEORY

As radical as it may seem, there are those who speculate that the biological system of Mars could be older than that of Earth, and Earth's biological systems actually originated on Mars. Conversely, it is more probable that life forms from Earth reached Mars.[8] The theory we originated from Mars has serious difficulties.[9] That Mars had an atmosphere favorable for life can only be postulated. Its surface is pitted with mountain-sized asteroid craters and scarred by planet-sized floods that scoured its surface. Extensive water-lain dunes and huge water-gouged canyon systems, larger than our Grand Canyon, indicate unprecedented global flooding similar to the biblical

Noachian flood on Earth, leaving behind pre-crater sedimentary layers. Later, large meteorites, supposedly destroying the atmosphere and oceans, again extensively pounded one side of Mars. Some of these craters also have what appears to be water-lain sediments in their bowls.

Evolution would be phenomenally impossible under these physical dynamics, and yet the Face of Cydonia stares silently up into the heavens. Would this suggest a technologically capable human-like species dwelt on Mars? Scientists, who base their philosophy on the theory of evolution, do not readily accept the startling possibility that the Face could be artificial.

Floodwater marks around the Face are philosophically assumed to be very ancient. However, what if water did exist on Mars until several thousand years ago? If the Face is very recent, its creation must somehow parallel human history, otherwise the only alternative is an ancient alien outpost.

In 1894, before the space probe observations of Mars made the theory of intelligent life incompatible with the theory of evolution, amateur

> **MARS LIFE**
>
> Water is required for evolution to propel inorganic elements into complex organic life. Yet scientists believe that several billion years ago oceans of water and favorable atmospheric conditions may have existed on Mars for only several million years. Life by evolutionary standards has existed on Earth for some 3.5 billion years; the theoretical several million years is not nearly long enough for complex life to evolve.

> **FACE OF CYDONIA**
>
> NASA satellite imagery suggests the Face was designed to be observed from space. Cleverly positioned rock knobs create shadows that appear as eyes and move with the angle of the sun.

astronomer Percival Lowell believed Martians were a highly advanced civilization millions of years older than humanity.[10] This belief fed the panic in the New Jersey radio audience initiated by the famous radio broadcast by Orson Welles in the 1930s, "War of the Worlds," of a spaceship invasion from Mars.

What happens if recent scientific assumptions are not correct and Mars had water and some sort of atmosphere until several thousand years ago? Dr. Gaverluk, in his book, *Did Genesis Man Conquer Space*,[11] considers the possibility that ancient mankind may have landed on Mars. The Bible, in the book of Genesis, states: *"The sons of God saw that the daughters of men were beautiful and they married any of them they chose,"* and, *"The Nephilim were on the earth in those days—and also afterward—when the sons of God went to the daughters of men and had children by them. They were the heroes of old, men of renown."* [12] The book of Numbers[13] in the Bible indicates a few Nephilim, in the time of Moses, were able to invade what is now Israel.

The Nephilim, meaning "fallen ones," may be the sons of God or the offspring of the sons of God. At the onset of Noah's flood, they possibly escaped to Mars, and the Face of Cydonia may represent their failed civilization. They may have had a limited chance to return from Mars. In addition, if ancient man or "the sons of God" traveled between the two planets, it is unlikely they undertook any contingencies for organic decontamination and/or deliberately took biological life with them to Mars.

Moreover, if bacteria or the presence of Earth-like organic molecules is found in

> **EPIC OF GILGAMESH**
>
> The story of the Babylonian flood as told in the Epic of Gilgamesh states: "The gods were frightened by the flood. They went off up to the heaven of the chief god. The gods cowered like dogs, crouching outside the door."[14]

near space, or even on Mars, this does not mean they evolved there. Donald Patton, a specialist in celestial mechanics, in his book, *The Long Day of Joshua*,[15] proposes that Mars' orbit at one time caused it to come in a close

> **MARS, GOD OF WAR**
>
> Mars is the ancient Roman god of war. The month of March is named after him. He was considered to be the father of Romulus, the founder of Rome.

encounter with Earth. In *Worlds in Collision*,[16] Emanuel Velikovsky suggests Mars and Venus were the gods of ancient Greek mythology that fought in the heavens, and that Typhon appeared in the heavens like a huge bloody red globe,[17] possibly bigger than the moon, streaming vaporous material. This may have been Mars shedding its oceans of mud and water as its gravity interacted with Earth's. If there were close planetary encounters with Earth, water and thus organic life may have been transferred through space to Mars.

> **TYPHON**
>
> Typhon, in Greek mythology, was a serpent-like, fire-breathing giant birthed by Gaia to overthrow the Titans.

ETHEREAL INVASION

The question of the artificiality of the Face and whether there was a creational history of Mars will only be settled by future space exploration. However, what if Earth has already been invaded by ethereal beings as outlined in the Bible? Particularly if the battle is focused on the spiritual component of the human being, the building of sophisticated technological armaments would be useless against such a foe. Local evolution has no premise for an argument of ethereal beings since, from their perspective, our species has only obtained its supreme position by a greedy gene and the survival of the fittest. The only position an evolutionist can take is that any such invisible intelligences are highly evolved hyperdimensional visitors trying to, or actually materializing in our dimension, which is the explanation of UFOs and paranormal communications. However, are they good, kind and loving? A television program interview with a number of abductees seemed to show only mental and physical abuse. Several of the participants made excuses similar to those made for spousal abuse: "Oh, I know they must be good and only trying to help us." Oh, really?

> **LUCIFER**
>
> Jesus authenticates Satan, the rebellious archangel Lucifer, as "the prince of this world" (John 14:30). He is the *"ruler of the kingdom of the air, the spirit who is now at work in those who are disobedient"* (Eph. 2:2).

There are many good people—Christians, secular humanists New Agers and others of many different religions—who are seeking some form of cosmic consciousness. The alternative to all this questioning is to say, "That's it; it really doesn't matter. I don't care if I'm only a bundle of molecules destined to be worms and dust; today is today and I'm going to do the best I can." Such concepts usually result in despair; the human spirit seems to want to be "of the something more," to have an eternal purpose. Strong natural desires of youth should be sufficient to overcome such negative thoughts, and for many they do—for a while. The 21st century should be an era of cosmic awareness and purpose, yet instead, it is an age of superficial virtual realities, spiritual delusions and family breakups.

SPIRITUAL CONCEPTS

The beauty of Earth and the vastness of space, to some, show a biological and cosmic complexity that speaks of intelligent design, yet the selfish indifference of the human spirit refutes design and therefore accountability to a just and holy God. Still, it is the awesome gap of spiritual awareness that separates man from the animals. God declares, *"Let not the wise man boast of his wisdom or the strong man boast of his strength or the rich man boast of his riches, but let him who boasts boast about this: that he understands and knows me, that I am the Lord who exercises kindness, justice and righteousness on earth, for in these I delight."*[18]

Jesus Christ taught His followers to love their enemies and to pray for those who persecute them. Christianity is not a belief enforced by rule of the gun, but a belief of the heart. Many secular philosophies say Christianity is intolerant with respect to its beliefs in morals and spiritual concepts; yet, such intolerance exists within the Church only against those who call themselves Christians but purport lifestyles and spiritual concepts contrary to the teachings of the God-man, Jesus Christ. Jesus called such people wolves in sheep's clothing.

These people have a deep moral guilt that their self-centeredness wants to quench by manipulated condemnations of others, whereas, in our various cultures, we can have a self-imposed psychological guilt versus a true, inner, moral, God-conscience guilt. It is the moral guilt that needs to be recognized and dealt with. Before I asked Jesus Christ for forgiveness and asked Him into my life, I encountered a feeling of guilt when confronted with the concept of salvation through the atoning death and resurrection of the God-man, Jesus Christ. This guilt left upon confessing my sin of rebellion to Jesus Christ in prayer.

MORAL GUILT

Moral guilt is not a result of situational ethics of evolution. It is the breaking of laws given by a higher order of being, such as creator-God. If God does not exist, then man is a law unto himself.

PSYCHOLOGICAL GUILT

Psychological guilt is relativistic guilt that comes from breaking rules and regulations of traditions or culture.

The Holy Scriptures declare that God has created man in His image and imparted a God-consciousness within man's inner being. Free will is the God-given choice of acceptance or rejection of the divine laws of God, His plan of salvation, His goodness and His enduring love. The rebellious ethereal army occupying Earth plays on man's selfishness, vanity and animal nature to convince him that God does not exist and, therefore, there is no "moral guilt."

The vastness of God's creation has been frustrated since mankind joined the cosmic rebellion. The Holy Scripture declares: *"The creation waits in eager expectation for the sons of God to be revealed. For the creation was subjected to frustration; not by its own choice, but by the will of the one who subjected it, in hope that the creation itself will be liberated from its bondage to decay and brought into the glorious freedom of the children of God."* [20] The most amazing story

OUR NATURAL CONSCIENCE

The great intellectual evangelist, Paul of Tarsus, refers to this inner natural conscience when discussing the law given by God through the writings of Moses versus the law of the Gentiles. *"Since they* [the Gentiles] *show that the requirements of the law are written on their hearts, their consciences also bearing witness, and their thoughts now accusing, now even defending them."* [19]

ever to be conceived is that God would offer His "life" to ransom a created creature. The whole of the story is Yeshua-Jesus, the God-man, who died and rose again purchasing our race from the clutches of Lucifer, the great deceiver.

It follows then, to understand the out-flowing of cosmological events, we should establish just who we are, who our ethereal adversary is, understand his maligned hate against us and see how the love of God, through His grace and mercy, sustains the cosmos and works to create celestial beings from amongst the rebellious sons of men. *"This is what the Lord says, he who made the earth, the Lord who formed it and established it— the LORD is his name: 'Call out to me and I will answer you and tell you great and unsearchable things you do not know.'"* [21]

CELESTIAL CITIZENS

That we should be celestials, and rule with Him throughout the Ages of Ages, is a concept that could only be conceived and implemented by an infinite omnipresent, omnipotent and omniscient, merciful, loving God.

NOTES:

[1] Matthew 6:10

[2] Ephesians 2:2

[3] Ephesians 6:12

[4] 2 Timothy 4:7

[5] Romans 8:28

[6] Crawford, Ian, "Where Are They," *Scientific American*, July 2000, p.38

[7] Coppedge, James F., *Evolution Possible or Impossible?* Zondervan Publishing, 1973

[8] <www.jsc.nasa.gov/pao/flash/>

[9] Schembrie, Joe, *A Hill on Mars*, Cydonia Books Inc., 1998, <cybooks.com>, chapter 4

[10] Ibid. chapter 9

[11] Gaverluk, Emil, Jack Hamm, *Did Genesis Man Conquer Space?* Thomas Nelson Inc., 1974

[12] Genesis 6:2,4

[13] Numbers 13:33

[14] Millard, Alan, *Treasures From Bible Times*, Lion Publishing, 1985, p. 43

[15] Patten, W. Donald, R. Hatch, L. Steinhauer, *The Long Day of Joshua and Six Other Catastrophies*, Pacific Meridian Publishing Co., 1973

[16] Velikovsky, Immanuel, *Worlds in Collision*, Dell Publishing Co., 1967, p.260

[17] Velikovsky, Ibid, p. 98

[18] Jeremiah 9:23–24

[19] Romans 2:15

[20] Romans 8:19–21

[21] Jeremiah 33:3

Who Are We?

edical technology and surgical skills are becoming more advanced every day. The television screen fills with a picture of pulsating organs interlaced with red blood vessels. Underway is a laparoscopy operation for a serious case of "heart burn." The scene switches, a clean-cut middle-aged doctor looks directly at the camera. He is dressed in a light green gown, a light green cap covers his head and a light green bandanna covers his mouth. Other gown-covered forms move around him. The cameraman directs the camera at the operating table. The lower chest and abdominal area of a man lies exposed on the operating table, four hollow tubes protrude from his stomach area; two tubes are on the left side and two on the right. Through these tubes into the abdominal cavity, the doctor has inserted his instruments and a miniature TV camera.

The doctor turns and looks at his television monitor. "See here," he says as the screen once more fills with the inner cavity of the man, "we can enter the area of the hernia with these small instruments instead of our large hands." As the doctor speaks, a pair of grabbers, like sharp-toothed pliers, comes in from the left and pushes aside some *translucent slimy material. A pair of shiny cutters then comes from the right and snips at the material. Steam hisses from the filmy material as what appears to be an electric knife makes a clean surgical cut. In the center of the screen, a blood-spattered, whitish corrugated tube comes down from the man's throat, enters the chest cavity at the top of the screen and extends across the screen down to his stomach. The surgeon continues, "Now, this is the protective material that we are looking for," his grabbers tap a sheath of white fatty flesh on the screen's right. "See here, I can take this protective material," now a pair of grabbers pushes the white, oblong flesh under the corrugated tube to the stomach, and the left grabber pulls the white material through, "and place it around this tube and it will stay."*

He continues, "Now this is the spleen," and his right grabber taps a dark purple blob on the right. At the top center of the screen a steady pulse beats through the red flesh of the cavity, reflecting the beat of the man's heart. A network of rubbery blood vessels comes out of this area to nourish the various organs of life.

"Now we have to sew everything in place," says the doctor as my television screen again fills with the operating room scene. The right grabber is withdrawn from a tube just under the man's rib cage. A nurse holds another probe ready to be inserted. On the end of the probe is a tiny crescent-shaped needle attached to black thread. The probe is plunged down the tube. Now the television shows the needle being manipulated through the oblong white material that has been wrapped around the tube to the stomach. The doctor skillfully sews the end of the wrapped material back onto itself, and then attaches the oblong white material to the entrance of the cavity to the throat. He explains that this will hold the material in place so that it does not push up into the man's throat area.

The holes into the abdominal cavity are cleverly sewn shut from the inside and the television camera withdrawn. Instead of a long incision in stomach muscles that take time to heal, the man will have four small scars with a much shorter recovery time. The next scene, several weeks later, is of a man in his late forties to early fifties eating hot peppers from his garden.

Indeed, medical technology and surgical skills are becoming more advanced—but what about the patient, that complex organic machine who lies on the operating table? Did he just evolve or, like medical technology, was he created by intelligent design?

News articles concerning the decoding of the human genome depict a greater scientific complexity with each new discovery. The deeper the cells of the body are probed, the more complex is the organization of the cell structure, and even more complex seem to be the protein machines operating in this biological regime. Darwin thought that life came from an amorphous blob. He had no modern concept of the complexity of the cell. Michael Behe, Professor of Biochemistry at Lehigh University, in his book, *Darwin's Black Box*, writes:

> Biochemistry has, in fact, revealed a molecular that stoutly resists explanation by the same theory so long applied at the level of the whole organism. Neither Darwin's starting points—the origin of life, and the origin of vision—has been accounted for by his theory. Darwin never imagined the exquisitely profound complexity that exists even at the most basic levels of life.[1]

Optimistic scientists project forward to the day when segments of DNA can be reassembled to benefit mankind. Scientist may very well be able to decode sections of DNA, but there is no guarantee totally new arrangements of amino acids (written by man), will not be toxic to our natural life forms. Genetically modified foods with natural genetic information are already a contentious issue.

The assumption of secular science is that an accidental jumble of proteins dictates who we are, but scientists are now finding that all life is built of efficiently operating components of the same protein arrangements. It is statistically impossible[3] for every separate species along the divergent theoretical phylum (branching tree) of life to have individually developed the same genetically constructed components (consider those species in which the complex eye, according to evolution, develops separately as they become more advanced along their phylum line). Superimposed on the functional aspect of biological life, from cell to macro form, is contextual information of what something is, or what it does, similar to the way, in the world of electronics, the computer chip is used and programmed into all sorts of machines. One type of machine does not

THE CODE OF LIFE

Carbon, oxygen, hydrogen and nitrogen combine to yield twenty precisely connected molecules, shaped like a left-handed glove, called amino acids. Various combinations of the twenty acids form proteins, the building blocks of life.

The DNA (deoxyribonucleic acid) molecule is the master document containing the code for the proteins. It is formed like a long twisted ladder (a double helix) whereby combinations of the twenty amino acids form the rungs of the ladder. The sides are composed of phosphate and sugar molecules. This coded information is packed into a small unit called a cell. In a human cell, the DNA is divided into forty-six segments called chromosomes. Each cell has about six feet of DNA. RNA is a copy of the master DNA which the protein machines use to build more proteins and keep the cell functioning correctly.[2]

suddenly become another type without intelligent design.

In this time of cosmic introspection, is it not possible our complex biological systems and intricate innate programming are of an intelligent design and creation? It appears this thought is more often than not negated by a self-will that rejects accountability to any sentient (thinking and analytic) being other than to oneself.

MAN: OF THE SOMETHING MORE

> **A DOG IS A DOG[4]**
>
> In the variety of its kind, a cuddly little dog in a woman's arms knows that it is a dog and is recognized as such, even by a large dog such as a Great Dane. The little dog does not make a macro evolutionary leap to become a cat.

The Holy Scriptures declare that the sophisticated programming and design of the human being is "of the something more" with a celestial destiny. Man is a composite spiritual-material being unlike the animals around him. The Bible reveals that some time ago in the space-time history of the Garden of Eden, the parents of the human race, Adam and Eve, under the temptation of a powerful ethereal being, made a historical decision not to trust in the goodness of God, their divine creator, effectually separating the eternal spirit of man from God's eternal Spirit source of energizing spiritual life.

The Bible, in Genesis 3:4, records this deceitful communication: *"'You will not surely die,' the serpent* [a physical animal possessed by Lucifer, the fallen angel of light] *said to the woman. 'For God knows that when you eat of it* [fruit from the tree of the knowledge of good and evil] *your eyes will be opened, and you will be like God, knowing good and evil."*

This was a real space-time decision; our human parents chose to be "like God," separating our race from our eternal destiny, thereby forfeiting the regency of planet Earth to Satan, the leader of the cosmic rebellion. This biblical scene is meaningless if man is only an evolved creature. However, if he is composed of both a natural and a spirit body, or spiritual essence, then this

interdimensional ethereal warfare is of major cosmological significance. Mankind, through Adam, lost round number one. The
Giver of Life no longer energizes our spirit body except through
being "born again" by the Holy Spirit of God.

SPIRIT AND SPIRITS

We need to be absolutely clear about the terms and usage of the
words Holy Spirit, ethereal spirits, human spirit and spiritual warfare. The Holy Spirit has no relationship to angelic spirits of any
sort, nor to human spirits, but is a transcendent personage of the
Holy Trinity. In his book, *The Holy Spirit*, Dr. John Walvoordex-
plains:

> It is a fundamental revelation of Scripture that the Holy Spirit is
> a person in the same sense that God the Father is a person and the
> Lord Jesus Christ is a person. The Holy Spirit is presented in
> Scripture as having the same essential deity as the Father and the
> Son and is to be worshiped and adored, loved and obeyed in the
> same way as God. To regard the Holy Spirit in any other way is to
> make one guilty of blasphe-
> my and unbelief. We tread
> therefore on most holy
> ground in thinking of the
> Holy Spirit of God and the
> truth involved is most sacred
> and precious.[5]

Angels are created ethereal
beings that can penetrate our
space-time realm from the
spirit dimension of the cosmos. There are good angels
that administer help to

JESUS IS GOD

The Holy Spirit sustained the
Second Person of the Trinity in
His incarnation as Jesus Christ.
Here, the Spirit of life met the
image of life He had created.
Such is the mystery of the incarnation; Jesus Christ was wholly
God and wholly man. Without
the incarnation of deity, the
ransoming blood of Jesus Christ
would have no meaning.

mankind and rebellious fallen angels that seek to destroy. Fallen angels and demons are invasive spirits that will try to invade the human body. The Holy Spirit as God is a sustaining Spirit through whom all things were created and have their being. God breathed the breath of life into man at his creation, and he became alive in the "image of God." This breath of life given by the Holy Spirit would suggest that God somehow gave something of Himself, and the human spirit is of eternal substance different from the angelic spirits. No wonder Satan seeks our demise.

ANGELS AND DEMONS

Angels and demons are of a different ethereal order. Pharisees,[6] who were elite Jewish intellectuals, believed in spirits and angels. For instance, Jesus cast out demons from possessed people; Michael and his angels will fight Satan and his angels in the heavens.[7]

The Holy Scriptures record, in Genesis 2:7, that after God had created all the plant life and animals, *"the LORD God formed the man from the dust of the ground and breathed into his nostrils the breath of life, and the man became a living being."* Dr. Walvoord writes:

In the case of human life, the Holy Spirit gives special significance and quality to life. God had said, "Let us make man in our image, after our likeness" (Gen. 1:26), and in this work, the Spirit imparts life in an operation distinct from the creation of all other life. Owen in speaking of this aspect writes: "Into this formed dust, 'God breathed the breath of life'; (divinae aurae particulam) a vital immortal spirit; something of himself; somewhat immediately of his own; not of any pre-created matter. Thus man became a middle creature, between the angels above and the sensitive animals below. His body was formed as the beasts from matter; his soul was an immediate production of divine power, as the angels were."[8]

31

The word "soul" can create confusion in its usage. Modern usage is that we have a body and a soul, that somehow, a soul gets plugged into a physical body. This opens up false concepts that animals have the same type of soul as man, or of an old soul coming into a body for an evaluation session in the physical world or the belief in reincarnation. Dr. Francis Schaeffer, in *Genesis in Space and Time*, comments:

> Lest we make too much of the word soul, we should note that this word is also used in relation to other living things with conscious life. So in reality the emphasis here is not on the soul as opposed to the body but on the fact that by a specific act God created man to be a living thing with conscious life. God made man in his image by a specific act of creation. This is strongly emphasized, as we saw before, by the fact that the special word create is used three times over, in both Genesis 1:27 and 5:1–2.[9]

To only use the words body and soul to describe a person is to miss the deeper teachings of Scripture. The Apostle Paul, in 1 Thessalonians 5:23, says to the Thessalonians: *"May your whole spirit, soul and body be kept blameless at the coming of our Lord Jesus Christ."* It is interesting that he starts with spirit, then soul and lastly body, in order of eternal significance.

Through the spirit we are God-conscious; through the soul we are self-conscious and through the body we are conscious of our physical reality. We are a trinity of being, even as God is Father, Son and Holy Spirit. Man has meaning in the spiritual and physical universe; he has been created in the "image of God."

THE SPIRIT BODY

The gates into our complex biological machine from the space-time world are those of sight, hearing, touch, smell and taste. These neurological inputs to the brain feed the self-consciousness of the soul through the portals of imagination, consciousness, memory, reason and affections. Even as we have a physical body, our spirit body has some form of substance. Pastor Clarence Larkin, a renowned theologian of the early 20th century, explains:

> While man differs from a beast in having a "spirit," yet he is as to his "body" only an animal. That is, his body, as to its functions, is like the body of an animal in its vital processes of respiration, digestion, assimilation and general makeup; so when the Apostle speaks of the "Natural" body he refers to the "animal" body of man. And when he speaks of man's "Spiritual" body, he means a "body" not some "ethereal substance," but a body with form and shape, but controlled and regulated by spiritual rather than natural laws. In

MANKIND'S TRINITY OF BEING

This trinity of being is symbolized in the design of the Israelite tent Tabernacle that God dictated to Moses and the Great Temple built by King Solomon. The design consists of an outer court encompassing a partition called the Holy Place. Within the Holy Place is the Holy of Holies, or the Most Holy Place, with its cherubim hovering over the Ark of the Covenant. It is in the Most Holy Place that the Shekinah Glory of God took up residence. The outer courtyard is the body, the Holy Place represents the soul and the Most Holy Place the spirit body. This symbolism makes sense as when Paul writes to the Corinthians, *"Do you not know that your body is a temple of the Holy Spirit, who is in you, whom you have received from God? You are not your own; you were bought at a price. Therefore honor God with your body."*[10] Each person is complete with body, soul and spirit; however, their spiritual nature will remain unregenerate until the Holy Spirit enters the spiritual compartment and begins the process. This happens when one is "born again."

other words both our "Natural" and "Spirit bodies" are composed of "matter," the only difference being that the matter of our "Natural" bodies is adapted to this "Physical" world, while the matter of our "Spirit" bodies is adapted to the "Spirit" world. It makes the subject clearer to speak of a "Spirit" body, rather than a "Spiritual" body, for the word "Spiritual" refers more to the "religious" attributes of a body, than to the material…So when a man's "body" is separated from his "soul" and "spirit" at death, the "spirit" is not "bodiless," it still has its "Soulish body." As this "Soulish body" can hear, and speak, and think, and feel, it must have some "tangible" form. It is not a "ghostlike" structure. There are doubtless limitations in its use, or there would be no need for it to recover its physical body at the Resurrection.[11]

Not only do the Scriptures give evidence of this spirit body, so do the extensive accounts of modern near-death experiences (NDE) recorded by medical researchers. In the Old Testament portion of the Bible, in 1 Samuel 28:13, God allows the witch of Endor to call the spirit of the dead high priest, Samuel, up from the compartment of Paradise. Samuel appears in visible form wearing a robe; there is verbal communication between Samuel and King Saul. In the New Testament, Peter, James and John see Jesus become transfigured in brilliant light; as well, Moses and Elijah, who have been dead for hundreds of years, appear and talk with Jesus.

In Luke 16:19, Jesus gives an account of a rich man and Lazarus, a beggar. The story is told in a factual way and not as a parable, implying that Jesus had personal knowledge of the pertinent details. Both the selfish rich man and the poor beggar, Lazarus, die; the rich man goes to the "compartment of torments" and Lazarus to "Abraham's bosom"—another name for Paradise. They can see, hear, feel emotions and recognize each other. The rich man calls out to Abraham; they hold a conversation. All have spirit bodies.

OUR FALLEN NATURE

The Holy Spirit of God strives with the spirits of men to awaken their God-consciousness. The book of Hebrews 4:12 declares: *"For the word of God is living and active. Sharper than any double-edged sword, it penetrates even to dividing soul and spirit, joints and marrow; it judges the thoughts and attitudes of the heart."* Here again is an illustration of the trinity of man. The soul is the abode of the spirit. The joints, which contain marrow, represent the body.

The spiritual you, in a pictorial sense, resides in an inner room with a single door guarded by the giant of self-will. The giant of self-will was born in the Garden of Eden when our first parents became self-taking rather than self-giving, believing the deceiver that they should be "as God." Even as Eve saw the fruit of the forbidden tree was good for food, she lusted after it for selfish pleasure; she saw it was pleasing to the eye and coveted it for herself. Lastly, she saw it was desirable for gaining wisdom, and in the pride of life she took and ate.

These three principles—lust, covetness and pride—govern our fallen nature. The fruit of these three principles are hate, jealousy, anger, covetness, sexual immorality, stealing, lying, deceitfulness and murder.

Picture now, two chairs in your inner room. One is very comfortable and was obviously made just for you; the other is very elegant and regal. What happens spiritually is the blackness of hopelessness and despair flood the soul from negative input to the physical senses, you leave your comfortable chair, shrivel into a corner believing there is no hope, no joy, no love and no peace. "You are nothing," is the cry of evolution, "you have no purpose, you are meaningless in the cosmos." "Shrivel up and die" wails the dragon of despair.

You can change all of this! Recognize that you are made in the image of God and He loves you so much that He came and gave

His life as a ransom for you. Call out to Him; you need His guidance and love. Ask His forgiveness and become "born again!"

When you do this, the Holy Spirit of God comes and sits beside you in the regal chair. The giant of self-will is slowly vanquished as the Holy Spirit begins the act of regeneration of your spiritual body. With Him come hope and the fruits of the Spirit.

Dr. Walvoord writes:

While the Scriptures are clear that a regenerated person can sin, and does sin, the lapse is traced to the sin nature, even though the act is that of the whole person. This must not be confused with various statements to the effect that a Christian can be sinless, or is unable to sin. The state of sinless perfection can never be reached until the sin nature is cast out, and this is accomplished only through the death of the physical body, or the transformation of the body without death at the rapture.[12]

HOPE

"May the God of hope fill you with all joy and peace as you trust in him, so that you may overflow with hope by the power of the Holy Spirit" (Rom. 15:13).

FRUIT OF THE SPIRIT

"But the fruit of the Spirit is love, joy, peace, patience, kindness, goodness, faithfulness, gentleness and self-control" (Gal. 5:22).

In this matter of sin, the Legions of Doom will attack and try to defeat you with guilt saying, "God does not love you any more." Your answer should be that which Adam and Eve should have cried out: *"Give thanks to the Lord Almighty, for the Lord is good; his love endures forever."* [13]

The alternative to asking the Holy Spirit of God into your life is to climb up on the regal chair yourself and declare, "I am god." If you truly believe in evolution, you will recognize the hollowness of this act, and all that is left is to follow the epigram, "I did it my way." However, rest assured, because you are a rebel and belong rightfully to the Prince of Darkness, his servants will knock gently and deceitfully at your spiritual door. It can start as simply as doing Yoga positions, reading astrology columns, reading tarot cards, visiting a fortuneteller, looking deep within yourself for spiritual guides and, most dramatically of all, seeking the presence of the ethereal through channeled séances. God has given you a will to open or close that door, and the Legions of Doom cannot violate your will; however, when you let them in they will occupy the regal chair, and it is only the ransoming blood of Jesus Christ that can remove them. Under full demonic possession, you will find your spiritual self forcibly shoved into a corner while the malevolent spirits defile your body. It is a sad reflection on our Western societies that many believe God is "dead," or He is a myth, while the gods of eastern mysticism and witchcraft are becoming entrenched. Thus, we are directly evidencing the spiritual battle taking place in our cosmos.

Spiritual battles wage all around us; at stake is our eternal destiny. In this world, when you least expect it, unwitting human servants of the Prince of Darkness will malign you through jealousy, pride, hate, greed and deceitfulness. You will then find that laws can be manipulated to selfish purposes, and justice can become twisted. In these attacks, God asks you to trust in His love and goodness, *that in all things God works for the good of those who love him, who have been called according to his purpose.* [14] It may take time, but take heart for God has promised, *"Do not take revenge, my friends, but leave room for God's wrath, for it is written: 'It is mine to avenge; I will repay,' says the Lord."* [15]

ETHEREAL ATTACKS

In the ancient book of Job, an evil ethereal being encroaches upon a man named Eliphaz. He records, *"Amid disquieting dreams in the night when deep sleep falls on men, fear and trembling seized me and made all my bones shake. A spirit glided past my face, and the hair on my body stood on end. It stopped, but I could not tell what it was. A form stood before my eyes, and I heard a hushed voice: 'Can a mortal be more righteous than God? Can a man be more pure than his Maker?'*[16]

Some time ago, I encountered a demon-possessed man; he came towards me, gaunt, with shabby clothes and long, stringy, unwashed hair, saying, "I am Jesus." He came up to me as if it was a spiritual challenge that could not be refuted: "I am Jesus." In compassion, I looked into his eyes and said, "Jesus loves you—He died to save you." That was as far as I got; he barked like a dog, pawed his foot and made a hasty retreat. Several days later, I noticed him coming down the sidewalk a block ahead of me and commenced to pray for his soul. The effect was immediate. His head came up; he saw me, turned and jaywalked across a busy street.

Modern missionaries also tell of frightening experiences with the demonic. The servants of the Prince of Darkness exhibit a deep hate for the children of light. A friend was visiting a small, friendly evangelical church in a South American country. While up on the platform with a group of other men, a physical force of deep malignant hate suddenly came over his body, momentarily freezing him. The spirit had no claim on him and soon departed.

Another friend shared with me a startling moment when he was confronted by a demonic being. He had been adopted as an infant by a Christian couple and had accepted the Lord as his personal Savior. As an adult, he met his biological father who had no idea my friend was a believer in Jesus. In one of their early meetings, his father was sitting beside him at the dinning room table. During a conversation about religion, his newfound dad said he hated "born-again Christians" and proceeded to list the reasons why. At that point, my friend said he was startled to see an ethereal face with malignant hate form around his father as he kept talking. He felt the hair on his neck stiffen and clearly heard the menacing words in his mind, "You will never get him," which, of course, referred to the spiritual state of being "born again."

A Christian lady related to me an experience that happened to her when her children were young. In an experience similar to that of Eliphaz, she awoke in the night to an ominous sound like rushing wings. A feeling of dark oppression forcibly pressed her against the mattress. Terrified, she was unable to move and felt as if she could scarcely breathe. In her spirit, she uttered a panic prayer to Jesus and instantly understood the quiet response of the Holy Spirit within: "You have committed yourself and your eldest child to me for protection but not your youngest one." Her prayer for that child was immediate and, just as quickly, the evil spirit of bondage left, having no more claim upon that household.

OUT-OF-BODY EXPERIENCES

There seem to be two types of out-of-body experiences: those associated with the death process or trauma, and those induced by eastern mysticism, drugs and the occult. Tal Brooke, who was once deeply involved in eastern mysticism and the occult, explains:

> Monroe and I tried to make sense out of the whole phenomenon of astral travel, catalyzing one another in the process. He was approaching the subject in terms of the "higher teachings" he had received while out of the body in his encounter with "higher beings, astral masters, and beings of light," combined with his diversified reading in yoga, eastern thought, and scientific theory. I was approaching his bizarre exploits and spirit encounters (plus a few of my own) from the viewpoint of nondualist Indian philosophy, through the perspective of my own 1966 mystical LSD experience—at which time I had experienced total unity of the universe—combined with a sort of mystical Christianity (along the lines of Ritchie, Cayce, Carl Jung, Paul Tillich,

and Teilhard de Chardin). But, to Monroe, perhaps my most important credential was that apparently I, too, had been able to leave my physical body. It had started when I was an eleven-year-old child battling the mumps in London. Half asleep in bed, I would become paralyzed, hear the sound of jets, and apparently go ripping through the roof to hover above our house. Occasionally the same thing happened during my teens, and it was starting again in college. Monroe's out-of-the-body symptoms matched mine point for point.[17]

NDE and out-of-body experiences (OBE) can only be explained if we are, in fact, "fearfully and wonderfully made," comprising physical and spiritual bodies. It appears that malevolent deceitful forces of the Legions of Doom can somehow use the natural phenomena of temporary destabilization of the body-spirit linkages to effect astral travel and communicate as masters of great wisdom. Tal Brooke reports that Monroe received technical information from spirit beings giving him success as a scientist and, later, to build an astral travel machine that gave startling spiritual viewing at a distance. In effect, the machine was only an elaborate hoax to affect the human will and spirit; the ethereal forces did the power linkages.

Scientists Professor Newberg, at the University of Pennsylvania, and Assistant Professor Gregg Jacobs, at Harvard Medical School, have discovered a small region of the brain that calculates spatial orientation and body-world or self-other awareness. During intense meditation brought on by prayer or chants, this area of the brain becomes an "oasis of inactivity" which creates a blurring of the self-other relationship. They state that, "if they go far enough they have a complete dissolving of the self, a sense of union, a sense of infinite spacelessness."[18] Followers of Eastern mystical religions seek this transcendental experience of cosmic oneness. Deceptive spirits likely access this area of the brain to achieve an allusion of dimensional unity, "godhood" and astral travel.

True Christian "born-again believers" do not experience one-ness with the cosmos; their prayers are praise and intercessory communication with their redeemer, Jesus Christ. Their relationship is person to person through the power of the Holy Spirit. The entering into deep meditation states through yoga, chants or any other such means is a permissive, willful opening of the inner spirit being to the unknown invasive spirit dimension. This is strictly forbidden by God since it is the self-seeking will for delusional spiritual power. Practitioners of eastern meditation try to void their minds. In contrast, follows of Christ are encouraged instead to be *"filled with the Spirit. Speak to one another with psalms, hymns and spiritual songs. Sing and make music in your heart to the Lord, always giving thanks to God the Father for everything, in the name of our Lord Jesus Christ."* [19]

The NDE fascination began with the publication of *Life After Life* in 1975 and *Reflections on Life After Life* in 1977, by Raymond A. Moody, Jr., MD. The forward to *Life After Life* was written by Elizabeth Kubler-Ross MD who became so involved in the occult that she had a spirit guide named Salem who would materialize in her room.[20]

In NDE, or OBE, many individuals see themselves attached to their physical body by a silver cord or tether. If this silver cord is broken, physical death occurs; in this sense, there is "nothing new under the sun." King Solomon, almost 3,000 years ago, records: *"Remember him—before the silver cord is severed, or the golden bowl is broken; before the pitcher is shattered at the spring or the wheel broken at the well, and the dust returns to the ground it came from, and the spirit returns to God who gave it."* [21]

NDEs have been much more common in our 21st century than in the past because of modern resuscitation methods. Medical doctor Maurice S. Rawlings has documented a number of these events in his book, *To Hell and Back*.[22] It would appear many people have

OF THE SOMETHING MORE

hellish experiences, but the mind quickly erases these memories. Reportedly, a typical NDE is accompanied by a rushing sound; the spirit body departs the physical body. The soulish body can see and hear as it hovers near the physical body. Suddenly the soulish body can be drawn through a dark tunnel or see the stars swirling by at a rapid rate. Next, there is a beautiful place where sometimes spirits of dead relatives arrive to help; but overall, there is this feeling of deep love. It is then that a being of light, with no identification or form, comes and assures you all is love there is no condemnation or judgement. Unfortunately, though, you must return and you do, to the thumping of the resuscitation unit. This experience can have a profound effect on how you view your life. The publication of these types of NDE has now evolved into the modern, New Age, "Omega Point," everyone-is-going-there religion.

SOULS AND CLONING

The question of the beginning of a soul is of deep theological interest in this age of cloning. From the perspective of either evolution or creation, cloning is not natural. Scientists decry the genetic decay of the cheetah in that there is no longer sufficient genetic variability to maintain it as a healthy species. In the same way, we hear of scientists searching the countryside for wild grains that have a healthy variation of genetic material. The question becomes self-evident: why, if evolution is true, is the genome of a species becoming less divergent? It would seem as if creation is a valid concept; God originally stacked the genome of each species with genetic variation and the law of entropy is now actively degrading each species. This is a more apt explanation than "evolution is not active anymore" and would explain the disappearance of so many species after the global catastrophes that have struck Earth.

The well-understood laws of sexual reproduction allow for the cross-linkage of genetic material between dominant and subdominant traits. A cell's protein mechanisms work to keep the cell in its pre-described genetic format by repairing damaging mutations. Cloning from a single stem cell generates a new creature from a fixed set of genetic instructions; thus, mutational damage will increase substantially with the clone of a clone of a clone. Furthermore, scientific research on cloned animals has shown that even though the clone appears genetically similar to its parent, it appears the RNA protein transcription engine might possibly be misreading the DNA blueprint sequence in its production of a cell's complex protein machinery (around 5,000 different kinds of molecules, many of them proteins, occupy a cell).[23] Serious health problems are showing up in both older and newborn clones, such as arthritis. "And there is plenty of anecdotal evidence of animals being born overweight, malformed and with damaged immune systems."[24] Evolutionary science with no morality should not be taken lightly. Sooner or later, some fiendish researcher will attempt to cross an animal genome with that of a human, such as a human stem cell within an ape egg.

Now, from the human perspective, where does the soul come from? Genetic twins each have a soul, not a portion of a soul. Susan Read, a genetic twin, writes, "Identical twins are living proof that identical DNA doesn't mean identical people. My sister and I may have the same hardwiring—and a wire that connects us. We have fun with our similarities, but at the end of the day, there's no confu-

NO MEANINGLESS CODE

Scientists refer to a genome as having meaningful code and reams of meaningless code; such is the assumption of evolution. Instead, it seems more likely "God created" and the assumed reams of so-called meaningless code is more like compact encrypted programming that defines, as Dr Francis Schaeffer would say, the "mannishness of man."

OF THE SOMETHING MORE

sion about who is who. Just as the fingerprints of all individuals, even identical twins, are unique, so are their souls. And you can't clone a soul."[25] All identical twins have subtle physical differences, which shows there are varying ways the RNA can transcribe the DNA in its production of living cells.

Some theologians propose that genetics predispose salvation. However, although one might inherit genetic characteristics of, for instance, a bad temper, it is how the self-will responds to the neurological input that determines a decision. The science of quantum mechanics (QM) has shown that this action of decision-making is not deterministic. Gerald Schroeder, a physicist-theologian, explains the thought process of free will in his book, *The Science of God*:

> Quantum mechanics has proven that the visible world is not a direct extension of the subatomic world from which it is constructed. By this it has laid basis for the biblical concept that the mind is not a mere extension of neurochemical reactions of the brain. QM does something much more important than destroy determinism—it provides the opening and the mechanism for choice.
>
> Through speech and body activity, the brain translates into physical manifestation the mind's thoughts. The conscious mind draws its inputs both from biochemically determined neurological activity and from what appears to be a partly random, nondeterministic surfacing of subconscious thoughts into the conscious. ....what might be described as a quantum wave function includes the range of an individual's subconscious information (this being the subconscious portion of the window of choice). The wave, in a manner that is not precisely predictable, then collapses, focusing on one concept and that surfaces as a conscious thought. But the collapse, while not deterministic, is also not totally random. It is highly skewed by the individual's history. If tension and anxiety underlie the experiences fed to the mind, then tension and anxiety will surface in thought.[26]

What we input through our neurological system can precondition our thought processes and ultimately create a bias toward our decisions. The actions of will, moment-by-moment, shape the soulish body through the life of an individual.

God breathed the breath of life into the genome; thus, a stem cell has in it the breath of life to manufacture a new independent soul placed in a body of predetermined genetic characteristics. There is no emplacement of a soul; we are unique individuals of eternal essence created in the image of God by the merging of the breath of life from each parent. Therefore, reincarnation is not a valid concept, nor is the idea of old souls entering new bodies. Cloning may be one of the violations of natural law God addresses when He says: *"The earth is defiled by its people; they have disobeyed the laws, violated the statues and broken the everlasting covenant. Therefore a curse consumes the earth; its people must bear their guilt."* [27]

Attempts by UFO aliens to create a physical body by which they can enter this space-time material world will fail because to be human is to be of body, soul and spirit energized by the eternal breath of life of God. Instead, they possess willing individuals and force the human will into a corner, or, as reported in Genesis 6:2, defy the prime directive of God and try to interbreed with humans. In an article on cloning, *TIME* reports that "the Raelians, a religious group committed to, among other things, welcoming the first extraterrestrials when they appear, have set up a lab and will attempt to bring a cloned human baby to term using a surrogate human mother."[28] If the Raelians are backed by an alien agenda, one would have to wonder just what this lab will be producing.

NOTES:

[1] Behe, Professor Michael, *Darwin's Black Box*, Simon & Schuster, 1998, p. 173

[2] Coppedge, James E., *Evolution Possible or Impossible?* Zondervan Corporation, 1973, pp. 58, 126

[3] Schroeder, Gerald L., *The Science of God*, Broadway Books, New York, 1997, p. 91

[4] "Wolf to Wolf," *National Geographic*, January 2002, p. 2

[5] Walvoord, Dr. John F., *The Holy Spirit*, Zondervan Publishing House, 1975, p. 5

[6] Acts 23:9

[7] Revelation 12:7

[8] Walvoord, Ibid. p. 41

[9] Schaeffer, Francis A., *Genesis in Space and Time*, Intervarsity Press, 1972, p. 39

[10] 1 Corinthians 6:19

[11] Larkin, Clarence, *The Greatest Book on Dispensational Truth in the World*, Revised edition 1920, Rev. Clarence Larkin Est., Forty-first printing, p. 97

[12] Walvoord, Ibid. p. 136

[13] Jeremiah 33:11

[14] Romans 8:28

[15] Romans 12:19

[16] Job 4:13–16

[17] Brooke, Ibid. p. 34

[18] *The Sydney Morning Herald*, May 10, 2001

[19] Ephesians 5:18–20

[20] Brooke, Tal, *The Other Side of Death*, Tyndale House Publishers Inc., Wheaton, Illinois, 1979, p. 51

[21] Ecclesiastes 12:6

[22] Rawlings, Maurice S. M.D., *To Hell and Back*, Thomas Nelson Publishers, Nashville, 1993

[23] Coppedge, Ibid. p. 149

[24] "Dolly's Arthritis Sparks Cloning Row," BBC NEWS, Friday, January 4, 2002

[25] "My Sister, My Clone," *TIME*, February 19, 2001, p. 47

[26] Schroeder, Ibid. p. 173

[27] Isaiah 24:5–6

[28] *TIME*, February 19, 2001, p. 44.

The Adversary

e self-controlled and alert. Your enemy the devil prowls around like a roaring lion looking for someone to devour." [1]

"The devil made me do it," the comedian would say, and the canned laughter stimulated the audience to one more "ha-ha." It was the 1960s; evolutionary enlightenment was slowly permeating the North American culture. Audiences tittered at the thought of the red-horned, long-tailed caricature depicting the devil. In their material abundance, they sneered at the rest of the world steeped in its religious mysticism. Prayer was merely psychological trapping used by the emotionally disturbed. God was dead, and many churches that were to reflect the glory of His name labored under a cloak of puritanical self-righteousness.

The sweet smell of freedom drifted in the air as the generation of flower children evolved; not that there was never any freedom before, but somehow it was different. The material blessedness of

49

the nation seemed evil, and Church beliefs outmoded religious restrictions. The flower children bloomed and were watered by "free love," by drugs and by eastern mysticism. Yet there was the fresh birth of newness for those who rejected these things. Some threw off the self-righteousness of dead churches and found spiritual freedom in Jesus Christ; a number continued in the hippie trend as "Jesus freaks." Many churches rocked with new light and life under the Holy Spirit, but the majority of this generation made pilgrimages to the countryside in mass gatherings, quivering to the beat of drums and the wailing of electric guitars as they worshiped themselves, Mother Earth, Mother Nature and the mysteries of the Prince of Darkness.

In the years spanning from the '60s to the 21st century, approximately four teenage generations have passed. What began as relatively innocent "I love you—you don't love me" music has evolved into crude, vulgar, licentious, rebellious, self-centered musical content. Differing age groups naturally throb to different beats, and Christian parents in particular blamed the messenger instead of the content. The vibrancy of youth passes through phases, and each generation begins afresh to accept or reject music, video content and lifestyle. Yet there is a disturbing overall trend towards increasing hopelessness, despair and a sense of foreboding anarchy.

No, we cannot see God or Satan; however, even as we cannot see the wind, we can still see its effects. Satan does not want to be seen. Evidence for his existence implies God exists. For most of us, the world seems to be a very normal place to live, operating under fixed natural laws. We may or may not like the circumstances of our lives, but, whatever they are, we attribute them to being natural. There is a perceived order in the world; aliens or bogey men do not harass us or even exist. Even though a wild animal may cause concern, it is those of our own kind who are the natural tormentors.

If we could somehow see the Legions of Doom operating from their ethereal web of darkness that surrounds Earth, it is possible many independent wills would cry out to Jesus Christ and be saved, but Satan does not want this since, by default, human civilization already belongs to him.[2] God wants individuals who come to love Him for who He is, out of their own free will. God does not put on a show of divine "magic." God came once as the God-man, Jesus of Nazareth. It was evident then, as it would be now, unless people have had a spiritual rebirth, they seek miracles only for selfish gain.

The physical world operates under fixed natural laws. Within this framework the individual will is given freedom of choice to accept or deny that God exists. It is a "free will choice" to believe by logical rational faith that He planned a means for redeeming mankind from the rebellion, that there is a judgment after death, that there is a resurrection, that there is an eternal life with purpose and meaning and that "God is good and His love endures forever."

EMOTIONAL PROBLEMS

Whether or not a person has been "reborn" by a spiritual new birth in their acceptance of Jesus Christ as Lord and Saviour, the pressures of life and the genetic decay of our biological systems can create psychological problems. These are natural illness that can be treated with the help of psychologists, psychiatrists and modern medicine, just like any other disease of the body.

Editors of evolution-based scientific magazines deplore, with just cause, the paranormal, pseudo-scientific and religious conjectures assaulting our modern society. What they and the true Church of Jesus Christ see, from different perspectives, is that all around the world there is a shift of cosmic consciousness such that the realm of mysticism is now considered natural. Indeed there is a definite plan in effect, not by man but by the ethereal forces waging war against us. It seems so innocent looking deep within oneself, thinking one is gifted with clairvoyance, ESP is natural and we have secret powers evolving us into beings that can flit around the astral planes. This deception is evil and is being effectively coordinated for a wicked purpose.

We live in a world where we can know good and evil and, like children in a room after a parent or teacher has left, can choose whether to obey or not. Humanistic psychologists can pontificate on many theories for the attitudes of man, from the extremes of love to hate and all that these emotions entail, but the biblical case is that we are subject to our self-taking human natures.

OUR SINFUL NATURE

Decisions made by our human will affect our spiritual wellbeing. Jesus Christ said to His close companions, Peter, James and John, *"Watch and pray so that you will not fall into temptation. The spirit is willing, but the body is weak."* [3] Paul of Tarsus recognized this schism in our spiritual natures; although he had experienced supernatural visions and a spiritual conversion, he exclaimed, *"I know that nothing good lives in me, that is, in my sinful nature. For I have the desire to do what is good, but I cannot carry it out. For what I do is not the good I want to do; no, the evil I do not want to do— this I keep on doing. …When I want to do good, evil is right there with me. For in my inner being I delight in God's law; but I see another law at work in the members of my body, waging war against the law of my mind and making me a prisoner of the law of sin at work within my members."* [4] Paul goes on to conclude victoriously, *"Who will rescue me from this body of death? Thanks be to God—through Jesus Christ our Lord."*

The chemical desires of our biological system are very powerful and designed to propagate the continuum of human life. It is the selfish misuse of these desires and emotions that Paul calls a part of our sinful nature. Secular scientists have no foundation for man's inner conflicts; instead, they study the lives of the chimpanzees and gorillas to try to determine what went wrong in the evolutionary leap to *Homo sapiens*. God created mankind to be sentient beings with cosmic free will. Since the fall, because our natures are now self-centered, we experience inner turmoil as we attempt to know good and

ALL SIN IS WORTHY OF DEATH

In the "wisdom" of our self-taking nature, we accord varying degrees of wrongness of sin, rebellion, or violation against God's holy nature. To God, any sin is worthy of death. Fortunately we are not stricken to death as were Ananias and his wife Sapphira.

It was in the early days of Christianity when, through the power of the Holy Spirit, Jesus was establishing His Church on Earth. Ananias and Sapphira sold some land which was rightfully theirs to sell. However, they coveted some of the money for themselves and, instead of being forthright, lied to Peter.

Satan once again was active in the decisions of the human self-taking will. Peter said, "'*Ananias, how is that Satan has so filled your heart that you have lied to the Holy Spirit and have kept for yourself some of the money you received for the land? Didn't it belong to you before it was sold? And after it was sold, wasn't the money at your disposal? What made you think of doing such a thing? You have not lied to men but to God.*'" At that point, Ananias dropped dead. Sapphira came to Peter later, not knowing what had happened, she, of her own free will, lied to Peter. "*Peter said to her, 'How could you agree to test the Spirit of the Lord? Look! The feet of the men who buried your husband are at the door, and they will carry you out also.'*" [5] Then the Holy Spirit of God withdrew the eternal breath of life and she, too, died.

evil without the power of the Holy Spirit of God. The well-meant intentions of secular scientists, psychologists, psychiatrists, and sociologists are only bandages for a diseased, hurting world.

Natural human emotions, whether they extend from jealously, pride, anger or sexual attraction, can be subjected to ethereal influences if we, in our conscious will, do not master them. Cain, the first son of Adam and Eve, was angry, and the Lord said to him: *"Why are you angry? Why is your face downcast? If you do what is right, will you not be accepted? But if you do not do what is right, sin is crouching at your door; it desires to have you, but you must master it."* [6]

Satan is not just a name for our alternate ego. He is very real. God has given us recorded evidence of a scene that happened in the heavens affecting a man on Earth named Job.

Job lived somewhere in the Middle East. Satan hated him because he worshiped God. During one of Satan's visits to the courts of Heaven, along with other heavenly beings, God questioned him:

HEAVENS OR HEAVENLIES

The terms "heavens," "heavenly" or "heavenlies" refer not to our atmosphere, but outer space and the dimension of the spirit world where God holds court in the "Great Assembly." [8]

"Have you considered my servant Job? There is no one on earth like him; he is blameless and upright, a man who fears God and shuns evil." [7] The ensuing story describes how God allowed Satan to use the natural forces and diseases on Earth to attack Job in an attempt to get him to curse God. At one point, Job sat in an ash pit scraping boils off his body, not knowing what was happening in the spiritual dimension.

The moral of the story is that although Job lost everything, he did not curse God. Why? He loved God for who God is, not for the material things He gave. After the testing, Job was rewarded with more than he had had before.

You can't blame the devil for your decisions. Temptations come from within your own nature; you must master them, or the evil one will use them to your destruction. James, the brother of Jesus, explains: *"When tempted, no one should say, 'God is tempting me.' For God cannot be tempted by evil, nor does he tempt anyone; but each one is tempted when, by his own evil desire, he is dragged away and enticed. Then, after desire has conceived, it gives birth to sin; and sin, when it is full-grown, gives birth to death."* [9]

INCREASING ENTROPY

Natural disasters and calamity shake the Earth as it groans in the throes of increasing entropy (disorder; erosion-corrosion) and people cry out, "Where is God?" as if they believe someone else is there. Holy Scripture is very clear someone else is there. Jesus called him the *"prince of this world."* [11]

The whole world is under the rule of Satan,[12] the *"god of this age,"* [13] the *"ruler of the kingdom of the air, the spirit who is now at work in those who are disobedient."* [14] Satan's cosmic plan is unfolding—he seeks to be worshiped as god of this world. The increase in UFO sightings and the whisperings and mutterings from the so-called "astral planes" suggest that the shift of cosmic consciousness, prophesied by adherents of the paranormal, may soon be implemented

ENTROPY

"Entropy is simply the name of a mathematical expression that measures the degree to which energy becomes less available for useful work with the passage of time.... Entropy always increases because, as time passes, the kinds of energy that do useful work continue to change into a form that is less available for such work."[10]

with the arrival of the transcendent masters. Don't be deceived. They (these rebellious angel beings) will appear as masters of higher learning to convince deluded mankind that they too, can be "as gods." Jesus was looking ahead in time to this period in the war of the cosmos when He said: *"For false Christs and false prophets will appear and perform great signs and miracles to deceive even the elect— if that were possible. See I have told you ahead of time."* [15]

Even as the world struggles with wealth inequities, poverty, social disorder, wars, terrorism, earthquakes, disease, epidemics and environmental problems, secular humanists and some religious orders will believe they have entered a period of spiritual enlightenment. Jesus again warned: *"Be careful, or your hearts will be weighed down with dissipation, drunkenness and the anxieties of life, and that day will close on you unexpectedly like a trap. For it will come on the face of the whole earth. Be always on the watch, and pray that you may be able to escape all that is about to happen, and that you may be able to stand before the Son of Man."* [16]

THE WAR OF THE COSMOS

Fear for your lives all of you who, in this age of grace and mercy, have rejected the sacrificial redeeming love of Jesus Christ your creator. Call out to Him and be saved! For the wrath of King Jesus will assail the rebellious beings in the heavens, and the war of the cosmos will explode on to Earth with supernatural fury. Michael, the protective

> **STARRY HOST**
>
> The word for "starry host" is the same Hebrew word *tsaba* that is used for "powers in the heavens above."

archangel of the nation Israel, and his angels will drive Satan, the great red dragon, from the heavens to the Earth.[17] Satan will be furious because he knows his time of freedom is coming to an end.

A large ice-asteroid may possibly hit the earth; it will shudder with earthquakes.[18] *"In that day the Lord will punish the powers in the heavens above and the kings on the earth below."* [19] The starry host will fall to the Earth.[20] When the rebellious angels have been driven to Earth, God will say: *"My sword has drunk its fill in the heavens; see, it descends in judgment on Edom."*[21] Then the carnage of war on Earth around the Middle East will cover the mountains with blood, and the stench of dead bodies will smother the air.

It is unlikely that angels bleed; thus, the imagery of the sword in the heavens is to show the intensity of the comic war. One can almost imagine from our space-age perspective, shimmering UFO-style spacecraft materializing in our local skies as they flee to Earth. The UFO inhabitants will then masquerade as enlightened beings.

The focus of the Bible is on the redemption plan for mankind, how the Son of God stepped into enemy territory by incarnating Himself as a human being. It does not explain much pre-human history yet, as we become more cosmologically aware, carefully placed references throughout its pages give shadowy glimpses of this ancient cosmic drama. We are not given any description of the "powers, principalities and dominions" of the heav-

THE LEADER OF THE REBELLION

The Bible explains that a beautiful archangel, anointed to a high celestial position as a guardian cherub, rebelled. He had power and authority and walked amongst "fiery stones,"[22] which may possibly be the galaxies of our universe, or even the planets of our solar system. He became proud of his beauty and sought to become as God, saying, *"I will ascend to heaven; I will raise my throne above the stars of God; I will sit enthroned on the mount of the assembly, on the utmost heights of the sacred mountain. I will ascend above the tops of the clouds; I will make myself like the Most High."*[23] It is postulated that he acted as a priest directing worship to God and that he, in his arrogance, sought some of this worship for himself.

ens. From the commingling of the sons of God with human women, we can cautiously deduce some of their order may be humanoid, which may explain the meaning of God's sword, "drinking its fill in the heavens."

A number of deeply spiritual, God-fearing biblical scholars have postulated that, through the arrogance of Satan and an alignment of rebel angels, a pre-Adam civilization became evil and was destroyed in a cosmic cataclysm. It is not known whether Earth, Mars or the hypothetical planet that once existed between Mars and Jupiter were involved. The face on Mars, if it is artificial, is certainly something that someone with a massive ego would construct. Spirit intelligences (demons) may be the bodiless spirits from this devastated civilization since they seek to possess humans. It is also proposed that demons may be spirits of the offspring of the sons of God and the daughters of men who were destroyed in the food of Noah.

The conclusion of the war in the cosmos will be when Satan, his angels, demons and all humans who have not accepted the gift of salvation provided by Jesus Christ are confined forever in Hell (the Lake of Fire). Modern secular thinkers scorn the concept of Hell. The Bible

LAKE OF FIRE

In Revelation 20:11–15 the Lake of Fire is the place that all evil angels and men are cast into after their judgment at the White Throne judgment. At present, the flames of the Lake of Fire are empty.

states that Hell, a place of eternal fire, was originally prepared for the devil and his angels.[24] Contrary to the belief of reincarnation or the Omega Point concept, God declares, man is to die once, and after that to face judgment.[25] In the Gospels, Jesus gave more warnings about judgment and Hell than he did about the attributes of eternal life and heaven. Dire must be the consequences of our separation from the love of God.

In the story of the rich man and Lazarus, the selfish rich man went into "Torments," a compartment of Hades. The God-fearing poor man went into Paradise. Hades is a jail for the spirits of dead people and evil angels awaiting trial at the White Throne judgment. Unfortunately, Hades has been loosely translated as Hell, creating confusion. Hades, at one time before Jesus arose from the dead, held Paradise and Torments, which were separated by an impassable chasm.[26] Upon the resurrection of Jesus, Paradise was emptied and now is in Heaven proper. In some horrifying NDE resuscitations, people have peered into the gates of Torments. In the supposed glimpses of Paradise, because the silver cord of life has not been broken, Satan can somehow manifest himself as a loving being of light[27] and his Legions of Doom as beings of enlightenment and goodness.

Satan, as this being of light in NDE, gives the impression there is no judgment after death, all is forgiven and all enter eternity as good souls; thus, those things done as a live human being are, all in all, meaningless. Counteracting this deception is a person's inner conscience which has been programmed by God. A young murderer, who was later shot and had a NDE, said to Dr. Rawlings concerning the loving being of light, "I was glad he didn't ask me about those things, but if he was from God, why didn't he? I thought about bringing it up, but said to myself, 'Why knock a good thing?' and kept my mouth shut. I knew I should be in Hell instead of this nice place, but I kept quiet."[28]

Angelology is everywhere—ornaments, cards, books and television pro-

> **ANGELS CAN LOOK LIKE PEOPLE**
>
> Angels can appear as normal human beings: *"Do not forget to entertain strangers, for by so doing some people have entertained angels without knowing it"* (Heb. 13:2). However, we are strictly forbidden to worship them.[29]

grams. The Internet is filled with angel sites. But are there "good" angels and "bad" angels? Can the innocent be deceived? It would appear that many people are being entrapped by their selfish desires of wanting something more on their own terms.

The Bible is clear that angels are involved in the lives of those who love and worship God: *"The angel of the LORD encamps around those who fear him, and he delivers them"* (Ps. 34:7). Moreover, God will *"command his angels concerning you to guard you in all your ways"* (Ps. 91:11). In the battle of the cosmos, we are told: *"Are not all angels ministering spirits sent to serve those who will inherit salvation?"* (Heb. 1:14).

Communication with angels can be so over-powering the reciprocator becomes absorbed in the self-satisfying power that it brings. This is idolatry to God and duplicates the rebellion of Satan and the Legions of Doom. Angels of Glory do not participate in endeavors that would detract from the worship of God because He sends them for a specific purpose to minister to those who worship Him. When one reads articles on the Internet of women being caressed at night by an angel, or groups of people gathering in candlelight in a perfume-scented room calling on "angelic energy," they are in a séance worshiping the god of this world, his demons and angel forces. One woman stated, "Angels help us with things God can't because he's too high up… you don't call on God when you want a parking space, you call on middle management: an angel."[30] The god of this world deceives those who, by their self-taking nature, want to be "as gods" and buy into the illusion of false spiritual power without accountability.

Prayer to God (particularly in the name of Jesus) has been dispelled from secular society, and yet school children are being taught to visualize, to assume the yoga lotus position and to channel the spiritual power of their inner selves while meditating.[31] Now we should ask ourselves, if evolution is true, why are these empty teachings being perpetrated upon our innocent children? If God does not exist, neither do other gods. If, by the implication of their actions, "gods" exist, then so does God. The worshiping of these gods is what the rebellion in the cosmos is all about.

THE GODS OF THIS WORLD

Do not be deceived; the gods of this world have supernatural power. Bruce Lockerbie, in his book, *The Cosmic Center*, describes how he witnesses their power in the Hindu festival of Thaipusam in India. Pilgrims fulfilling acts of devotion suffer intense pain and agony as they are impaled with lances and have articles hooked into their flesh which they drag to an idol in a huge temple. Accompanied and encouraged by friends, they struggle, gouged and bleeding in the intense heat, uphill to the temple.

> I follow the procession into the temple. Once inside the great doors, a blast of sound like a fire storm envelopes me. At the arrival of each devotee, the mob's cries of greeting reverberate with such deafening hollowness, I feel as through my own voice were being sucked out of me. I am overwhelmed by noise, by dissonance so powerful, so infernal, I feel almost swept away. For the first time I know for a certainty that I am a spiritual alien on hostile ground. …These instruments of death have all been removed and the spell broken by priests in the Sri Bala Murugan temple at the end of the march. Victorious, these supplicants of the Lord Subramaniam pass within arm's reach, carrying overhead, like a laurel wreath, the barbs and hooks of their humiliation. And on their tortured bodies there is no blood and there are no wounds.[32]

Satan has the power of false miracles; there was no blood and no wounds. No matter which religious system it is, mankind struggles with accountability.

All religions have some sort of acts of works or humiliation that must be accomplished for spiritual justification. This may be why the all-in-all redeeming sacrificial act of humiliation and death by the God-man, Jesus Christ, is a stumbling block to many; their human pride wants to earn their salvation. The great prophet Isaiah cried out, *"How then can we be saved? All of us have become like one who is unclean, and all our righteous acts are like filthy rags."* [33] The answer is given in the accomplished death and resurrection of Jesus Christ. *"For it is by grace you have been saved, through faith— and this not from yourselves, it is the gift of God—not by works, so that no one can boast."* [34]

Are the good angels active? Of course they are; most people know someone who has a mysterious story to tell. In the ancient days of the 1940s, my parents were chugging over a narrow high mountain pass in British Columbia in an early 1930s vehicle. The road was very narrow; one bank dropped off hundreds of feet to the valley below. My father was driving with a thick roll-your-own cigarette streaming blue smoke hanging out of the side of his mouth. My mother, a young God-seeking woman, was hanging on for fear of her life on the steep bank side. Suddenly an angel floated along side the car, on her side, and put his hand on the front fender. She stared, aghast, hardly believing what she was seeing. She looked at Dad. He was intent on driving and obviously saw nothing. She did not know what to say and could only stare in apprehension. The angel held the fender until they reached the flat valley floor and then suddenly disappeared. The moment he took his hand off the fender, the front axle and wheel departed the car.

A SPIRITUAL AWAKENING CALL

The scene played briefly on the Seattle evening news; not only had the city suffered a violent earthquake, the inner city Mardi Gras celebrations had turned destructive. The colors of the television scene matched the emotion of despair. Framed between two buildings in an alley lit with pale-pink and greenish overtones was a teenager, his back to the camera, kicking: kicking at a garbage can, kicking at a wall, kicking at doorjambs, kicking-kicking-kicking!

How close is anarchy? It is as close as the Legions of Doom can get it. Violence in the cities turns to looting and destruction. Schools are battlegrounds of violent delusions as students are gunned down.

In the wake of the rash of school shootings, a general e-mail that speaks to the ethereal war of the cosmos was circulated amongst concerned people:

On Thursday, May 27, 1999, Darrell Scott, the father of Rachel Scott, a victim of the Columbine High School shootings in Littleton, Colorado was invited to address the House Judiciary Committee's sub-committee. What he said to our national leaders during this special session of Congress was painfully truthful. They were not prepared for what he was to say, nor was it received well. It needs to be heard by every parent, every teacher, every politician, every sociologist, every psychologist and every so-called expert!

These courageous words, spoken by Darrell Scott, are powerful, penetrating and deeply personal. The following is a portion of the transcript:

> "Since the dawn of creation there has been both good and evil
> in the hearts of men and women. We all contain the seeds of
> kindness or the seeds of violence. The death of my wonderful
> daughter, Rachel Joy Scott, and the deaths of that heroic teach-
> er, and the other eleven children who died must not be in vain.
> Their blood cries out for answers.

The first recorded act of violence was when Cain slew his brother Abel out in the field. The villain was Cain, not the club he used. Neither was it the NCA, the National Club Association. The true killer was Cain, and the reason for the murder could only be found in Cain's heart. In the days that followed the Columbine tragedy, I was amazed at how quickly fingers began to be pointed at groups such as the NRA. I am not a member of the NRA. I am not a hunter. I do not even own a gun. I am not here to represent or defend the NRA—because I don't believe that they are responsible for my daughter's death. Therefore, I do not believe that they need to be defended. If I believed they had anything to do with Rachel's murder, I would be their strongest opponent. I am here today to declare that Columbine was not just a tragedy—it was a spiritual event that should be forcing us to look at where the real blame lies! Much of the blame lies here in this room. Much of the blame lies behind the pointing fingers of the accusers themselves.

I wrote a poem just four nights ago that expresses my feelings best. This was written before I knew I would be speaking here today:

> Your laws ignore our deepest needs,
> Your words are empty air.
> You've stripped away our heritage,
> You've outlawed simple prayer.
> Now gunshots fill our classrooms,
> And precious children die.
> You seek for answers everywhere,
> And ask the question "Why?"
> You regulate restrictive laws,
> Through legislative creed.
> And yet you fail to understand,
> That God is what we need!

Men and women are three-part beings. We all consist of body, soul, and spirit. When we refuse to acknowledge a third part of our make-up, we create a void that allows evil, prejudice, and hatred to rush in and wreak havoc. Spiritual influences were present within our educational systems for most of our nation's history. Many of our major colleges began as theological seminaries. This is a historical fact. What has happened to us as a nation? We have refused to honor God, and in so doing, we open the doors to hatred and violence. And when something as terrible as Columbine's tragedy occurs—politicians immediately look for a scapegoat such as the NRA. They immediately seek to pass more restrictive laws that contribute to erode away our personal and private liberties. We do not need more restrictive laws. Eric and Dylan would not have been stopped by metal detectors. No amount of gun laws can stop someone who spends months planning this type of massacre. The real villain lies within our own hearts. Political posturing and restrictive legislation are not the answers. The young people of our nation hold the key. There is a spiritual awakening taking place that will not be squelched!

We do not need more religion. We do not need more gaudy television evangelists spewing out verbal religious garbage. We do not need more million dollar church buildings built while people with basic needs are being ignored. We do need a change of heart and a humble acknowledgment that this nation was founded on the principle of simple trust in God!

As my son Craig lay under that table in the school library and saw his two friends murdered before his very eyes—he did not hesitate to pray in school. I defy any law or politician to deny him that right! I challenge every young person in America, and around the world, to realize that on April 20, 1999, at Columbine High School, prayer was brought back to our schools. Do not let the many prayers offered by those students be in vain.

Dare to move into the new millennium with a sacred disregard for legislation that violates your God-given right to communicate with Him. To those of you who would point your finger at the NRA I give to you a sincere challenge. Dare to examine your own heart before casting the first stone! My daughter's death will not be in vain! The young people of this country will not allow that to happen!"

Be courageous enough to do what the media did not—let the nation hear this man's speech. Please send this out to everyone you can.

On September 11, 2001 sudden violent destruction descends on New York City; two large commercial aircraft commanded by radical Islamic terrorists slam into the World Trade Towers, and a third into the Pentagon, creating great balls of fire. The mighty Twin Towers of trade and commerce collapse into a massive pile of burning ruins. Some people imagine they saw a large, evil face form in the rising billows of smoke and fire. Yet this terrible world-shattering tragedy was a major spiritual wake-up

> **TRAGEDY**
>
> Secularism is a deception of pride until the bells of tragedy toll for souls.

call to the free world and, in particular, the United States of America whose motto is, "In God we trust."

In the days that followed it became apparent God had quietly worked in the carnage and destruction to miraculously rescue many people. Hard-working people in all walks of life gave their lives as heroes, and untold millions of people around the world prayed.

Unnatural rage is aflame in the hearts of many people around the world. All around us as the angelic battle is fought, Satan seeks to deceive and destroy while God seeks to redeem. McCandlish

Phillips, author of *The Spirit World*, quotes from the diary of a First World War German soldier on the unnatural madness that permeated the battlefield. Ernest Junger, the soldier, wrote:

> My right hand embraced the shaft of my pistol, my left a riding stick of bamboo cane. I was boiling with a mad rage, which had taken hold of me and all the others in an incomprehensible fashion. The overwhelming wish to kill gave wings to my feet. Rage pressed bitter tears from my eyes. …The monstrous desire for annihilation, which hovered over the battlefield, thickened the brains of the men and submerged them in a red fog.

Mr. Phillips comments:

> This account reveals nothing less than the presence of possibly thousands of evil spirits gathered in the air at the site of battle, determined to turn it into a scene of maximum carnage. "The monstrous desire for annihilation… hovered over the battlefield." It "thickened the minds of the men and submerged them in a red fog." Satan's policy of death had been put into peculiarly intensive effect, at a moment when the opportunity for bringing death to many men was ripe, by a concentration of evil spirits—spirits of destruction—at the scene of battle.[35]

Even as the battle raged in the material space-time world, the Angels of Glory held the Legions of Doom at bay. Counteracting the concentration of evil spirits during this war were the apparitions known as the "Angels of Mons."[36] These apparitions appeared in the sky to hold back the Germans from butchering the British as they retreated from the Belgian town of Mons. Needless to say, this was proof to war-weary Britain that the heavens were on their side.

Similar supernatural events occurred during the surprise attack of Syria and Egypt on Israel in the 1973 Yom Kippur war, as Satan mobilized the Arab armies in an attempt to annihilate the Jewish people. Lance Lambert, a reporter, in his book, *Israel: A Secret Documentary*, describes the war. Syria attacked on the twenty-mile wide Golan Heights with 1,200 tanks and helicopters loaded with assault troops. This was more tanks than the combined force of Britain and France. "Egypt attacked with 3,000 tanks, 2,000 heavy guns, 1,000 aircraft and 600,000 men." Israel's army were peacefully at prayer on the most holy day of the year, Yom Kippur, by noon, Syria had taken the Golan Heights while the Egyptians had crossed the Suez Canal and taken the Bar-Lev line. Inexplicably, both armies stopped and waited which gave Israel time to regroup and reorganize. Lambert reports:

> An Israeli captain, again totally irreligious, said that at the height of the fighting on the Golan, he looked up into the sky and saw a great gray hand pressing downwards, as if it were holding something back. In my opinion that was exactly what happened. Without the intervention of God, Israel would have been doomed.[37]

The Lord called many people around the world to intercessory prayer before any of the events happening in Israel were known. Samuel Howells was one of these. "He felt a tremendous burden and anguish come upon him and asked the Lord 'What does this burden mean?' The Lord told him, 'My enemy is seeking to precipitate Armageddon.'"[38] Armageddon is described in the book of Revelation as a time when all the armies of the world under the command of the antichrist surround Jerusalem to annihilate the nation Israel, God's chosen people.

THE DESTRUCTION OF JERUSALEM

The enemy, Satan the rebel archangel, has tried to destroy the Jews for thousands of years. In the 1930s, Germany turned to mysticism and the occult. The result was World War II and the Jewish Holocaust. At the time of the Maccabees, in 168 BC, Antiochus Epiphanes persecuted the Jews and desecrated the altar in the temple by offering a sow. The ensuing preternatural is reported in 2 Maccabees:

> And then it happened, that through all the city for the space almost of forty days, there were seen horsemen running in the air, in cloth of gold, and armed with lances, like a band of soldiers. And troops of horsemen in array, encountering and running one against another, with shaking of shields, and multitude of pikes, and drawing of swords, and casting of darts, and glittering of golden ornaments, and harnesses of all sorts. Wherefore every man prayed that apparition might turn to good.[39]

Jesus told His disciples that He would be rejected and that Jerusalem would be destroyed. Subsequently, He was killed and arose again from the dead. Forty years later, in 70 AD, the Roman army sacked Jerusalem. However, during a lull when Titus temporarily withdrew the Roman army from around the city, all the Christians fled based on Jesus's warning. Shortly before the Roman onslaught, a series of incredible signs happened in the temple during the period of the feast of Passover to Pentecost. Josephus, the famous Jewish historian of that era, writes:

> On the eighth day of the month Xanthicus (Nisan), and at the ninth hour of the night, so great a light shone round the altar and the holy house, that it appeared to be bright day time; which light lasted for half and hour.
>
> At the same festival also, a heifer, as she was led by the high priest to be sacrificed, brought forth a lamb in the midst of the temple.
>
> Moreover, the eastern gate of the inner (court of the temple), which was of brass, and vastly heavy, and had been with difficulty shut by twenty men, and rested upon a base armed with iron, and had bolts fastened very deep into the firm floor, which

was there made of one entire stone, was seen to be opened of its own accord about the sixth hour of the night.

Besides these, a few days after that feast, on the 21st of the month of Artemisius (Jyar), a certain prodigious and incredible phenomenon appeared; I suppose the account of it would seem to be a fable, were it not related by those that saw it, and were not the events that followed it of so considerable a nature as to deserve such signals; for, before sunsetting, chariots and troops of soldiers in their armor were seen running about among the clouds, and surrounding of cities.

Moreover at the feast, which we call Pentecost, as the priests were going by night into the inner (court of the) temple, as their custom was, to perform their sacred ministrations, they said that, in the first place, they felt a quaking, and heard a great noise, and after that they heard a sound as of a great multitude saying, "Let us remove hence."[40]

Josephus, a Jewish traitor, knew nothing of Christianity, nor did he seem to fathom the ethereal war of the cosmos; thus, there must be a core of truth to the signs. The signs he reported have tremendous import. First, a great light representing the Shekinah glory of God shone around the altar in the Holy of Holies on the ninth hour. According to biblical numerology, nine is the number of judgment. Second, a heifer miraculously gave birth to a lamb. A lamb is a symbol of Jesus, the Lamb of God, whose blood was shed on Passover for the sins of the world. God was clearly telling the priests the sacrificial system

> ### SHEKINAH GLORY
>
> The Shekinah glory comes at Exodus 40:34 and departs at Ezekiel 10:18. The word is not in Scripture but is used later by Jews and Christians to express the visible divine Presence, especially when resting between the cherubim over the mercy seat of the Ark in the Tabernacle.[41]

is no longer effective. Third, the heavy eastern gate opened of its own accord at the sixth hour. Six is the number of man. Symbolically, the Shekinah glory departed leaving Judaism to its own rules and regulations; now the open door to salvation is through the Lamb of God.

Pentecost means fifty and occurs fifty days after Passover. Fifty is comprised of five, the number of grace, and ten the number of fullness. The feast of Pentecost is special to believers because, on this day, Jesus sent the Holy Spirit from Heaven and the Church was born. The signs recorded by Josephus of the shining chariots and soldiers in the sky, and the words, "Let us move hence" at Pentecost, were the departure of the protectorate of Israel, Michael, the archangel, with his army. The words of prophecy were fulfilled: Jerusalem was sacked and the temple burnt by the Roman war machine.

What is even more startling, these signs may have meaning in our own church and times. We know that Jesus is the open door to salvation and believers in Him all over the world await His return accompanied by the possibility of the much-debated "rapture of the Church." Jesus says, in Revelation 3:7–10:

> These are the words of him who is holy and true, who holds the key of David. What he opens no one can shut, and what he shuts no one can open. I know your deeds. See, I have placed before you an open door that no one can shut. I know that you have little strength, yet you have kept my word and have not denied my name. I will make those who are of the synagogue of Satan, who claim to be Jews though they are not, but are liars—I will make them come and fall down at your feet and acknowledge that I have loved you. Since you have kept my command to endure patiently, I will also keep you from the hour of trial that is going to come upon the whole world to test those who live on the earth.

Is it possible that some day, at the time of Pentecost, the Holy Spirit of God will say, "Let us remove hence," and take all Spirit-filled believers home to Heaven? Then would fall the hour of trial upon the whole world, a time of great apostasy and spiritual delusion as people are possessed by demons and appear to have supernatural abilities.

The battle of the cosmos is fought in the heavens, on the Earth and in the hearts and wills of men. This battle may soon merge into the visible realm as Satan seeks to delude the human race that they were not created by God to be of the "something so much more." A magnificent "UFO" may very well land with an ambassador from the council of the galaxies welcoming Earth into a new age. All dissonant voices will be stilled.

NOTES:

[1] 1 Peter 5:8
[2] John 12:31
[3] Matthew 26:41
[4] Romans 7:18–25
[5] Acts 5:1–9
[6] Genesis 4:6–7
[7] Job 1:8
[8] Psalm 82:1
[9] James 1:13–15
[10] Gange, Dr. Robert, *Origins and Destiny*, Word Books, 1986, p. 42
[11] John 12:31; 16:11
[12] 1 John 5:19
[13] 2 Corinthians 4:4
[14] Ephesians 2:2
[15] Matthew 24:24
[16] Luke 21:34–36
[17] Revelation 12:7–9
[18] Isaiah 24:18

[19] Isaiah 24:21

[20] Isaiah 34:4

[21] Isaiah 34:5

[22] Ezekiel 28:14

[23] Isaiah 14:13–14

[24] Matthew 25:41

[25] Hebrews 9:27

[26] Luke 16:19–26

[27] 2 Corinthians 11:14

[28] Rawlings, Maurice S. M.D., *To Hell and Back*, Thomas Nelson Publishers, Nashville, 1993, p. 62

[29] Revelation 19:10

[30] Colt, George Howe, "In Search of Angels," *LIFE*, December 1995, p. 88

[31] Nadya, Labi, "Om a Little Teapot…" *TIME*, February 26, 2001, p. 51

[32] Lockerbie, Bruce, *The Cosmic Center*, Multnomah Press, 1977, p. 98

[33] Isaiah 64:5–6

[34] Ephesians 2:8

[35] Phillips, McCandlish, *The Spirit World*, Victor Books, 1970, p. 123

[36] Hellen, Nicholas, *Sunday Times*, London, England, March 11, 2001

[37] Lambert, Lance, *Israel: A Secret Documentary*, Tyndale House Publishers, 1975, pp.8–29

[38] Lambert, Ibid. p. 27

[39] 2 Maccabees 5:2–4, *Apocryhpha: The Authorized Version*, Oxford University Press, p. 267

[40] Whiston, William, *The Works of Josephus Complete and Unabridged*, "The Wars of the Jews, Book 6, Chapter 5.3," Hendrickson Publishers, p. 742

[41] *Unger's Bible Dictionary*, Moody Press, 1973, p. 1008

The Lion of Judah

eople who believe that God exists and came into this world as the God-man, Jesus Christ, recognize there is a spiritual adversary. Others deny accountability for their actions and/or seek self-satisfying spiritual delusions. If one does not accept the claims of Jesus Christ that He is God and died to redeem our human race, neither will one understand the magnitude of the invisible war of the cosmos and its eternal consequences to our existence.

Lee Strobel, who holds a Master's degree from Yale Law School, examined the extensive evidence for Jesus Christ in his book, *The Case for Christ*. He concludes:

> Resolve that you'll reach a verdict when you've gathered a sufficient amount of information, knowing that you'll never have full resolution of every single issue. You may even want to whisper a prayer to the God who you're not sure exists, asking him to guide you to the truth about him. And through it all, you'll have my sincere encouragement as you continue your spiritual quest.
>
> At the same time, I do feel a strong obligation to urge you to make this a front-burner issue in your life. Don't approach it

casually or flippantly, because there's a lot riding on your conclusion. As Michael Murphy aptly put it, "We ourselves—and not merely the truth claims—are at stake in the investigation." In other words, if my conclusion in the case for Christ is correct, your future and eternity hinge on how you respond to Christ. As Jesus declared, "If you do not believe that I am the one I claim to be, you will indeed die in your sins" (John 8:24).[1]

At this juncture, one might pause and ask: "If God is a God of love and He died to redeem us, why do all the bad things happen? Who is in control?" This question is usually asked from our "poor me" corner of the world. The answer lies in looking at our cosmos from God's perspective. God's love is not a bland permissive love. Very few people around you continue to wait expectedly for someone who does not "love them any more," yet this is what God has been doing throughout the ages. One day God's time of waiting expectedly will be over.

McCandlish Phillips puts God's love into perspective:

> Because He is love, God is consistently intolerant of everything that violates His own intention in creation. God hates evil with a pure and furious hatred because He sees that it is constantly at work to destroy what He has made—at work to destroy man, to destroy society, to destroy nature, to destroy civilization, to destroy harmony, to destroy joy. He does not look upon it as man does, that is, relatively, because He sees it not limitedly but in the whole path of its effective ruination.
>
> The intention of Satan is to make moral, spiritual, and physical chaos and wreckage out of as much of God's creation as he possibly can. Satan enlists man in that attempt, by appealing to his lawless lusts and passions. We can see the effects of that all around us, in the nation, in the world.
>
> Man is infected with the moral disease that God calls sin.

God is not tolerant of human sin because He knows that if it were allowed to go unarrested it would ultimately destroy every- thing in its reach. …God's love is expressed in the creation, but it is supremely expressed in the redemption. God cannot go far- ther in loving man and in dealing with sin than to die for sin.[2]

God could have destroyed His creation—man—at its rebellion. However, He chose to take His wrath upon Himself as the God- man, Jesus Christ. If we cannot comprehend the horror and awfulness of our sinful rebel- lion, then neither will we take to heart the deep redeeming love of God in this cosmic act.

The illusion of the world's religious systems is that there are many ways to God, and after death, all will somehow enter a state of peaceful bliss. In contrast to this, the Old Testament is filled with God's wrath against sin. In the New Testa- ment, Jesus expands upon the consequences of man's self- centered rebellion: there is judgment after death for the things done in life. So decep- tive are Satan's allurements to man's self-seeking will that, without the help of the Holy Spirit, no man would be saved. Jesus states: *"Enter*

SPRING IS COMING

You might laugh at this brief lit- erary interlude. As I sit looking out over patches of snow cover- ing meadow and trees in the glow of a setting sun, and try to contemplate an infinite God's view of the cosmos, my wife is joyfully writing her children's story on Charlie the cricket in Grandma Joy's garden. Charlie is awaiting the warm days of spring when he can sing his song in the sweet smell of clover amongst a rainbow cascade of flowers. In a simple yet pro- found way, we are like Charlie as *"creation waits in eager expecta- tion for the sons of God to be revealed."* The dark winter of the war of the cosmos may soon be over, then all of creation will sing with wondrous joy.

through the narrow gate. For wide is the gate and broad is the road that leads to destruction, and many enter through it. But small is the gate and narrow the road that leads to life, and only a few find it," [3] and, *"No one can come to me unless the Father who sent me draws him, and I will raise him up at the last day."* [4] The book of Revelation, dictated by Jesus to the apostle John, details the fearsome wrath of God on a rebellious world and the joys of the redeemed at being raised up in the last day.

In order to understand God's actions in the cosmos, we need to humbly appreciate that He acts in love with kindness, justice and mercy,[5] we are but creatures of dust and He is God. It is through His deep redeeming love we are to be "of the something more." God is infinite; He is creator and sustainer of all there is—of our space-time world and the dimensions of dimensions of the "spirit world." He states: *"For my thoughts are not your thoughts, neither are your ways my ways.... As the heavens are higher than the earth, so are my ways higher than your ways and my thoughts than your thoughts."* [6] Though at most times we cannot appreciate the sorrows or disasters that befall us, we must trust that "God is good and that His love endures forever," as He works through the complexities of this world to bring His sons and daughters to glory.

WHY DO GOOD AND BAD THINGS HAPPEN?

There are several cosmological premises that must be accepted before one can put order into what seems to be daily chaos on Earth. These are:

1) God created.
2) There was a spiritual rebellion in the cosmos.
3) Mankind joined the rebellion.
4) God implemented the curse of hardship and death.
5) God incarnated Himself as the God-man, Jesus Christ.

6) He died to redeem mankind, and

7) He rose again from the dead as proof that He will again bring order into the cosmos.

Now, what we need to do is to try and put all of the interactions in the cosmos into perspective. There is spiritual strife in the cosmos caused by the divergent will of Lucifer, the rebellious archangel, against the holy will of God. On Earth there are billions of individuals who think they shall be "as gods" and will either continue their alignment with Satan or repent and let Jesus be the God of their lives. At the same time, the battle of the ethereal takes place around, in and through the spiritual bodies of men.

We live after the crossroads of Calvary. Jesus, the God-man, the Lion of Judah, sits at the right hand of the Father in Heaven interceding for believers while Satan accuses us before the Father. At the same time, we can have a personal relationship with Jesus because He is omnipresent as God the Father, and He indwells believers since their bodies are temples of the Holy Spirit. Finally, there are calamities in the natural world because of the law of increasing entropy (disorder), in other words, things are wearing out.

In the physical realm, God says He is the One who: *"created the heavens and stretched them out, who spread out the earth and all that comes out of it, who gives breath to its people, and life to those who walk on it."* [7]

"He sits enthroned above the circle of the earth and its people are like grasshoppers." [8]

"All men are like grass and all their glory is like the flowers of the field. The grass withers and the flowers fall, because the breath of the LORD blows on them." [9]

"I am the LORD, and there is no other. I form the light and create darkness, I bring prosperity and create disaster." [10]

God is saying that adversity or calamity come from the effects of the law of entropy and are the fruits of spiritual rebellion against

Him. Therefore, through good and evil, God is the creator and sustainer of all there is.

HAVE HOPE—GOD HAS A PLAN

The difficulty we have, from our "poor me" perspective, is that the philosophy of evolution has so degraded our concepts of who we are, we have difficulty overcoming our feelings of hopelessness and despair. Hope becomes a foundationless abstract, yet, in the chaos of the war of the cosmos, we know we have meaning because we are made in the image of God who died to redeem us.

The Bible is very clear that we have cosmological significance in this space-time world. It is written in the Psalms: *"For you created my inmost being; you knit me together in my mother's womb. I praise you because I am fearfully and wonderfully made; your works are wonderful, I know that full well. All the days ordained for me were written in your book before one of them came to be."* [11] However, in our self-taking wills, we rebel against our creator. God says, *"Woe to him who quarrels with his Maker, to him who is but a potsherd amongst the potsherds on the ground. Does the clay say to the potter, 'What are your making?'"* [12]

There is no doubt, based on the experience of Job, in the war of the cosmos God has foretold Satan He will pluck certain people from his evil grasp. This is sometimes why our lives can have conflict and disaster similar to Job. Along this line of thought, the great evangelist, Paul, writes in the book of Romans: *"Does not the potter have the right to make out of the same lump of clay some pottery for noble purposes and some for common use? What if God, choosing to show his wrath and make his power known, bore with great patience the object of his wrath—prepared for destruction? What if he did this to make the riches of his glory known to the objects of his mercy, whom he prepared in advance for glory—even us, whom he also called, not only from the Jews but also from the Gentiles?"* [13]

THE LAW OF RETRIBUTION

Just as physical laws govern the physical world, the moral laws of God, codified in the Ten Commandments, govern the spiritual realm of sentient beings. To jump off a cliff without a safety devise is to ignore the physical law of gravity; to violate one of the Ten Commandments is to commit a spiritual felony. Jesus says of God the Father's impartial actions in the physical world:, *"He causes the sun to rise on the evil and the good, and sends rain on the righteous and the unrighteous."* [14] With respect to the spiritual, Jesus states: *"So in everything, do to others what you would have them do to you, for this sums up the Law and the Prophets."* [15] Jesus illustrates His point further: *"Be merciful, just as your Father is merciful. Do not judge, and you will not be judged. Do not condemn, and you will not be condemned. Forgive, and you will be forgiven. Give and it will be given unto you."* [16] This is God's spiritual law of retribution.

The complexities of our lives are wrapped up in this spiritual law of retribution as God works in His "just ways" to bring members of the rebellion into the kingdom of light. God states: *"It is mine to avenge; I will repay. In due time their foot will slip; their day of disaster is near and their doom rushes upon them."* [17] Likewise, even though it is not readily apparent, we are informed: *"that in all things God works for the good of those who love him, who have been called according to his purpose."* [18]

Man's self-seeking nature brings cultural and religious strife on an individual and national basis. Superimposed on these hidden spiritual dynamics are the natural physical laws. The sun provides heat, light and gravitational-electromagnetic energy to the Earth, moon and solar system. Climatic conditions can vary rapidly around the world. Earth shudders as it slowly cools and shrinks causing tectonic plates to shift as they ride plumes of molten lava deep within its core. The law of entropy is active biologically as it degrades the genetic viability of the genome with destructive mutations which is reflected in physical abnormalities and diseases. Excessive habitat, resource and environmental abuses are bringing disparities and emotional stresses. Societies are in a moral abyss as they reap the empty rewards of the philosophy of evolution, the survival of the fittest. The earth groans with earthquakes; bridges and buildings collapse, and people are killed. The scientifically enlightened may cry out in meaningless despair, "Oh God, why?" while the spiritually enslaved beat themselves and offer sacrifices to appease the gods. Amazingly, a few Christians also fall into the delusion that it is a cosmological punishment. Similar to the Twin Towers calamity in New York, but in a microcosmic way, when a tower fell on eighteen people in the town of Siloam, Jesus asked the religious leaders a rhetorical question: *"Do you think they were more guilty than all the others living in Jerusalem?"* He then answered: *"I tell you, no! But unless you repent, you too will all perish."* [19] His meaning is clear: natural disasters and contrived evils can take your life, but unless you repent of your sins while you have the opportunity, you will perish in the flames of Hell.

As the physical and spiritual dynamics are interwoven each day, we know that *"God is a righteous judge, a God who expresses his wrath every day."* [20] In the sense of God's daily wrath, He is making sure we bear the consequences for the actions of our selfish wills according to His moral law of retribution. The Scriptures declare: *"He who is pregnant with evil and conceives trouble gives birth to disillusionment. He who digs a hole and scoops it out falls into the pit he has made. The trouble he causes recoils on himself; his violence comes down on his own head."* [21]

Paul of Tarsus, who wrote the book of Romans, was an expert in Judaism and a missionary servant of Jesus Christ to the Gentile nations. He wrote: *"The wrath of God is being revealed from heaven against all the godlessness and wickedness of men who suppress the truth by wickedness, since what may be known about God is plain to them, because God has made it plain to them. For since the creation of the* world God's invisible qualities—his eternal power and divine nature—have been clearly seen, being understood from what has been made, so that men are without excuse."[22]

Paul goes on to describe what happens to people who reject the knowledge of God: "Furthermore, since they did not think it worthy to retain the knowledge of God, he gave them over to a depraved mind, to do what ought not to be done. They have become filled with every kind of wickedness, evil, greed and depravity. They are full of envy, murder, strife, deceit and malice. They are gossips, slanderers, God-haters, insolent, arrogant and boastful; they invent ways of doing evil; they disobey their parents; they are senseless, faithless, heartless, ruthless. Although they know God's righteous decrees that those who do such things deserve death, they not only continue to do these very things but also approve of those who practice them."[23]

The battle of the cosmos begins with the will of each of our hearts. God created each one of us with a plan in mind though it may never come to be due to circumstances of our free will decisions. God has said: "For I know the plans I have for you... plans to prosper you and not to harm you, plans to give you hope and a future. Then you will call upon me, and I will listen to you. You will seek me and find me when you seek me with all you heart. I will be found by you,"[24] and: "My eyes will be on the faithful in the land, that they may dwell with me; he whose walk is blameless will minister to me."[25]

Yet our walk is not blameless, so how can God love us? Therein is the mystery of salvation: "We love because He first loved us."[26]

King David of Israel, so long ago, knew the anguish of sin because he committed adultery with one of his chief soldier's beautiful young wife, and then manipulated her husband into battle so that he was killed. In deep remorse and repentance, David prayed to the Lord and later penned these words for our encouragement: "The LORD is compassionate and gracious, slow to anger, abounding in love. He will not always accuse, nor will he harbor his anger forever;

he does not treat us as our sins deserve or repay us according to our iniquities. For as high as the heavens are above the earth, so great is his love for those who fear him; as far as the east is from the west, so far has he removed our transgressions from us. As a father has compassion on his children, so the Lord has compassion on those who fear him." [27]

The law of retribution is both national and individual. God said to Abram: *"I will make you into a great nation and I will bless you; I will make your name great, and you will be a blessing. I will bless those who bless you, and whoever curses you I will curse; and all peoples on earth will be blessed through you."* [28] Later, God came to Abram and renamed him Abraham ("father of many"): *"No longer will you be called Abram; your name will be Abraham for I have made you a father of many nations. I will make you fruitful; I will make nations of you, and kings will come from you."* [29] God, through Moses, amplified this law of retribution in Deuteronomy 27 and 28 as the blessings and cursings which the people later pronounced at Mount Gerizim, the Mount of Blessings, and Mount Ebal, the Mount of Curses.

The cursings and the blessings begin with the individual. If the individual follows God's moral laws, blessings come individually and, subsequently, to the nation. Therefore, actions of individuals lead to growth or disintegration of their nation. In accordance with God's pronouncement to Abraham, Jews over the centuries, as they moved from nation to nation, have been a rock of testing to various people groups. Where they were hated and persecuted, curses fell and/or will fall upon those nations. Canada and the United States, to date, have been blessed culturally, scientifically and economically due to their treatment of the Jewish people and Israel.

Many scholars who study biblical prophecy consider Europe to be home of the future New World Order lead by a man with supernatural talents. The Bible is clear that Russia and Europe will suffer a great holocaust under the wrath of God. Over the centuries, ethnic groups in these areas have had pogroms against the Jews; the 1940s holocaust drove them to seek a homeland. Britain, under its Palestine mandate, maintained a Mediterranean blockade with ruthless internment of the refugees on Cyprus and planned for their forcible return to the refugee camps in Europe,[30] some of which were the extermination centers of Germany holding over 2 million European Jewish survivors. The very nations where these people had lived rejected them. Even Canada and the United States allowed only limited migration; thus, the nation Israel was born in great travail on May 15, 1948.

Even as the Arab nations continue to seek Israel's demise, there are increasing undercurrents of hostility amongst the European countries. Lance Lambert reports what happened openly in the 1973 Yom Kippur war:

> The American airlift did not begin until the tenth day of the war. Each plane carried 100 tons of ammunition, tanks, and weapons. The Israeli army was actually running out of ammunition by the time the airlift began. The delay was almost completely caused by the refusal of America's so-called allies, particularly Britain, to grant facilities to the United States for refueling her planes. Britain was so bitter about the airlift that she persuaded her NATO allies to fight it. Germany refused to allow the United States to take weapons from her bases on German soil and put them on Israeli ships in Bremen and Hamburg. Finally Portugal opened up the Azores to United States transport planes, and Israel was saved. Planes then came in almost nose to tail. There was no time to lose. If they had not come, Israel would have been totally lost.[31]

"Let Israel say—if the LORD had not been on our side when men attacked us, when their anger flared against us, they would have swallowed us alive; the flood would have engulfed us, the torrent would

85

have swept over us, the raging waters would have swept us away. Praise be to the Lord, who has not let us be torn by their teeth. "[32] This conflict is not going to magically disappear. The 21st century has already been marred by violence as the PLO manipulates world sympathy with rocks, bullets, mortar fire and martyr homicide bombers resulting in Israel's military incursion into Palestine territory. No nation, least of all the United States, would stand for this type of irrational violence within its borders. With the 2001 terrorist actions against the World Trade Towers in New York and the call for a coalition against terrorists and countries that harbor them, this war, and the Israel-PLO conflict, will intensify.

Unfortunately, this is the ongoing war of the cosmos. Dave Hunt succinctly explains:

> Why should there be such hatred against Israel and anyone Jewish? The answer to that question unlocks the whole puzzle of Bible prophecy and the destiny of nations. All of God's promises are inextricably intertwined with Israel's destiny. Destroy Israel and you have discredited the God of Israel and the Bible. The Messiah had to be born of King David's family, then rejected and crucified by the house of Israel. It was to Jerusalem that the resurrected Savior would return to rescue the Israelis, now back in their homeland and besieged by the armies of the world. Had Satan been able to destroy Israel in time, there would have been no Messiah (He had to come before the temple in Jerusalem was destroyed).
>
> If Hitler, or anyone else before or since, could destroy world Jewry, there would be no Israel, no seed of Jacob to return to their land, as promised. Without Israel as a nation today, the God of Abraham, Isaac, and Jacob—the God of the Bible—was dead indeed. That is how important Israel is. **Conversely, for those who are willing to face the facts, the very existence of Israel today proves the existence of her God.*** Moreover, He has

greater proof yet to demonstrate in Israel, so that at least all the nations, the unbelieving Israelis included, will know for certain that the God of Israel is the God of history written in advance [*emphasis mine].[33]

God says of the nation Israel: *"You are my witnesses... that I am God."* [34] Prophecy is history written in advance to prove in all the events that happen in the world, the infinite God creator of all the Heavens and the Earth is in control. He is a just God and holds the actions of individuals and nations in the balance scales of judgment, just as Sodom and Gomorrah were destroyed by fire and brimstone for their wickedness.[35]

God also told Abraham that the wickedness of the Amorites, the people that lived in Canaan, had to yet reach its full measure before judgment.[37] This happened some 400 years later with the return of the Israelites under the leadership of Joshua. Eventually, when Israel went "whoring" after false gods, the Medes and Persians, in turn, defeated the Babylonians destroyed them as a nation—so it goes through history.

God is patient. Satan is already under sentence of judgment for his role in the great cosmic rebellion, yet he is still free. God measures the actions of nations; He states: *"The day of the Lord is near for all nations. As you have done, it will be done to you; your deeds will return upon your own head."* [38]

The plains of Megiddo in Israel become the focus point

CANAANITES

The Amorites were part of a group of peoples living in the Middle East around Israel and Jordan several thousand years ago. Archaeologists refer to them as Canaanites. They believed human and animal sacrifices had magical powers which brought the worshipper into sympathy and rhythm with the physical world. Joshua led the Israelites back into *the land* around 1400 BC.[36]

for all the nations of the world as they combine to annihilate Israel in the great battle of Armageddon. The prophet Joel has recorded this future scene for us: *"'Come, trample the grapes, for the winepress is full and the vats overflow—so great is their wickedness!' Multitudes, multitudes in the valley of decision! For the day of the LORD is near in the valley of decision. The sun and moon will be darkened, and the stars no longer shine. The LORD will roar from Zion and thunder from Jerusalem; the earth and the sky will tremble. But the LORD will be a refuge for his people, a stronghold for the people of Israel."* [39]

Trouble boils in the world and in our lives just as quickly as a tornado can manifest itself on a peaceful countryside. Yet God says to our fearful hearts: *"Strengthen the feeble hands, steady the knees that give way; say to those with fearful hearts, 'Be strong, do not fear; your God will come with vengeance; with divine retribution to save you.'"* [42]

TRUST AND FAITH IN GOD

Though we might not understand complexities woven into each day, we are assured: *"Blessed are all who fear the LORD, who walk in his ways. You will eat the fruit of your labor; blessings and prosperity will be yours."* [43] Yet we have to be careful a belief in God is not one that expects wealth, health and prosperity as a normal course of one's faith. In the difficulties that assail us, God works in all circumstances in justice, love, mercy and goodness to bring about prosperity; however, with these come persecutions. [44]

Faith that "God is good and His love endures forever" is the difference between the righteous and the unrighteous. God says: *"The righteous will live by his faith,"* and of the unrighteous: *"See he is puffed up; his desires are not upright… indeed, wine betrays him; he is arrogant and never at rest. Because he is as greedy as the grave and like death is never satisfied."* [45] What then, is the key to God's blessings? The prophet Isaiah tells us the Lord: *"will be the sure foundation for your times, a rich store of salvation and wisdom and knowl-*

TIME

Time seems to be flowing slowly like a gentle river, yet the rapids and waterfalls lie ahead. Anti-Semitism is on the rise. Christians are being persecuted and martyred around the world. The scale of wickedness is filling up rapidly; maybe all too soon the masters of enlightenment will be revealed as they are driven from the heavens, and the wrath of God will explode upon this rebellious planet. Russia and an alignment of Arab nations will attack Israel and be destroyed. Fire, likely representing nuclear warfare, will ensue upon Russia and the coastlands (possibly America?).[40] Europe, likely the kingdom of the super-ruler, will suffer intensely. The Bible records, *"The fifth angel poured out his bowl on the throne of the beast, and his kingdom was plunged into darkness. Men gnawed their tongues in agony and cursed the God of heaven because of their pains and their sores, but they refused to repent of what they had done."*[41]

edge; the fear of the LORD *is the key to this treasure."* [46] The word "fear" means a reverent trust in God's undertakings.[47]

Matthew, a disciple of Jesus, records Jesus's teachings on worldly worries: *"Therefore I tell you, do not worry about your life, what you will eat or drink; or about your body, what you will wear. Is not life more important than food, and the body more important than clothes? Look at the birds of the air; they do not sow or reap or store away in barns, and yet your heavenly Father feeds them. Are you not much more valuable than they? Who of you by worrying can add a single hour to his life? And why do you worry about clothes? See how the lilies of the field grow. They do not labor or spin. Yet I tell you that not even Solomon in all his splendor was dressed like one of these. If that is how God clothes the grass of the field, which is here today and tomorrow is thrown into the fire, will he not much more clothe you, O you of little faith? So do not worry, saying, 'What shall we eat?' or 'What shall we drink?' or 'What shall we wear?' For the pagans run after all these things, and your heavenly Father knows that you need them. But seek first his kingdom and his righteousness, and all these things will be given to you as well. Therefore do not worry about tomorrow, for tomorrow will worry about itself. Each day has enough trouble of its own."* [48]

In contrast to the fear (reverent trust) of the Lord, the religious systems of the world set up rules and regulations that often detract from the faith-provisions of the kingdom of God. In Luke 11, Jesus chastises the Pharisees (religious socialites) and the experts in Judaic law (religious leaders) because they: *"have taken away the key to knowledge. You yourselves have not entered, and have hindered those who were entering"* (v.52). In same way, in our own era, scientific humanists and followers of religious systems are blind to the concept of God as creator-sustainer of the universe. The former negate Him in favor of evolution, the latter consign Him, or their gods, to their self-serving needs as a cosmic hotel bell boy. A woman in a liberal Catholic country placed her patron saint so that he was looking into a corner like a disobedient child because he had failed to help her find her keys. [49]

MIRACLES AND SYNCHRONICITY

Miracles are, by definition, wonders or events of such statistically low probability they either appear to be supernatural or are supernatural. They are of two types: miracles of design and miracles of deception. A miraculous recovery by prayer to God from a terminal illness is a miracle of design. These are much debated and go largely unnoticed. The magic of witchcraft is an appeal to the spirit world for self-satisfying power and is a miracle of deception. Reverent trust in the Lord is not a self-seeking desire for spiritual power. One does not stand naked in a field with hands raised crying out, "Clothe me like this lily, oh Lord!" and expect God, like Cinderella's fairy godmother, to mystically create attire.

In our busy world, we seem to have no time for miracles, nor do we willingly admit a statistically unique event is one when it happens. Yet, if God is active in our cosmos, miracles (of design and not those of deception) are a natural consequence of His sustaining the universe. To a Christian, life is a miracle; to an evolutionist, we exist because luck overcame statistical probability. To a Christian, life has hope because God, miracle of all miracles, instituted new spiritual-physical laws in that Jesus Christ was resurrected from the dead, whereas an evolutionist can only hope statistical probability will not overcome "luck" in some sort of cosmic annihilation.

If we think carefully about a miracle in our physical space-time world, it is, in its simplest form, the direction of divine intelligent thought upon the movement of random energy. Since God is the creator-sustainer of all there is, there should be a flow of intelligent thought and synchronicity in the development of events in our lives.

Most people have interesting events to relate whether it is about synchronicity or miracles. A radio announcer friend tells of the time he was doing interviews at a scenic lookout in the Okanagan region of British Columbia, Canada, questioning where people were from and to where were they traveling. He had just interviewed a man from England who said he was on his way to Australia to surprise his sister. Just as they finished the interview, a car pulled into the lookout area and out of it stepped the sister who was visiting beautiful British Columbia—talk about surprise!

Several years ago, when disaster wreaked havoc on my life, I was commuting weekly from Vancouver, on the Pacific Ocean, over the Coast Range Mountains to my hometown of Vernon in the sunny Okanagan. It is a distance of some 300 miles. My almost-twenty-year-old Ford Country Squire station wagon usually hummed along quietly in cruise control. Suddenly the alternator light went on which meant it was no longer working. I knew the battery would, sooner or later, go dead. I was still on the delta farmlands with 200 miles to go but with only a few dollars and no credit cards.

Life is full of calculated choices, and I am sure God smiled at the one I was about to make, for what He did was statistically unique. Fortunately, it was early summer and I knew the battery was in good condition. Turning off all electrical power, I decided to see if could at least make it into the Okanagan area where either I could find a real garage with a battery charger or call my family to come and help me. The smell of the trees and alpine flowers in the high country almost made me forget my predicament as I thanked the Lord for His goodness.

SYNCHRONICITY

Synchronicity can be described as the area of common interest surrounding our lives such as family, friends and associates. It is like concentric ripples spreading outward from a pebble dropped into a flat pond. In a sense, a harsh gust of wind that disturbs the pond's symmetry is like the malevolent force of Satan seeking to destroy our lives. This is a simple explanation of why amazingly coincidental events happen to us, both to the righteous and the unrighteous. God is just; however, the righteous person gives glory to God, and the unrighteous calls it a statistical coincidence.

One hundred miles rolled by; soon it was 150. Now I was in the Okanagan, passing through Kelowna, praying, "Lord, I need a real gas station," but all were closed or were self-serve stations with only pop and candy. At least I was getting closer. Then the trusty old Ford hiccuped, and I knew it was about to quit. As I passed through a stoplight, the engine died. Quickly, I put it into neutral and fought the dead power steering as I coasted into a small Turbo gas station on my immediate right. Two people, a man and a woman, were standing just in front of the car as it slowly stopped, now off of the road. Amazed, I looked and could not believe my eyes: the man was holding the connections for one of those large battery chargers. All he would have to do is open the engine hood and hook them up. I explained my predicament and said I had been praying for a real gas station. "Well," said the woman, "I always tell people we serve gas and not them slurpees."

Was God in control? Was it a miracle? My inner response was that even though my life was in turmoil God wanted me to know He was in control—down to the smallest detail.

God plans ahead in time and space; if the event seems improbable enough, we may call it a miracle. Whatever you want to call it, He is doing miracles every day. The answer to our initial question—why do bad things happen?—is that life is an ongoing set of interconnected complexities within our physical-spiritual existence. From God's perspective, He created man with a free will and man rebelled; therefore, all of mankind is lost. Instead of destroying mankind in the Garden of Eden, He instituted physical laws of hardships and the spiritual act of retribution. His desire is that we, of our own free will, admit our rebellion and, by His grace and mercy, return to Him.

Few people who are prosperous and at peace seek God. The pride of self-prosperity stands in opposition to humility and forgiveness. It is the turmoil in our spiritual and physical being that pushes us to seek the "something more" to our lives, to seek the salvation provided by Jesus Christ.

Jesus, just before His death by crucifixion and later resurrection, met with His disciples and assured them: *"I have told you these things, so that in me you may have peace. In this world you will have trouble. But take heart! I have overcome the world."* [50]

NOTES:

[1] Strobel, Lee, *The Case for Christ*, Zondervan Publishing House, 1998, p. 366

2 Phillips, McCandlish, *The Spirit World*, Victor Books, 1973, p. 68

3 Matthew 7:13–14

4 John 6:44

5 Jeremiah 9:24

6 Isaiah 55:8

7 Isaiah 42:5

8 Isaiah 40:22

9 Isaiah 40:6–7

10 Isaiah 45:6–7

11 Psalm 139:13–14, 16

12 Isaiah 45:9

13 Romans 9:21–24

14 Matthew 5:45

15 Matthew 7:12

16 Luke 6:36–38

17 Deuteronomy 32:35

18 Romans 8:28

19 Luke 13:4–5

20 Psalm 7:11

21 Psalm 7:14–16

22 Romans 1:18–20

23 Romans 1:28–32

24 Jeremiah 29:11–13

25 Psalm 101:6

26 1 John 4:19

27 Psalm 103:8–13

28 Genesis 12:2–3

29 Genesis 17:5–6

30 Hunt, Dave, *Peace Prosperity and the Coming Holocaust*, Harvest House Publishers, 1983, pp. 225-228

[31] Lambert, Lance, *Israel: A Secret Documentary*, Tyndale House Publishers, Wheaton, Illinois, 1975, p. 17

[32] Psalm 124:1–6

[33] Hunt, Ibid. p. 228

[34] Isaiah 43:12

[35] Genesis 19

[36] Packer-Tenny-White, *The World of the Old Testament*, Thomas Nelson Publishers, 1982, pp. 46, 86, 107

[37] Genesis 15:16

[38] Obadiah 15

[39] Joel 3:13–16

[40] Ezekiel 38 and 39

[41] Revelation 10:16

[42] Isaiah 35:3–4

[43] Psalm 128:1–2

[44] Mark 10:30

[45] Habakkuk 2:4–5

[46] Isaiah 33:6

[47] *Unger's Bible Dictionary*, Moody Press, 1973, p. 348

[48] Matthew 6:25–34

[49] Peters, Dan, Missionary to Belgium, personal communication

[50] John 16:33

Twisted Arts and Science

The reverberant noise was somewhere between the smashing of glass and the amplified crunching of cornflakes, mixed with jubilant jumping and yelling. As each CD of rap, metal and rock music hit the pile on the floor, the new-millennium teenagers stomped. Hundreds of dollars worth of CDs, including a complete set of Metallica, lay smashed on the floor. Why would a teenager deliberately destroy his valuable music collection?

Dustin,[1] a graduating grade twelve student, sits across from me in a little coffee shop booth with soft cushion seats. Casual sports clothes attire his solid football-player style body. A backpack lies on the seat beside him; the curved peak of his baseball cap, which is pulled tightly down on his head, forms an intense semicircle just above the bridge of his nose. His dark eyes look intently at me through round glasses. "Why," I ask, "did you smash those CDs?"

His answer is simple and straightforward. "I couldn't do it by myself," he states quietly. "Since I became a believer in Jesus

Christ and accepted Him into my life, my life has changed." Pausing, deep in thought, he reflects on how much of a different person he has become. As I watch his face, the image of him standing with Tim, the youth pastor, in the baptismal tank reading his testimony is clear in my mind's eye. Dustin is a teenager of the make-it-happen '90s, a teenager of the spiked, colored hair, hanging clothes, loud incomprehensible screeching music and adult-indifferent generation. A generation, if you really took time to get to know them, of deep feelings caught in a cascade of cross-cultural ideologies and capitalistic marketing glamour; a generation living out the fruits of the '60s, '70s and '80s—a deliberate, malevolent, spiritually controlled cosmic agenda.

Dustin continues: "I couldn't break them myself; I tried. There is some great music, but the content is wrong."

"What do you mean?"

"The beat is great, but Christian music can also have a great beat. The content is not right. It's all sex, drugs, violence, hate, 'stuff authority' and foul-mouthed language. It gets to you inside. I felt rebellious and gloomy. I didn't want to go to school," he says. "Sometimes after a party, when I was walking home drunk or stoned, I would wonder what I was doing. I found myself living for the next time—always the next time. Maybe it would be better."

As he pauses to take a drink of root beer, my mind wanders back to the olden days of the late '50s, early '60s, the teen dances—"sock hops" with bunny hops and twist—where booze was the main problem, throbbing with rock and roll "you-love-me-I-love-you" music. Marijuana, LSD and "snow" were largely a problem of the larger more-sophisticated American and Canadian cities. Yet sometimes, when a soft scented sparkly-eyed little honey twirled in a hot jive, finger to finger, my nasty intellect would clobber my emotions with, "Is this all there is, just one beat after another?"

Reflecting back to that era, it is apparent that the Beatles and Rolling Stones were symptomatic of a spiritual dissonance that began in the early '60s with the "God is dead" generation.

"I love rap," Dustin continues, "but it and heavy metal made me feel angry and aggressive. The whole message was that it was okay to do drugs and have free sex—after all, everyone is doing it. The artists would give special thanks to fellow stoned musicians. You know, 'keep doing it, there is no limit.'" Dustin leans back in his seat and wraps his strong hands around his root-beer glass. He smiles, more relaxed as he ponders his thoughts. "The whole thing is about rebellion; defying your parents and authority, you know, stuff the cops. I used to think the dealers were cool, sort of family. They had nice cars and clothes as they hung around the school."

As he pauses, I ask, " What about the music videos?"

His response is quick. "Sex, violence, drugs and 'hate the cops.' The drugs and visual images were a turn-on. Naked girls dancing—you know, you could be doing it. The images were never quite finished; the heavy emotional urges filled in the visual." He hesitates, then comments, "It was all so empty. The next time never led to a bigger next time, only to more drugs to fill the emptiness until I was no longer sure of who I was any more."

I ask, "What would be a summary statement of how your generation thinks?"

"Do it my way or the highway; you stay out of my way and I out of yours; if you cross me, I will beat you senseless," he replies. "Matter of fact, several days ago a couple of Christian friends and I were listening to Christian rock as we drove and were waving our arms and having a great time. Some guys in a nearby car thought that the way we were waving our hands gave the 'you suck' symbol and followed us to the beach." He laughed as he finished. "That took some sorting out!"

"Okay, now how did you get to become a Christian?"

Dustin leans forward and smiles. "My cousin asked me to a church weekend young people's retreat, and, to my surprise, I said yes. Next thing I know, I am dancing to the sound of Christian rock with "Open the Eyes of My Heart" pounding into my head. Here is a whole bunch of teens having fun and laughing. I could be myself. The music and thoughts were of happiness and joy."

"Then what happened?"

"After that weekend, I got to know more of this group of kids my own age who were alive with no drugs, booze or sex and no feelings of anger or aggression. I knew deep inside I wanted to find out more, and eventually Pastor Tim showed me how to ask Jesus Christ for forgiveness and ask Him into my life."

"So has it been easy?" I ask.

"No, the hard part was shaking the drugs and vivid sexual imagery, but inside I felt a peace, a strength to commit to this new beginning. That's why I had my friends help me smash my collection. The beat is great, but the words are wrong. Now I start my day with some great Christian rock—with good words and meaning—and feel so much better. Life is not empty and gloomy."[1]

As I drop Dustin off at the church parking lot for Friday night young people's action, his new group of friends comes and drags him into their scene. The sound of laughter echoes in my ears as I drive away thinking, "Dustin, you have found the beginning of the something more, of the so much more."

THE TERMS OF THE REBELLION

Does music really leave a "self-image imprint" on a generation? Scott Thompson of the '90s generation, a former member of the comedy troupe Kids in the Hall, had his gig abruptly terminated while performing at a gala dinner for the inaugural Griffin Poetry Prize. The dinner was attended by a number of Canada's top literary figures. "Mr. Thompson performed a raunchy skit full of references to sex acts and told explicit jokes," said the reports. "He also wagged a sex toy in the face of" a respected lady author. Scott Thompson commented, "Basically it's about being an animal; bodily fluids are not obscene, in my mind. I guess the audience didn't have a sense of humour."[2]

Richard Lacayo looks at rock music of the Generation Ys for *TIME*. He writes:

> All the same, as a means to reach kids, rock is more complicated than pets and baseball. It has never been completely domesticated by age and commercial calculation. One way that rock bands keep their distance from respectability these days is by shouting "F___" a few dozen times on every album. (Or even "I wanna (*) ___ you like an animal," as Trent Reznor famously offered on one of his Nine Inch Nails albums.) Rock is still tied up with sex and drugs, and it's a supremely subtle parent who can share all kinds of music with her kids without seeming to endorse the troubling stuff.[3]

Looking back, it is apparent the rock beat did, and still does, make one feel youthfully alive and was a break from the creamy crooner traditions that dominated the '40s and '50s. From my older perspective, having lived through this rift, it was the status quo, materially conscious, emotionally insecure parents who suffered the cultural shock. Many parents enjoyed the music, and most of their teens slipped through the great transition wondering what the fuss was all about. It seems the beat and the screaming teenies, from the insecure-parent viewpoint, was the precipitation of rebellion. From a teenager's viewpoint, the complexities of their hormone changes, self-awareness and the desire to be alive left them feeling misunderstood and was also interpreted as rebellion.

The subversive spiritual forces of the Legions of Doom quickly supplied the terms of the rebellion. In this sense, after the early '60s, the subtle sex and drug undertones in the music became descriptive, eventually progressing to violent rebellion against authority and to the use of coarse language. Some Christian teenagers suffered under the same disillusionment as their hypocritical parents, in their protective religious straightjackets, blindly condemned "rock" as the devil's music yet worshiped the almighty dollar. Thus, rock music became the medium of the misunderstood baby boomer flower children.

Baby boomer parents have a lot more in common with their children than their parents had with them. Richard Lacayo comments, "A lot of baby boomers have figured out that it's a short trip from the Pink Floyd they once loved to the Radiohead their kids now love." Teenagers and parents are always going to misunderstand each other more or less; it is the nature of growing up. Every teenage generation will have its subcultures and terminology as they relate to each other in the transition from youth to adulthood. Music opens doors of communication for parents taking time to relate to their children and their musical interests. Mr. Lacayo writes about a female executive and her two daughters:

> Her daughters Nnyla, 23, and Rayna, 13 love some kinds of rap. So does she. And the parts she doesn't love—the trash talk, the relentless treatment of women as nothing more than walking booties—give her a chance to discuss with her daughters just why she doesn't love them. "We discuss things openly about sex and relationships... What's tacky and what's not tacky. Sometimes the kids are more embarrassed by things they see in music videos than I am."[4]

This discussion is not about being critical of musicians or teenage subcultures. Teenagers only exist in affluent societies of the world. Poor areas of the world have children and adults—adults being those over the age of fourteen. When it comes to music, whatever the age, whether one loves melody, jazz, blues, rock, rap, country or any other beat, music reflects the yearnings of the soul. The question becomes "is there a subliminal content that is psychologically preparing our society for something?" The beat emphasizes the dynamic reality of the musical content. What is the spiritual content of the throbbing rhythm in a body-packed sensually filled mosh pit? What is the spiritual content of the lively beat in a church congregation clapping their hands and praising Jesus?

In one sense, the misunderstood baby boomer generation of parents, and even their children as parents, have failed their modern teenagers. Where can teenagers go to be themselves, to rap and have fun? What can they do? The commercial focus is on violent video games, on music videos and movies with sex, drugs, violence and rebellion. Is this all there is to growing up? Is it all one big circle of life with no meaning? No wonder there is despair. No wonder there is a seeking of the transcendental; maybe humans are not just animals, maybe there is a possibility we are "of the something more." Nevertheless, in the battle of the cosmos, which drummer will we dance to?

THE EVOLUTION OF ART

"I turned and there were the bison, three feet from my eyes. 'Oh my God,' I exclaimed. What a moment what an impact. I could not believe my eyes. The bison are incredibly beautiful incredibly powerful and immensely full of Religious Purpose," writes John Robinson.[6] Hidden deep in the Tuc D'Audoubert cavern in France are two carefully sculptured bison measuring two feet by eighteen inches by four inches thick—art from 15,000 years ago. The artist

CAVE ART NOT RARE

Randall White, York University anthropologist, points out that more than 200 late Stone Age caves bearing wall paintings and engravings have been found. Since the find of Lascaux in 1940, an average of one a year has been discovered.[5]

left the bison leaning up against a small rock protrusion, one behind the other. Mr. Robinson has assumed they represent an ancient fertility rite. Writes Sharon Begley for *Newsweek*:

> The Grotte Chauvet is one of hundreds of natural caverns cut into the pale limestone cliffs that form the Ardeche Gorge (in France). But it is unique. Its stone etchings and 416 paintings are, at 32,000 years, the oldest cave art known to science. The find consists of mural after mural of bold lions, leaping horses, pensive owls and charging rhinoceroses that together make up a veritable Louvre of Paleolithic art.... A string of three chambers, 1,700 feet long, as well as one connecting gallery and three vestibules, are all covered with masterworks breathtaking in their use of perspective (as in overlapping mammoths) and shading, techniques that were supposedly not invented until millenniums later. And eons before Seurat got the idea, Stone Age artists had invented pointillism: one animal, probably a bison, is composed of nothing but red dots.[7]

These magnificent finds certainly indicate *Homo sapiens* were capable of sophisticated art well into antiquity which has upset modern evolutionary concepts of cavemen. Now enthralled scientists are studying every aspect of the cave art for "spiritual" content, when maybe the artist, or progression of artists, were naturalists like many artists of today and just wanted to depict life around them without having them ruined. Archaeologists were surprised to see the sophistication of cave art since they based their concepts on the philosophy of evolution by which cave art should have gotten progressively complex. In contrast, the Bible describes early man as having musical instruments and knowledge of metallurgy[8].

Certainly, art through the millennia has reflected religious and philosophical beliefs of human culture and yet, at times, may only image segments of an ethnic group or the artist's personal concepts.

Art galleries of the Western world contain both natural (general view rating) to sexually explicit works. Many societies, over the centuries, have had sexually explicit fertility figurines and artwork as part of their cultural settings. The difference between these cultures and those that follow the principles of the Judean-Christian God is that there are no moral absolutes against which to judge art.

Therefore, this discussion is not about how art (or music) has changed with various cultures through the ages, but about how it has shifted in Western civilization against the moral principles of Jehovah-God. It is only against this moral basis that we can judge the progression of the war of the cosmos into our 21st century.

The 20th century was remarkable for many technical accomplishments, one of which was the ability for self-visualization through sound and film tracks. Henceforth, art, just like science, has evolved. Art is communication through skilled human accomplishment and can be thought of as static or dynamic. In previous centuries, sculpture, paintings and literature were the principle form of static art, whereas music, drama and dance constituted dynamic art.

Works of art may or may not be aesthetically pleasing and may or may not communicate a message. Aesthetically pleasing artists usually survived, while those with only a message starved: that is, until the 20th century. The audio and film industry has prostituted art by propelling the aesthetically pleasing art forms into a mass entertainment industry and art with a message into commercials and propaganda. Movies and music videos are powerful art forms. Not only are they entertaining, but their content can mold the thought patterns of society. The money-driven entertainment industry uses film and sound along with video games to promote sexual liberties, promiscuity and violence in the guise of individual freedoms with no accountability. Occurrences of road rage, school shootings and irrational violence become symptomatic of a society in despair.

Music videos, some using coarse language, sing of lovers' despair, drugs, sexual freedoms, rebellion and violence. The message is bombasted into your subconscious: you are nothing but an animal dancing to the beat of your uncontrollable hormones and emotions. Situation comedies poke fun at marriage, family, and religious values, further eroding the fabric of a loving, caring society. The commercially driven entertainment industry seems to suggest that, somehow, children are just supposed to have morals and know there is a sociological right and wrong. The paradox is that, since evolution has no morals, and if we are creatures with no preprogrammed moral conscience by God, then the entertainment industry, a large supporter of evolution, is defining our morals and would appear to be promoting a quantum leap into social anarchy.

MEANINGLESS

"Man now realizes that he is an accident, that he is a completely futile being, that he has to play out the game without reason. I think that even when Velasquez was painting, even when Rembrandt was painting, they were still, whatever their attitude to life, slightly conditioned by certain types of religious possibilities, which man now, you could say, has had cancelled out for him. Man now can only attempt to beguile himself for a time, by prolonging his life—by buying a kind of immortality through the doctors. You see, painting has become—all art has become—a game by which man distracts himself" (Francis Bacon, the English painter).[9]

Static art suffers from the same disillusionment. In the name of great art, artists may smear paint (and some not-so-nice stuff) on their canvases in meaningless streaks and splashes. Abstract art can have form and balance and be aesthetically pleasing to individual perceptions; sometimes the point is not what is depicted but how it was produced. However, as drugs, rebellion, sexual freedoms, poverty and violence engulf our Western culture, artwork has become increasingly grotesque and, once again, the message is loud and clear: society is in the grasp of hopelessness and despair.

The mystical, the magical and the alien are clever fundamentals for storytelling, but why have they reached such a dominant position in literature and the movie industry at the same time as record companies are pumping out sounds of rebellion and hate? Should an observer from a parallel universe have only our movies as a basis to examine our galaxy, he could only conclude that the human race and all other intelligent creatures are at war for the survival of the fittest and that we are evolving into mystical, magical beings. We know that it is not the case, but it would seem most successful movie scripts are predicated on violence, as if the authors are still emotionally unstable children, devoid of empathy, who attack their environment with temper tantrums, maliciousness and guile. Somehow, they cannot artistically construct an alien society that permeates love and goodness through its realm of galactic space.

Does the word boring describe their attitude to this concept of a civilization? Is there an underlying philosophical belief denying artists and authors the mental attitude to reach for this kind of concept? Certainly, there is no unified desire to create static or dynamic art that will inspire our civilization to this kind of greatness. Nor has any past civilization on Earth managed to achieve it. In the Western world, the great Roman Empire collapsed of moral decay, and it is likely the magnificent dynasties of China collapsed from the same peril. Certainly, Confucius, Buddha and Mohammed sought a more virtuous way to the eternal. The God-inspired theocratic society of the Jews drifted into idolatry. Similarly, advanced technological countries of our world struggle with moral attitudes fed by empty philosophical concepts, drugs, prostitution, licentious living, deceit, hate, lying, stealing, murder, adultery, the worship of self and aspiring to monetary, physical and spiritual power. This, to the entertainment industry, is not boring.

Dynamic and static arts are not obscure icons of a society but, like frosting on a cake, are symptomatic of philosophical, religious and scientific premises of a civilization. The Reformation of the 16th century brought an aspect of spiritual hope into people's lives which was reflected in the static and dynamic arts and architecture of the following centuries. Science had its roots with Christian men of learning who believed in a supreme creator; thus, nature had order and its laws were determined by empirical evidence. In contrast, the philosophy of evolution, originating with Charles Darwin in the 19th century, has dragged the religion, art and science of the 21st century into directionless despair.

> **THE RISE OF MODERN SCIENCE**
>
> "The years from 1500 to 1700 saw not one but two profound upheavals in Western thought. In religion Luther, Calvin, Zwingli and Knox were replacing a man-centered view of the world with a God-centered one. In science Copernicus, Galileo, Brahe, Kepler and Newton were replacing a universe centered on the earth with one centered on the sun. A religious reformation and a scientific one went hand in hand" (James R. Moore).[10]

THE EVOLUTION OF THEORIES

Strong evolutionary opinions and hypotheses were formulated in the early to mid 20th century such that theory became promoted and taught as fact. Ernst Mayer, Professor Emeritus of Zoology at Harvard University, described by *Scientific American* as "one of the towering figures in the history of evolutionary biology," reached the zenith of his career during this period. He concludes an article for *Scientific American* as follows:

Let me now try to summarize my major findings. No educated person any longer questions the validity of the so-called theory of evolution, which we know to be a simple fact. Likewise, most of Darwin's particular theses have been fully confirmed, such as the common descent, the gradualism of evolution, and his explanatory theory of natural selection.[11]

Now, we are to understand one is not educated unless one subscribes to the concept of evolution. Moreover, it is this age group of intelligentsia who, in the 1950s, labeled Emanuel Velikovsky as a heretic for proposing the earth had suffered major catastrophic events. Geologists have since found that periodically major catastrophic events over Earth's ages have annihilated phylums of species. This upset the theory of gradualism, so that punctuated evolution and other aspects of rapid mutational theory were proposed to shore up Darwin's hypothesis. Professor Mayer accurately states, "And no biologist has been responsible for more—and for more drastic—modifications of the average person's world view than Charles Darwin."

GRADUALISM assumes life began from inorganic matter and through small changes over eons of time produced Earth's diversity of life.

MUTATION is sudden genetic changes. They need to be consistently favorable to explain the rapid complexity of life.

PUNCTUATED assumes that after a cataclysm life suddenly mutated to fill biological niches.

Darwin's idea that molecules of inorganic matter could, by hapless chance, unite, and, over boundless time, become living creatures with form and context by the process of natural selection and survival of the fittest, was starkly at odds with a number of prevailing world views. Other world views were offended that evolution did not require God, or any supernatural spiritual directive force; nothing was deterministic, everything was randomness and chance, thus eliminating the boundaries between species or essences. Yet evolution has to assume that somehow the genome of each species gets stacked by chance with variation and innate programming such that natural selection can eliminate weaker variations.

Moreover, mankind is now only one expanding branch of the evolutionary tree and is therefore no longer a unique being. Professor Mayer reiterates one of modern science's greatest assumptions:

> But biologists Thomas Huxley and Ernst Haeckel revealed through rigorous comparative anatomical study that humans and living apes clearly had common ancestry, an assessment that has never again been seriously questioned in science. The application of the theory of common descent to Man deprived man of his former unique position.

Professor Mayer then reflectively admits:

> Ironically, though, these events did not lead to an end to anthropocentrism. The study of man showed that, in spite of his descent, he is indeed unique among all organisms. Human intelligence is unmatched by that of any other creature. Humans are the only animals with true language, including grammar and syntax. Only humanity, as Darwin emphasized, has developed genuine ethical systems. In addition, through high intelligence, language and long parental care, humans are the only creatures to have created a rich culture. And by these means, humanity has attained, for better or worse, an unprecedented dominance over the entire globe.[12]

He concludes, evolution has "placed our fate squarely in our own evolved hands," mimicking Satan's deceptive statement in the Garden of Eden: *"you will be like God"* (Gen. 3:4).

How does the philosophy of evolution affect religion and our philosophical world views? Some religions have the concept they can have their spiritual beliefs and still believe in evolution, but this is a shallow understanding of what evolution entails. In the evolutionary world view, there is no spiritualism or supernaturalism. God, or any other form of intervening spiritual energy, is not permitted in our material cosmos of space and time. So global consciousness is effectively impossible and any religious gods, including the Jehovah-God of Judaism and Christianity, have never existed.

Likewise, the concepts of Satan as a marauding interdimensional being, the Gaia force, Mother Earth, or any other channeled spiritualities would be only illusionary weakness of our evolving minds. Any such spirit would be locked into our space-time world like electricity and could not account for any of the modern NDE or OBE experiences grabbing media attention. Moreover, any such spirit would have to be directionless and random with no purpose since this is the principle of evolution. Death, to the evolutionist, is the door to oblivion.

The New Age religion, the pinnacle of humanism, has glamorized the concept of this inner force such that we are evolving into evolutionary gods. However, their philosophies have entwined the paranormal with its alternate energy planes and mystical voices.

FALSE SPIRITUALITY

A young woman who had a number of rings inserted in her ears, nose and belly button, made the statement, "It's a feeling of total empowerment... I crave the feeling. It's a big adrenaline rush." The owner of the body piercing shop commented, "I think it has a lot to do with the spiritual awakening in society."[13] This is a loosely used term suggesting something mystical, of the transcendent, is happening when all they are doing is feeling good about themselves and their peers.

These mystical voices state they are coming to assist humanity in a quantum leap of spirituality. True scientists of evolution deplore flirtations with such spiritual concepts because they open up the possibilities of the supernatural and the inevitable accountability to creator God outside of our space-time world. Equally unpalatable is the alternative: our evolution is aided and abetted by superior alien beings.

In an article on evolutionary paleontology for *TIME*, Lemonick and Dorfman commence their article with the headlines: "One Giant Step for Mankind—Meet your newfound ancestor, a chimplike forest creature that stood up and walked 5.8 million years ago." They continue in the article:

> And it was here too that nature indulged in what was perhaps her greatest evolutionary experiment. For it was in eastern Africa at about this time that a new type of primate arose—an animal not so different from its apelike ancestors except in one crucial respect: this creature stood on two legs instead of scurrying along chimplike on all fours. Its knuckle-walking cousins would stay low to the ground and never get much smarter. But while it wouldn't happen until millions of years in the future, this new primate's evolutionary descendants would eventually develop a large, complex brain. And from that would spring all of civilization, from Mesopotamia to Mozart to Who Wants to Be a Millionaire.[14]

The article continues with the usual somehow evolution, with "her" being a synonym for the force of Mother Earth, brought modern man into being. The geological find consisted of "fragmentary fossils" of five different individuals in the main Ethiopian rift valley of Africa some eighty kilometers from the 1974 hominid find of "Lucy." This new creature has been named "Kadabba." Based on the limited number of bones found, it would appear to be the size of a modern common chimpanzee. Since the skull usually consists of a number of fragments, artistic license, based on philosophical premises, is evident in how it looks when it is pieced together. Lucy (*Australopithecus afarensis*, meaning southern ape from Afar, Ethiopia) represents a population of chimp-like animals that contemporary evolutionists believe evolved into humans. And yet, as Dr. Gish noted, a living baboon "Theropithecus galanda, has a number of dental, mandibular, and facial characteristics which are shared with the australopithecines. This fact is particularly damaging to the dental evidence for a hominid (man and man-like apes) status for the australopithecines."[15]

In 1978, Mary Leakey discovered three parallel trails of footprints remarkably similar to modern man at site G, Laetoli, thirty miles south of the Olduvai Gorge in northern Tanzania. These are known as the Laetoli footprints. They have been dated between 3.6 and 3.8 million years ago, close to the age of Lucy. The evolutionist community has ascribed them to the Lucy-type hominid.[16] However, in a study of footprints of modern habitually unshod peoples, Russel H. Tuttle explains: "In discernible features, the Laetoli G. prints are indistinguishable from those of habitually barefoot *Homo sapiens*;"[17] yet, because they are so old, evolutionists conclude they can not belong to humans. Marvin Lubenow writes:

> The real problem—the only problem—is that to ascribe those fossil footprints to Homo does not fit the evolutionary scenario timewise. According to the theory of evolution, those footprints are too old to have been made by a true human. It is a classic case of interpreting facts according to a preconceived philosophical bias.[18]

The African rift valley is famous for its fossils. Since geology is a highly subjective science, the sedimentary sequences can be viewed with any bias desired to fit any hypothesis. The valley is a continental rift in-filled with volcanic ash and sedimentary debris. The rhythmic banding and interlayering of the sedimentary units suggest high density silt-laden flood waters played an important part in the infilling of the rift. However, an evolutionist wants these sediments to represent ancient lake beds, forests or savannas whereby the volcanic ash quietly covered the bodily remains. The volcanic ash is dated using the argon-argon radioactivity method. In this area of Africa, the surface rocks are highly weathered and any water movement through the sediments will reset the age of the rocks. Radiometric age dating on blind control samples of various volcanic rocks of known age has given dates that are out by millions of years.[19] This difference has a huge impact on the evolutionary philosophical interpretation of human fossils.

French and Kenyan paleontologists Senut and Pickford announced, in December 2000, they found biped bones dated at 6 million years ago. It has been named "Millennium man" and designated as a hominid because, philosophically, *Homo sapiens* could not have lived then. In July of 2001 a French-Chadian team announced the discovery of a 6 million-year-old skull with a very large cranium and well-developed teeth. The discovery was made in the Djourab desert of northern Chad, west of the African rift valley. The large cranium and well-developed teeth suggest that it is possibly a human fossil, but it does not fit the evolutionary time frame.

A possible geological model for the rift valley is that it has undergone periods of immense flooding along with intense volcanism and ash falls. The bones of various ape species and mankind would then be distributed throughout the sedimentary sequences. It is not hard to be prophetic; once unbiased paleontology gets underway, true human bones will be recognized for what they are, intermixed with chimpanzees, apes and other similar species eliminated by catastrophic events. In the meantime though, scientific degrees and prestige mandate the philosophy of evolution be maintained at all cost.

Lemonick and Dorfman write:

> Establishing the precise path of human descent might be very hard. For most of the past 6 million years, multiple hominid species roamed the earth at the same time—including a mere 30,000 years ago, when modern humans and Neanderthals still coexisted. We still can't figure out exactly how Neanderthals relate to the human family; it's all the more difficult to know where these newly discovered species, with far fewer fossil remains to study, belong.[20]

Modern science has shown that it is the genetic variation within the genome that gives the multiple characteristics of a species. Professor Mayer writes: "Because of the importance of variation, natural selection should be considered a two-step process; the production of abundant variation is followed by the elimination of inferior species (by natural selection)." Professor Mayer, an evolutionist, is trying to account for variation within a species; however, his statement refutes "gradualism" and implies that all the characteristics of modern man

MICRO AND MACROEVOLUTION

Evolutionists do a first-class job of confusing the layman between microevolution and macroevolution. Microevolution concerns the small genetic variations within a species as it adapts to a different environment or interbreeds with others of it's own kind. A moth, through microevolution, does not become a dragonfly; that would be macroevolution. A small dinosaur does not become a bird by running and flapping appendages for millions of years—otherwise cats could fly like flying squirrels.

lie latent within the developing hominids. Otherwise, all apes, gorillas, chimpanzees, monkeys, hominids and man coexisted and only the interconnecting hominids, as inferior species, did not make it into the present.

SCIENTIFICALLY NEANDERTHAL

God states, in Genesis, that He made all living things according to its kind, which implies contained genetic variability. Dogs are living examples of multiple characteristics within a kind. Would a future paleontologist equate a pug-nosed British bulldog with a long-nosed German shepherd based on skull characteristics? Likewise, based on various interpretations of skull characteristics, Neanderthal man has gone through an amazing artistic evolution since January 2000. Before January 2000, he was considered to be of stocky frame with a heavyset skull containing protruding eyebrow ridges and jaw structure. Most artists depicted him as semi-hairy like an ape, and slightly stooped, holding a club—inferring quasi-intelligence.

On January 2000, Neanderthal man appeared on the cover of *Scientific American*[21] along with a bearded human wearing a bandanna. Mr. Neanderthal is now standing upright, is less hairy and has a modern but still slightly apish coarse-looking face. He is holding a roughly fashioned spear and appears to have some sort of ornament around his neck. By the April 2000[22] issue, he has evolved to having a handsome Nordic look with blond hair and a non-hairy natural light skin texture. He lived in caves; he left evidence of culture, he coexisted and likely interbred with humans.

By August 1, 2001, Neanderthal man made a quantum evolutionary virtual artistic leap! Dr. Christoph Zollikofer and Marice Ponce de Leon of the University of Zurich, Switzerland, using digital computer imaging techniques on a variety of skulls rather than the artistic coarse stereotype, produced a very modern-looking young female with fair skin, bluish eyes and light brown hair. However, Dr. Zollikofer maintains: "The finds support the idea that Neanderthals did not interbreed with early humans and contributed little or nothing to the present human gene pool." No logical conclusion was given for this statement other than what appears to be a philosophical bias. Dr. Zollikofer then states: "Neanderthals are a sister species that died out 30,000 years ago."[23]

It is the concept of evolution that gives the basis for a philosophical belief that God does not exist and our space-time world is not of intelligent design. The 1960s proclamation "God is dead" thrust the arts into rapid moral decline, culminating in hopelessness and despair. The progression into the 21st century has continued with an increase in coarse language and irrational violence amongst the youth. The concept of the female as a stable loving mother endowed with empathy and compassion is also being systematically eroded by the alcoholic beverage and entertainment industry. Beautiful tough female cops who can kick, punch and handle any killing machine slowly came into vogue. Female wrestling and boxing are drawing larger audiences. Scantily dressed, well-endowed, alluring women saturate the film industry with wanton violence,[24] and society wonders why

ANCIENT DNA

Statements have been made that ancient DNA extracted from 29,000-year-old Neanderthal fossil bones has no resemblance to human DNA. Other scientists say this cannot be determined. Logically, if modern science is having problems supporting DNA identification as forensic evidence in the courtroom, how can supposedly ancient DNA retain its identification? DNA is organic matter that rapidly decomposes upon death and is easily degraded by bacteria.

there has been a dramatic increase in schoolyard violence amongst teenage girls.

The message "survival of the fittest" rings loud and clear. This leaves women with less alluring body features with the psychological impression they are not as evolutionary fit. Evolutionary scientists maintain, after all, we are only animals subject to our hormones and only the fittest animals will successfully breed. The driving force of life, according to the philosophy of evolution, is successful evolutionary breeding. Some evolutionary scientists depict the human female as being reproductively successful because she can have sex at any time. Is it any wonder there is such hopelessness and despair in the world of women? Men also suffer from subliminal feelings of despair that they will not be evolutionary successful studs. These ideas feed further feelings of inadequacy.

- "All-women colleges saw a 125 percent increase in frequent drinking."
- "Among women who drank, there was a 150 percent increase in 'unplanned' sexual activities, date rape and sexual assault."
- "Women arrested for aggravated assault has increased a staggering 46 percent."
- "On a recent episode of the Fox sitcom Undeclared, several college coeds go out to a bar, where one woman gets so drunk, she flashes her breasts" (Amanda Bower).[25]

A SPECIAL CREATED BEING

Fortunately, in all of this, God did create man in His image; we do have a built-in conscience, and our existence does have meaning. Each generation, at least in our Western culture, has a fresh "show me" attitude towards life's philosophies and religions. However, to use religion as a theocratic power base is a denial of freedom the same way the saturating of society with the philosophy of evolution has preconditioned people's attitudes and values. The consequence of this philosophy is the denial of the uniqueness of mankind, the breakdown of interpersonal relationships and values, the lack of commitment to marriage, the animalizing of culture and sexual relationships and the removal of absolute moral laws.

The belief in God, a divine loving creator, restores the special relationship of man to his world. The concept of man as a special created being made in the image of God with a cosmic purpose and accountability to his creator restores a higher order to the concept of his eternal soul to its future existence and authenticates man's attributes, culture, personal relationships, moral values and religious desires.

The world is filled with many "good" people who choose not to believe in God and so exercise their God-given freedom of spiritual belief. Their lives are filled with family, careers, sports and activities of all sorts. However, though their lives may be good and honorable, subtle major problems exist. There is a broad psychological shift consuming the civilizations of the world. It would appear that Satan and his Legions of Doom, from their ethereal city surrounding Earth, are directing the "alien plan" in preparation for their visual manifestation to Earth's citizens. Jesus informed His disciples that, when He comes back to Earth, the times would be like the days of Noah before the flood. This was a period of human history when the rebellious angels deceived humanity with supernatural powers and took wives of human women.

News of the paranormal and the unusual increases each day, particularly on the Internet where there are no restricting editors. The difficulty is sorting the possible truth from the chaff. Herbert Vander Lugt comments:

> Many people around the world claim they have been abducted by extraterrestrial beings. Researchers call it a "new psychological disorder." Jeff Kanipe, an authority in this field of study, says that some people become so obsessed with the desire for help

from another world that they "hallucinate help coming from the skies in the form of alien saviors—saviors, I might add, that oftentimes behave sinisterly.[26]

Is it reasonable to believe a person would intentionally harm him or herself by the delusion of an extraterrestrial abduction? It is more likely they have indeed tangled with interdimensional forces since such people are usually willing seekers of the paranormal, of witchcraft, tarot cards, astrology, fortune telling and séances and may even belong to Satanic cults. It is these people who have most of the UFO experiences. Paranormal researcher, Bob Larson, writes:

> Even the most cursory analysis of UFO encounters suggests that the message carried from out there to down here is consistent with an occult/metaphysical view of cosmology. As I have already mentioned, studies show that those who experience UFO encounters believed in extraterrestrials before their experience. In addition, most UFO contactees and abductees were already involved in some form of occult practice or psychic experimentation prior to their initial encounter with aliens.[27]

HOAX OR MESSAGE

The biblical viewpoint is that these ethereal intelligences exist. There is increasing empirical evidence they are manifesting their presence in our space-time world for a psychological purpose. For instance, the crop circles appearing around the world have increased significantly in mathematical complexity; so much so that it would take a mathematician to design them and hours of meticulous measuring and flattening of plants to construct them, which is difficult to do without being discovered. Furthermore, it seems they are associated with the paranormal and would appear to be generated by balls of light.

Researcher Fredy Silva, a believer in the paranormal, has published a book, *Secrets in the Field*, based on his examinations of these worldwide phenomena. He writes:

> In 1988, during the days when crop circles were only sporadically mentioned in the local press, a channeler named Isabelle Kingston was given a series of communications from a group consciousness called The Watchers. These ascended masters were responsible for guiding humanity through its most difficult moments; references to them exist in ancient Egypt as the Neteru, the Shining Ones.
>
> Among many predictions The Watchers gave were of signs in the fields that would shortly be manifesting around Europe's biggest man-made 'pyramid' Silbury Hill (hill of the Shining Beings). These signs would help humanity gain awareness of its greater responsibility in the Universe; these signs would also be carrying codes of energy for imprinting the Earth, and cleansing the ancient sites which lay upon an invisible electromagnetic (EM) grid around the world. Twenty years later, this prophecy has certainly taken form in the crop circles, whose EM fingerprints are now known to charge the energy grid of ancient nearby sites, and interact with the biophysical rhythms of people who enter them.
>
> But one further prophecy concerned the gradual deciphering of the glyphs, through which new technology could be built to help humanity. This was to be achieved by 2007. And it appears that some progress is now being made as we draw nearer this date.[28]

There seems to be a suggestion that some of these complex two-dimensional drawings on farmer's fields reflect designs of futuristic three-dimensional machinery. It would appear by the increase in anti-gravity articles, a revolutionary discovery might be close at hand. Some people believe these glyphs are messages from a benevolent alien. Ms. Brigitte Boisselier,[29] a member of the Raelian Sect that has been attempting to clone a human being, addressed a meeting of the National Academy of Scientists in Italy in August 2001 on cloning. She maintains life on Earth was originally created by extraterrestrials through cloning and their group has received messages from these creatures.

People are wondering if the complicated crop glyphs are indeed messages or a well-planned hoax. On August 12, 2001, a large circle composed of six spirals, like spokes on a wheel, appeared at Milk Hill near Alton Barnes, Wiltshire, England.[30] The spirals were formed by 409 various-sized circles. The glyph covered some 700,000 square

ALIENS

The grays are drawn with large slanted eyes in a pear-shaped hairless gray skull. They reportedly fly the UFOs.

feet. It has been estimated it would take thirteen people nine hours to construct the pattern which would have to be done in darkness in a farmer's field with restricted access. Five days later, two more complicated-glyphs occurred at night in a field by the Chilbolton Radio Telescope near Wherwell, Hampshire in the UK.

One of these glyphs was a face somewhat like an alien "gray," the other a strip message looked similar to the digitally encoded schematic beamed from the Arecibo Radio Telescope on Puerto Rico in 1974. The message was aimed at the star cluster M13 some 20,000 light years away. A return message would take another 20,000 years. Fintan Dunne[31] compared the two schematics. He believes the aliens are saying they are of the same hydrocarbon life form, they have a different DNA, they have smaller bodies and larger heads, they inhabit three planets and one moon of a star system, they intercepted the Arecibo message and have responded telepathically through hyperspace.

In August and September of 2001, and again in February 2002, an alert was posted amongst crop circle enthusiasts calling for "meditation" for the alien intelligences that created the crop circles (see chapter 7 for the unusual events of September 11, 2001). This type of meditation becomes worship and is

> SHERMER'S LAST LAW
>
> "Any sufficiently advanced extraterrestrial intelligence is indistinguishable from God."[32]

religious in nature. Since Satan desires to be worshiped as God, it appears the war of the cosmos is intensifying. In an amazingly well-timed warning article in *Daily Bread* for August 24, 2001, published well in advance of the unusual glyphs, Mr. Lugt writes:

> After spending millions of dollars in a 40-year project, scientists have still made no contact with extraterrestrial beings. But their search continues. Robert Jastrow, director of the Mount Wilson Institute, says that he expects to find "beings superior to us ... not only technically, but perhaps spiritually and morally."
>
> Jastrow and his fellow scientists hope that an alien civilization billions of years old will be able to tell us why we are here and how to overcome our destructive tendencies, which make advances in weapons technology so terrifying. This fear that humanity might destroy itself, as well as the innate desire for meaning in life, may account for the many popular books and movies about extraterrestrial beings.[33]

Mr. Lugt goes on to say the author of life, Jesus Christ, is *"The Word became flesh and made his dwelling among us"* (John 1:14) so we can have meaning to our existence and inherit eternal life. Whether or not the glyphs are real or a hoax, it is apparent a segment of our society is willing to believe the paranormal is the answer. We have now gone from "God is dead" of the 1960s to worshiping the alien. The wills of mankind are under spiritual siege. Who will you worship, God or Satan?

NOTES:

[1] Dustin McKay, personal interview, June 1, 2001

[2] "Kid in Hall defends gig," *National Post*, Vol. 3, NO. 190, Saturday, June 9, 2001

[3] Lacayo, Richard, "Rock of Ages," *TIME*, February 26, 2001, p. 56

[4] Ibid. p. 56

[5] Hughes, Robert, "Secrets of the Stone Age," *TIME*, February 13, 1995, p. 44

[6] Robinson, John, sculptor-artist for the Bradshaw Foundation, <www.bradshawfoundation.com/bison>

[7] Begley, Sharon, *Newsweek*, May 25, 1999
<www.hominids.com/chauvetcave.html>

[8] Genesis 4:19–22

[9] *Eerdmans' Handbook to the History of Christianity*, Wm. B. Eerdmans Publishing Co., 1987, p. 31

[10] *Eerdman's Handbook to the History of Christianity*, p. 42

[11] Mayer, Ernst, "Darwin's Influence on Modern Thought," *Scientific American*, July 2000, pp. 79–83

[12] Mayer, Ibid. p. 82

[13] Broughtor, Dean, "Points of Beauty," *Vernon Sun Review*, January 20, 2001, p. 13

[14] Lemonick, Michael, Andrea Dorfman, "One Giant Step for Mankind," *TIME*, Canadian Edition, July 23, 2001, p. 48

[15] Gish, Duane T., Ph.D., *Evolution: The Fossils Say NO!*, Creation-Life Publishers, 1978, p. 112

[16] Lubenow, Marvin L., *Bones of Contention*, Baker Book House, 1992, p. 173

[17] Tuttle R.H. and D.M. Webb, "The Pattern of Little Feet," (abstract) *American Journal of Physical Anthropology* 78:2 (February 1989): p. 316

[18] Lubenow, Ibid. p. 175

[19] Blick, Edward F. Ph.D, *A Scientific Analysis of Genesis*, Hearthstone

Publishing Ltd, pp. 36 and 96

[20] Lemonick, Ibid. p.48.

[21] Tattersall, Ian, "We Were Not Alone," *Scientific American*, January 2000, p. 56

[22] Wong, Kate, "Who Were the Neandertals" (sic), *Scientific American*, April 2000, p. 56

[23] Helen Briggs, "Meet the Neanderthals," BBC News Online, Wednesday, August 1, 2001

[24] "Go Ahead Make Her Day," *TIME*, Canadian Edition, March 26, 2001, Show Business, p. 52

[25] Bower, Amanda, "Women on a Binge," *TIME*, Canadian Edition, April 1, 2002, pp. 42–43

[26] Lugt, Vander Herbert, "Help From Above," *Our Daily Bread*, August 10, 2001, RBC Ministries, Grand Rapids, MI

[27] Larson, Bob, *UFOs*, Thomas Nelson Publishers, 1997, p. 73

[28] Silva, Fredy, "The Unfolding Technology of Crop Circles," <www.lovely.clara.net/technology>

[29] *San Francisco Chronicle*, August 8, 2001

[30] <www.monmouth.com>

[31] <www.rumormillnews.com>

[32] Shermer, Michael, "Shermer's Last Law," *Scientific American*, January 2002, p. 33

[33] Lugt, Ibid. August 24, 2001

Man: Alive

The soft red glow of the setting sun seems to reach into tomorrow as it paints the silhouette of the far side of the ocean bay. Wisps of warm breezes dance to the swish of silvery orange ripples as they play along the shore. Alluring perfume floats from yellow and pink flowers that peek around flickering leaves kissed by the twirling air. A single note from a guitar waves into the moment and hangs in anticipation. Then, as if in answer to an eternal question, the musical twitter of several birds surrounds the note. Once more, the question vibrates into the glowing expanse, and again the songbirds respond. Only now, a woman's voice rises in accompaniment to nature's chorus. Melodious harmony spills out into the evening warmth as several more voices join in praise and worship to Jesus, King of Kings and Lord of Lords.

There is no doubt man is an animal, but is man a progressive evolution of the monkey, chimpanzee or gorillas families? It is often glibly said that "man evolved from monkeys" because some of the bone structures are anatomically similar, yet that is like saying a computer evolved from a television because it uses a television monitor. What took it to get from the television screen to the computer was intelligent design and operation programming. You may have not paid any attention to the man-from-monkey statement, but it makes it seem as if there were monkeys, apes and/or chimpanzees, and we evolved from one of their kind while they remained genetically stable. I recently visited an evolutionary-minded Web site where a monkey sat facing the viewer. Underneath was written: "we evolved from monkeys."

Typical of this thought is the statement by Lemonick and Dorfman in *TIME*: "The newest fossils have brought scientists tantalizingly close to the time when humans first walked upright—splitting off from chimpanzees."[1] Their best guess is that it happened at least 6 million years ago. Their accompanying time chart shows the postulated hominoid lines but nothing in the chimpanzee or gorilla lines, not because the focus of the article was on hominids, but because there are no interconnecting fossils in the chimpanzee-gorilla phylum lines to illustrate. If scientists cannot find fossils from the original proto ape-human animal through to modern monkeys, chimpanzees, or gorillas, then the evolutionary human line is one of philosophical conjecture. The proto ape-human animal was not a chimpanzee. The Bible states that God created each animal in its own kind.

Primatologists are finding that the ape families, in particular the chimpanzees, have habits or traits that can be passed from one generation to another which is the definition of human culture. Needless to say, evolutionists who suggest we indeed came from the chimpanzee, champion this anthropomorphism (the ascription of human characteristics to animals). From an evolutionary viewpoint, the proto ape-human had to exist prior to 6 million years ago. This creature would have had to have these traits fully developed to pass them on genetically. Any characteristics that the modern chimpanzee may have are only shadows of human traits, traditions and cultures, yet Professor McGrew writes concerning the variability of grooming techniques and the use of stone and wood tools amongst chimpanzees:

> These sorts of differences seem to be the sorts of things that if they occurred in human beings we would call them traditions. There is evidence that other apes such as gorillas and orangutans show cultural differences as well as creatures such as whales and dolphins. Chimp culture could help us understand the evolutionary origins of human culture.[2]

Older evolutionary literature proposed that the survival of the fittest came through selfishness, that there was no room for empathy, sympathy or complex social organization within an animal group. This is a philosophical assumption of the evolutionist; from a creationist viewpoint, God is love and all He created is good, so social complexity amongst animals is logical, yet an evolutionist would have it that, because the study of primates has shown social complexity, this is somehow supposed to show that we evolved from them. Frans de Waal, a primatologist and author of the book, *The Ape and the Sushi Master*, arrives at the conclusion:

> Instead of being tied to how we are unlike any animal, human identity should be built around how we are animals that have taken certain capacities a significant step further. We and other animals are both similar and different, and the former is only sensible framework within which to flesh out the latter.[3]

Meredith Small, in a book review for *Scientific American* of *The Ape and the Sushi Master*, summarizes de Waal's thoughts as follows:

> For decades, anthropologists and others have come up with various traits that separate humans from chimpanzees in an effort

to define what is uniquely human. But chimpanzees keep nudging into our territory: tool use, complex social relationships, empathy and sympathy, sophisticated communication—they seem to have bits of it all. And now it seems they have culture, the last bastion of separation. …And we emerge as an unpleasantly self-important species. We pretend that struggle for social power, which is a common behavior pattern among other primates, is "self-esteem" and therefore that it is found only in humans. We assume that humans are the only one whose behavior is influenced by learning and experience and that we are the only ones who are altruistic, caring beings—such kindness exhibited by other animals is misguided pathology.[4]

Since an evolutionist cannot allow for a creator, he can only conclude that kindness, empathy, complex social organization and selflessness (altruism) must be a law of natural selection which once again is a reversal of Darwin's thesis. Professor Mayer concedes:

Such selection for altruism has been demonstrated in recent years to be widespread among many other social animals. One can then perhaps encapsulate the relation between ethics and evolution by saying that a propensity for altruism and harmonious cooperation in social groups is favored by natural selection. The old thesis of social Darwinism—strict selfishness—was based on an incomplete understanding of animals, particularly social species.[5]

It is apparent that we can manipulate our philosophical approach by seeing what we want to see so we can believe what we want to believe. Typical of this is de Waal's comment that "culture, the last bastion of separation" has been breached. The implication is that this proves we came from the apes. Yet primatologists are in no hurry to attribute to humans other characteristics of the apes such as harem breeding, social pecking order, grooming for lice or that male chimpanzees gather together to kill monkeys for "male bonding."

Anthropologist David Watts of Yale University comments, "Chimps aren't necessarily good models for humans—we don't hunt in the canopy, and we don't have large canine teeth. The main importance for human evolution is in the social realm—the networks of male bonding. Like it or not, the old-boy network is an essential part of life in the jungle and in the boardroom."[6]

THE DISTINGUISHING TRAIT

Yes, we are animals, but to believe that is all we are is the road to hopelessness and despair. God has created us for "something so much more," and it is time to see who we really are. It is in the

CLEVER ANIMALS

Many animals have unique traits and the ability to observe and mimic, yet we do not extend to them anthropocentric characteristics such that we evolved from them. Our family dog, Molly, a cross between a golden Labrador and a German shepherd, was exceptionally clever. Upon observing my kicking a racquetball for her, she mimicked me by placing her foot on the ball and zapping it with considerable force. Pets of all kinds can be loving andfaithful, and may have saved their masters from death. Animals can do amazing things. In the summer of 2001 a female duck in the city of Vancouver, British Columbia, Canada, tugged on a policeman's leg and led him to where her ducklings were trapped beneath a storm grate.

realm of the mind, of thought and will, which separates us from the animals. Man created in the image of God is rational with a sense of morality, but what totally distinguishes us from other animals is our fear of non-being. We are an animal of unprecedented body design, endowed with intelligence and sentience. Our intelligence and specially designed voice box allows for speech and singing. As a result, humanity has diverse language capability with intricate syntax and grammar. We voice laughter, have complex emotions and thoughts (no one has ever reported a group of cows standing around telling udderly funny jokes). Yet we run and play like animals and grieve death. Animals also have complex ways of being submissive and saying they are sorry, though groups of apes have never yet brought food and gifts of sympathy to one of their own that has lost a young one or mate. Likewise, long-term memory of birthday parties, weddings and funerals do not seem to be meaningful occasions in any other animal species than man. If we view life as evolutionarily simplistic (coming from time-plus-chance), we will not appreciate our biological complexity or the ultra complexity of a God who could create the "heavens and earth."

Our free will gives rise to individual thoughts subliminally guided by innate programming as to ethics and morality which we call our conscience. We live as communities in complex social structures. Our animalistic nature to mate and reproduce can be tempered by our intellect, unlike a female cat or dog that, in heat, will mate with any male she can find. Evolutionists take the position that "love" is purely a sexual aspect of human nature. Robert Wright, an evolutionary psychologist, writes: "The good news from evolutionary psychology is that human beings are designed to fall in

BASE PAIRS

At the time of this general statement in the late 20th century, there was thought to be only one billion nucleotide sequences, or base pairs, in the human DNA strand. The decoding of the human genome in the early 21st century has shown that there is upwards of 3.5 billion base pairs. Biological body design and operational programming context indicate that there is a vast difference between ape and man.

love. The bad news is that they aren't designed to stay there."7 Yet there are many animals that mate for life; why don't evolutionists assign the possibility of this attribute to humans?

There are major body differences between apes and man, even in the way they mate. Yet there is a commonality of body parts amongst all animals. It is often quoted that there is only some 10 percent difference in human DNA to that of the apes. There may be little differences in some organic parts, but what the parts comprise and the programming that runs the biological machine can be vastly different.

A major difference in the ape species and humans is that humans reproduce face to face so that there is eye contact, sentient being to sentient being. Sensations of happiness and trust coming from the sexual attraction between a man and a woman, spoken of as being "in love," is hopefully only the surface of a deeper emotional experience of affection of one sentient being for another. This type of deep affection is the love we should have for each other; it is this love God desires. God seeks a deep love, affection, or adoration which we call worship. The emotions of empathy, sympathy, compassion, selflessness, joy, hope, trust and willingness to give all have their roots in the emotion of love.

In contrast to love, we have the conscious will to hate and therefore suffer all the devastating emotions and actions that it entails. It has been established in earlier chapters that we have an eternal spiritual component that animals do not have. The eternal destiny of the spiritual body, or soulish body, is a direct consequence of the will of the intellect during physical life in the interactions of love versus hate. One thing dramatically separates the triune being of man from all other animal species on Earth is the ability to "willfully worship." Jesus told the Samaritan woman: *"Yet a time is coming and has now come when the true worshipers will worship the Father in spirit and truth, for they are the kind of worshipers the Father seeks. God is spirit, and his worshipers must worship in spirit and truth."* [8] The battle of the cosmos is about whom you will affirm in worship, God the creator or Satan the deceiver, usurper of mankind's dominion.

Birds and humans were created to sing. Birds, by innate programming, fill the earth with inspiring and soothing sounds. Mankind is also programmed to be musical (some more than others) but can choose whether or not to lift their voices in adoration and praise. A great heritage of inspiring music in the Western world is that of worship and praise written by composers such as Beethoven and Bach. Music of mourning, despair and the shallow, temporarily thrilling beats of yesterday and today disappear into the abyss of time.

Primatologists have not yet found a group of apes in a jungle clearing creating rhythm and music by pounding on hollow logs or coconut shells, singing in worship and praise to their creator. To worship in spirit and truth is free will adoration that comes from an unprogrammed sentient being. No matter how many anthropocentric traits scientists assign to other animal kinds or aspects of culture anthropologists give to creatures in the ape phylum, it is only mankind that was created in the image of God and given the breath of life. In common with the animals, man has three basic instincts: to hold territory, to gain substance from the territory and to reproduce. Only man has the fear of non-being and a further instinct to worship, to seek the "something more" which is his "God-consciousness." Because of the spiritual dissonance that began in the

> **SUBTLE EVOLUTIONARY ASSUMPTION**
>
> "Drumming is primal," says Kulu Spiegel, who conducts circles for at-risk youth and corporate honchos out of his World Beat Rhythm Circles in Durango, Colorado. "It brings people together in a trusting way they often have never known before."[9]

Garden of Eden, the three basic instincts of man (termed temptations of the flesh) interfere with his spirituality.

Without our animal body with its five senses feeding our psyche, we could not grasp the concept of love and hate as spiritual truths. It is through our suffering of death and decay in this world that we wrestle with the counterparts of love and hate: hope and despair. Religion is the attempt by mankind to gain some sort of spirituality by overcoming temptations of the flesh with rules and regulations. The philosophy of evolution is an attempt by the intellect to deny the spirituality of a human being; this removes any reason to separate the man from the monkey, yet anthropoids do not practice religion.

Naturalists have no answer to the spirituality of man, or to the paranormal interdimensional cosmic conflict, other than they could be a more-advanced, evolved species that will either help us or subjugate us. Since God created whatever multidimensional cosmos might exist, He is outside of our space-time world and the world of spirits. Because man is of body, soul and spirit, he is of both the natural and the supernatural. It is only by being "born again" that an individual can understand and be part of the supernatural of God. Mankind has the destiny to challenge the universe as eternal celestial beings while anthropoids will only serve their purpose in the vast biological diversity of Earth.

CAN A CLONE GO TO HEAVEN?

Our scientific world is becoming like the days of Noah. Women abductees have reported alien experiments with their reproductive organs, and scientists are meddling with animal-human genetics. However, should a pure human clone be born, it (he or she) would be like a genetic twin and therefore would contain the breath of life and, though it may be genetically unstable, it could know the redeeming love of Jesus.

Our Kinsman-Redeemer

Jesus Christ is our kinsman-redeemer. He did not die for any other power, dominion or principality. He did not die for the fallen angels or Nephilim. He did not die for the anthropoids or any other animals. It is awesome to be a unique human being with the potential to be an eternal, celestial citizen. It is almost unbelievable that the infinite Almighty God, our creator, came to Earth in the incarnation of Jesus Christ as our kinsman-redeemer. That we should be called sons and daughters[10] of God, like our kinsman-redeemer, Jesus Christ, is too glorious to fully comprehend.

Yet none of this would have happened if Adam and Eve had not joined the angelic rebellion by their willful act. "The only difference between our relationship with God now, and that which man's would have been if he had not sinned, is that now it is under the covenant of grace, and not under the covenant of works; therefore, it rests on the basis of Christ's finished mediatorial work."[11] Through our salvation, God is showing His justice, love, grace and mercy to the powers, dominions and principalities. Moreover, mankind of the new birth has the joy and hope, guaranteed by the resurrection of Jesus Christ, to rule over powers, dominions and principalities in the heavens and mankind on Earth as they expand into the universe.

Is it any wonder there is a life-and-death battle in the cosmos centered on mankind? The Bible infers a history to the cosmos in that there was a rebellion by the powers, dominions and principalities in the heavens. It may well have involved our solar system and a once-devastated Earth.

In the ancient realm of angels, there was freedom of choice. However, by the disease of vanity, one third of the angelic forces followed Lucifer, the rebel leader.[12] This period of free will choice for angels is past. Their allegiances and destinies are eternally fixed.

If you are not a Bible believer, consider the rising evidence of the paranormal and reported NDE and OBE experiences. These alone suggest that there is something unusual happening and, combined with the ideas that we evolved from Mars or were created by governing aliens, adds up to an anti-created-by-God spin. This is typical psychological manipulation that is used in warfare.

If people do not believe they have a spiritual component and were created in the image of God, they are already defeated because, upon death, our eternal destinies are fixed.[13] Since mankind has joined this rebellion, it is the free will decision of the intellect that brings about a spiritual rebirth. It is by faith one believes Jesus is God and loves us so much that He died on the cross to redeem all who will believe in Him and ask for forgiveness, and that He arose again in the resurrection as proof of our eternal inheritance.[14]

When we examine the deception scene in the Garden of Eden, we understand the decision by Adam and Eve was made through the human will. They desired to be as God and, as a result, forever became self-taking rather than self-giving because they did not trust that God was good and that His love endures forever. Thus, we—the human race—know good and evil but, by our spirits, do not have the power to refute evil. If Satan and his Legions of Doom can keep us believing we evolved from monkeys, Martians or whatever—with no spiritual essence—then we have forfeited our opportunity for salvation. If he can convince us we have some sort of mysterious "all-get-to-heaven" spirituality—that there are many ways to God, or that we can somehow, by our own efforts of goodness, gain entrance to the eternal—then we have denied God's mercy and grace.

THE FIFTH CHERUBIM

The stupendous event in the Garden of Eden can only be approached from a supernatural viewpoint. At this time, in the beginning of human history, the rebellion of some of the heavenly beings—possibly including destructive planetary events of war within our solar system—is already underway.

Lucifer is the leader of this revolt. He is a magnificent archangel, thought by Hebrew theologians to be the fifth cherub that accompanied the four cherubim seen by Ezekiel, or living beings described in the book of Revelation. He is like a dragon adorned in glittering jewels and precious stones. Oblivious to the pair in the garden, he watches astounded by God's pronouncement that these insignificant creatures—made in the image of God,[15] a little lower than God[16] (Ps. 8:5, see note next page) and created of the dust of the earth—would displace him in power and authority.

It was obvious that they have been given a freedom of will that was formulating concepts. He has observed, on numerous occasions, how the Creator[17] lovingly walks and talks with His loved ones in the picturesque garden effervescing with life, color, sound and scent. "How simplistic is their simple trust," he smirks. If he can deceive them to doubt God, they would be under his authority and this beautiful dominion will be his.

> **THE SERPENT**
>
> In the real space-time world, a flying serpent hovered close to Eve. There has been considerable speculation as to what this creature looked like. Because of the negatives of God's curse upon this creature, it is postulated it had legs and possibly wings. It may have stood upright. Its body may have been covered in highly reflective scales that glistened in the sun.

At this point in time, the Holy Spirit of God is sustaining the human pair with transcendent glory. The natural and the supernatural are in a harmonious link; there is no concept of nakedness or disharmony between the flesh and spirit bodies, yet the pair have free will-thought since the Holy Spirit of God is a sustaining spirit not an invasive spirit.

ANGELS, HEAVENLY BEINGS OR GOD?

Psalm 8:5, Kings James Version, says "angels;" The New International Version says "heavenly beings" and notes, "or as God" which is the correct translation. This is important in the understanding of who we are and the virgin birth of Jesus. The Hebrew word is *elohiym* as in Genesis 1:26: *"Then God said, 'Let us make man in our image, in our likeness.'"* Psalm 95:3 states: *"For the Lord* [Yehovah (the) self Existent or Eternal; Jehovah, Jewish national name of God] *is the great God, the great King above all gods* [elohiym]." King David writes, in Psalm 138:1: *"I will praise you, O LORD, with all my heart; before the 'gods' (elohiym) I will sing your praise."* In Psalm 82:1, God presides over the great assembly giving judgment amongst the elohiym. In verse 6, God says: *"You are 'gods'* [elohiym]; *sons of the Most High."* Jesus authenticates this statement in John 10:34, only He uses the Greek word for God, *theos*. The Jews are accusing Jesus of saying He is God; Jesus references this verse as being in their sacred law. The word *elohiym* is occasionally applied by way of deference to magistrates and sometimes as a superlative, so it is important to see in what context that it is used. In all these cases, "god" is not referring to human magistrates, otherwise humans would be created a little lower than human magistrates and Jesus would be saying He is a magistrate. The word for angels, as in Psalm 34:7 where angels encamp around those who fear God, is *mal'ak*, a messenger. The Greek word for angel is *aggelos* as in Hebrews 1:4 where Jesus is described as being superior to angels. Mankind, though we do not have the superior attributes of angels, are of the "image" of God wherein flows the eternal breath of life of the living God. Thus in the virgin birth of Jesus, the divine eternal Son merged with His eternal breath of life given to man and therefore became "wholly God and wholly man." Angels do not have this eternal breath of life of God. Now do you understand why Satan hates you and is using evolution to deceive you?

The fallen cherub moved from the supernatural into real space-time history and possessed the body of the serpent. The serpent addressed Eve: "Did God really say, 'You must not eat from any tree in the garden?'" and so the conversation of deceit began. Covetousness to be like God seeped into the human will. This brought doubt that "God is good and that His love endures forever."

Once the act of completion (taking and eating of the fruit) followed the thought, the will was solidified. The sustaining Spirit of God departed as the God-conscious human spirit shriveled. Now the human pair, experiencing the concept of nakedness and the overwhelming dread and emptiness of the knowledge of good and evil, stood in the garden

> ### THE TENTH COMMANDMENT
>
> The tenth commandment given by God to Moses is: *"you shall not covet."* It is interesting that all the other commandments precede outward from this commandment like spokes of a wheel (Deut. 5:21).

almost alone. Wings flapped and the yellow eyes of the shimmering scaly creature, which had seemed so alluring, now looked at them intently.

THE SERPENT

Like legends of an ancient world flood, motifs of flying serpents exist in many ancient cultures of the world. In our modern paranormal world, UFO abductees report encounters with humanoid like beings known as Reptilians. The whisperings and mutterings of the Internet suggest the Reptilians supercede the Grays in power and authority. Do the motifs of flying serpents and paranormal reports of Reptilians descend from a biblical truth in the Garden of Eden?

The principle focus of the Bible is on Christ's redemptive actions in our cosmos, yet there are other mysteries dealt with in only a line or two of Scripture. We can only conclude these mysteries will be illuminated as we move forward in time. The question of the serpent is one of these.

Genesis 3:1 records: *"Now the serpent was more crafty than any of the wild animals the Lord God had made."* After the dastardly deed, the Lord God pronounces to the serpent in the realm of the natural: *"Cursed are you above all the livestock and all the wild animals! You will crawl on your belly and you will eat dust all the days of your life"* (v.14). When we examine the Hebrew words for the description of the serpent—*aruwm chay*—the mystery begins to unfold. The Hebrew word *aruwm* means crafty or cunning in a "bad" sense. The word *chay* means "alive" or "living things" whether literally or figuratively, hence the words "wild animals." We know the second portion of God's pronouncement is to Satan in the supernatural because He defines the terms of the cosmic war and its outcome: *"And I will put enmity between you and the woman, and between your offspring and hers; he will crush your head and you will strike his heel"* (v.15). This means, at some point in real space-time history, an offspring of the woman, Jesus Christ, will defeat Satan.

We assume this beautiful winged and legged serpent was of the earth because, to this point in the biblical record, there is no reference to powers or principalities, and he is reduced in status and compared to other animals. The major question then becomes how could he be cunning in a "bad" way, as the fall of Adam and Eve in earthly history had not yet happened? Although snakes wriggle in the dust, they do not eat it, nor are they exceptionally cunning or crafty above any other animal. This opens up several ponderous questions. How did the serpent become bad and/or was it an alien being already aligned with the rebellion? Next, it refocuses on the mysterious process of free will underway in Adam and Eve. Maybe God had given them a counterbalance in their decision-making.

When we examine Genesis carefully, we see that God did not

create Adam in the Garden of Eden but put him in the garden to tend it. Genesis 2:15 says: *"The LORD God took the man and put him in the Garden of Eden to work it and take care of it."* Now it is curious the Hebrew word *shamar* has been philosophically interpreted as "take care of it" when the main meaning is to "hedge about" (as with thorns) or to guard or protect. If this is the case, God forewarned Adam that there was something unusual—he was to be on guard. Adam's intellect would have been given a warning to process in the will of his mind. He, in turn, would have communicated this to Eve.

Contrary to the naturalistic viewpoint, Adam and Eve were of superior intellect. It is the thought of the intellect in our space-time world that governs the processes of the will. The will, in turn, is embedded in the supernatural of our spiritual body.

Adam and Eve were sustained by the Holy Spirit and fellowshipped with the Lord God, and, although they did not "know good and evil," they should have observed

> **CAVEMEN**
>
> "Cavemen" are a product of later history—after the fall of Adam and Eve and again after Noah's flood in the worldwide dispersion of humanity.

that the serpent was somehow different, in spirit or in actions, otherwise the Lord's instructions to "guard" the garden would have had no meaning.

Eve she saw the fruit was pleasing to the eye, good for food and gaining wisdom. The physical act of seeing would activate cognitive reasoning in the mental realm. Did Adam and Eve know, even though the serpent was mysterious and glittering, there was cunningness about him their rational minds knew was different? Since God is a just and Holy God, some counterbalance may have been in place. Thus, when they ate of the fruit of the knowledge of good and evil, they would have had to let what they saw in the physical suppress the formulating counterbalance of conscience in the intellect of their wills, and then doubt the goodness of God. It is no wonder that we, the human race, became as trash. How great and wondrous is the mercy and grace of our Lord and redeemer!

In taking the position that the serpent was an earthly created being, we still have not been able to resolve how the serpent became crafty and what happened to its kind at the fall, as there may have been untold numbers of them when Adam and Eve were cast out of the garden. One possibility is that, because the serpent was not created in the image of God for an eternal destiny, God allowed its nature to be subverted by Satan outside the Garden of Eden and thus to be a means of counterbalance to the testing of Adam and Eve. Then, under God's curse, its species, which had served its purpose, was reduced to the serpent species we see today.

The Legions of Doom may have assimilated those serpents that existed before the fall to gain access into our physical realm. If these creatures appeared in the days between Adam and Noah, humanity should have known there would be terrible consequences.

A second tenet is that the serpents were physical aliens already in the rebellion. They may be classified under the mysterious dominions of the heavens and were exploring Earth. The curse upon the serpent creatures (*"Cursed are you above all the livestock and all the wild animals"*) then degraded their alien life form to that of our modern reptiles with complete loss of sentience. Since God created life from the "dust" of the earth, the judgment to eat the "dust" of the earth was to now subsist on biological matter. This would be a dramatic warning to the rest of their kind not to manifest themselves into our space-time realm. Any reported modern encounters with the reptilians have been by people flirting with the paranormal in violation of God's command. John Rhodes, in his book, *Dragons of the Apocalypse*, analysis various UFO theories:

These brief descriptions of each theorized reptilian "alien" origin reflect the current perceptions within the UFO community. Many investigators/researchers have observed evidence supporting each particular theory, suggesting that all three may in fact be correct. Some reptilians come from far distant solar systems; others evolved here on Earth and have remained hidden in their underworld empire, while others permeate through the dimensional barrier that separates humanity from the astral realms of the dead. If even one of these theories is true, then humanity is headed towards a revelation of which only the wildest imaginations could ever conceive.

We have been told by the Hebrew, American Indian, Aztec and Hindu prophets that at the "End of Days" we will encounter Dragons, Leviathans and serpent-gods. They shall, we are told, arrive as the harbingers of terror, death, redemption and salvation. From where they will come is a question that has eluded the finest scholarly minds that study these passed down prophesies. One thing we do know, however, and that is that there is more than enough evidence to suggest that they are here, on and in... EARTH... now.[18]

Whether or not we consider the above to be paranormal nonsense, we do know three factual things given to us by the Bible. First, there was something unusual about the serpent in the Garden of Eden and, upon encountering its guile, Adam and Eve joined the rebellion. As a result, they

ANGELIC OCCUPATION

Beings of the heavens who left their first estate and consorted with human women did so against the prime directive of God. This second event was extremely serious in that we are informed: *"the angels who did not keep their positions of authority but abandoned their own home—these he has kept in darkness, bound with everlasting chains for judgment on the great Day"* (Jude 6).

were dispatched from the garden. Cherubim and a flashing sword prevented their return to the garden and the tree of life.

Second, in the days between Adam and Noah, fallen angels called sons of God consorted with mortal women. Through (or because of) the actions of man's self-taking nature and the union with rebellious beings, God declared the world evil and regretted He had made mankind. The Noachian flood was God's judgment of this evil.

AS IN THE DAYS OF NOAH

G. H. Pember, an insightful theologian of the 19th century, notes seven causes of the antediluvian apostasy (Noah's flood) which are apparent in our modern society of the 21st century:

1) A tendency to worship God as Elohim, that is, merely as the creator and benefactor, and not as Jehovah, the covenant God of mercy, dealing with transgressors who are appointed to destruction and finding a ransom for them.

2) An undue prominence of the female sex, and a disregard of the primal law of marriage.

3) A rapid progress in the mechanical arts, and the consequent invention of many devices whereby the hardships of the curse were mitigated and life was rendered more easy and indulgent.

4) A proficiency in the fine arts which captivated the minds of men and helped to induce an entire oblivion of God.

5) An alliance between the nominal Church and the world which speedily resulted in a complete amalgamation.

6) A vast increase in population. The rejection of the preaching of Enoch [and Noah] whose warnings thus became a saviour of death unto the world and hardened men beyond recovery.

7) The appearance upon the earth of beings from the Principality of the Air, and their unlawful intercourse with the human race.[19]

Third, Jesus has told us that before He returns it will be like the days of Noah with all sorts of signs and wonders being done to deceive people. Those people will suffer God's wrath because they will prefer false magic rather than repenting and worshiping their creator.

Mankind's encounters with paranormal forces have invariably led to evil. The last encounter, yet to come, will also be devastating. We do not know in what form the Legions of Doom, at God's timing, will be allowed to manifest themselves in our space-time realm. It is likely that they will appear as very handsome humans. If the appearance of signs in the heavens, the face on Mars or the unusual crop circles on Earth are any indication, then that time may be rapidly approaching. The increasing occurrence of weird animal mutilations suggests that, if they are not caused by evil humans, then sinister aliens are involved, possibly the Reptilians who have to feed on the "dust" of the earth.

In spite of terrifying experiences of abductees and weird animal mutilations, there is a prevailing mindset that alien contact will be beneficial to mankind. These people believe extraterrestrials have come to help in our evolutionary growth, whether physical or spiritual. This third contact will bring deceptions that go against the laws of God. The Scriptures warn: *"The coming of the lawless one will be in accordance with the work of Satan displayed in all kinds of counterfeit miracles, signs and wonders, and in every sort of evil that deceives those who are perishing. They perish because they refused to love the truth and so be saved. For this reason God sends them a powerful delusion so that they will believe the lie and so that all will be condemned who have not believed the truth but have delighted in wickedness."* [20]

> **ALIEN-HUMAN LOVERS**
>
> The sci-fi movie industry has psychologically prepared humanity for alien-human lovers in violation of God's creative plan. This third encounter will deceive those who desire to be "as gods."

It is only when we consider the specific purposes of man that we can make any sense of this schism of the cosmos. Man functions in the space-time world as an animal, yet he is of the supernatural through his eternal spirit given by the "breath" of God. Mankind, as a sentient creature, has been created with free will; he is not a biological automaton programmed to worship his creator. Why would God, being just and fair, force someone to spend eternity with Him who had never sought Him during his life on Earth?

We are created in the image of God. God seeks a relationship of trust, fellowship and worship from a willful heart. This is reflected in the commandment given to Moses: *"Hear, O Israel: The LORD our God, the LORD is one. Love the LORD your God with all your heart and with all your soul and with all your strength."* [21]

Jesus, when tested by the experts in the law as to the greatest commandment, answered: *"'Love the Lord your God with all your heart and with all your soul and with all your mind.' This is the first and greatest commandment. And the second is like it: 'Love your neighbor as yourself.' All the Law and the Prophets hang on these two commandments."* [22]

OUR FUTURE AS BELIEVERS

It is through the willful acceptance of the death and resurrection of Jesus Christ that we have the spiritual power to fulfill God's purposes for us. Satan will make every effort to keep us from making this eternal decision of the will since our future is to be ruling celestial citizens. The technological achievements, freedoms and prosperities of this 21st century should cause us to give praise and honor to God, however the spiritual needs are blinded by the desires of the body. Pember writes:

> And the law of Satan is this:—That we seek all our pleasures in, and fix all our heartfelt hopes upon, this present age over which he presides; and that we use our best endeavors—by means of

various sensuous and intellectual occupations and delights, and countless ways of killing time which he has provided—to keep our thoughts from ever wandering into that age to come, which will see him a fettered captive instead of a prince and a god.[23]

The day will soon come when the battle of the cosmos will be brought to a violent conclusion. The prophet Isaiah was given such a glimpse when God inspired him to write: *"In that day the LORD will punish the powers in the heavens above and the kings on the earth below."* [24] The book of Revelation, dictated to the elderly apostle John by the glorified Son of Man, Jesus Christ, describes all the concluding details of the wrath of God upon an unrepentant world occupied by Satan and his Legions of Doom.

Abraham is known as the father of all who believe by faith. He lived in a time when it seemed as if God did not exist. Men were building a civilization by the effort of their own works and worshiping the gods of mysticism and astrology. The articulate theologian, Paul of Tarsus, writes in his book of Galatians: *"Consider Abraham: 'He believed God, and it was credited to him as righteousness.' Understand, then, that those who believe are children of Abraham. The Scripture foresaw that God would justify the Gentiles by faith, and announced the gospel in advance to Abraham: 'All nations will be blessed through you.' So those who have faith are blessed along with Abraham, the man of faith.... You are all sons of God through faith in Christ Jesus, for all of you who were baptized into Christ have clothed yourselves with Christ. There is neither Jew nor Greek, slave nor free, male nor female, for you are all one in Christ Jesus. If you belong to Christ, then you are Abraham's seed, and heirs according to the promise."* [25]

Abraham believed by faith there was something more; *"he was looking forward to the city with foundations whose architect and builder is God."*[26] *"Therefore God is not ashamed to be called their God, for he has prepared a city for them."* [27] We know through the power of the resurrection our *"citizenship is in heaven. And we eagerly await a Savior from there, the Lord Jesus Christ, who, by the power that enables him to bring everything under his control, will transform our lowly bodies so that they will be like his glorious body."* [28] Paul describes this transformation scene: *"For the Lord himself will come down from heaven, with a loud command, with the voice of the archangel and with the trumpet call of God, and the dead in Christ will rise first. After that, we who are still alive and are left will be caught up together with them in the clouds to meet the Lord in the air. And so we will be with the Lord forever."* [29]

Where will we be with the Lord forever? Jesus reassures His disciples: *"Do not let your hearts be troubled. Trust in God; trust also in me. In my Father's house are many rooms; if it were not so, I would have told you. I am going there to prepare a place for you. And if I go and prepare a place for you, I will come back and take you to be with me."* [30] In the book of Revelation, Jesus shows the apostle John a vision of an incredible city existing in heaven. It is home to the Bride of Christ, a term used for believers. This city will be our celestial home. Later in the ages of time, it will come out of Heaven to the Earth. [31]

The prophet Isaiah was given a foreshadowing of the perilous times that may soon be upon the world. He describes the resurrection and the translation of believers into heaven, to the places prepared for them before the wrath of God comes to judge the world for its wickedness. *"But your dead will live; their bodies will rise. You who dwell in the dust, wake up and shout for joy. Your dew is like the dew of the morning; the earth will give birth to her dead. Go, my people, enter your rooms and shut the doors behind you; hide yourselves for a little while until his wrath has passed by. See, the LORD is coming out of his dwelling to punish the people for their sins."* [32]

Once the wrath of God has been completed against Satan, his Legions of Doom and rebellious humanity, the Bride of Christ as celestial citizens will rule and fellowship with Jesus *"who has gone into heaven and is at God's right hand—with angels, authorities and powers in submission to him."* [33] In the awesome might of His transcendent glory, Jesus reassures John: *"To him who overcomes, I will give the right to sit with me on my throne, just as I overcame and sat down with my Father on his throne."* [34] Again: *"To him who overcomes and does my will to the end, I will give authority over the nations."* [35]

Inspired by the Holy Spirit of God, Paul writes: *"Do you not know that the saints will judge the world? ...Do you not know that we will judge angels?"* [36] (dominions, powers and principalities of the heavens). It is no wonder humanity's coming third encounter with the paranormal is so devastating; the freedom of Satan and his Legions of Doom to be as gods is at stake.

Yes, man is an animal, and he functions in our natural world as such; yet, he is "of the something more"—of the spiritual. It is by repentance and faith that each one is empowered by the Holy Spirit of God to be come a celestial citizen. Dr. Francis Schaeffer writes:

> The first point which we must make is that it is impossible even to begin living the Christian life, or to know anything of true spirituality, before one is a Christian. And the only way to become a Christian is neither by trying to live some sort of a Christian life nor by hoping for some sort of religious experience, but rather by accepting Christ as Saviour. No matter how complicated, educated, or sophisticated we may be, or how simple we may be, we must all come the same way, insofar as becoming a Christian is concerned. As the kings of the earth and the mighty of the earth are born in exactly the same way physically as the simplest man, so the most intellectual person must become a Christian in exactly the same way as the simplest person. This is true for all men, everywhere, through all space and all time. There are no exceptions. Jesus said a totally exclusive word: "No man cometh unto the Father but by me."[37]

This is the great cosmic mystery! *"God so loved the world that he gave His one and only son, that whoever believes in him shall not perish but have eternal life."* [38] Personal repentance comes when we realize all of us have self-taking natures and *"all have sinned and fall short of the glory of God, and are justified freely by his grace through the redemption that came by Christ Jesus."* [39] To be justified before God the Father means Jesus took upon Himself our punishment, thus—justified—"just-as-if-I-had-died." No matter who we are or what we try to do, we will not be saved by our own efforts: *"For it is by grace you have been saved, through faith—and this not from yourselves, it is the gift of God—not by works, so that no one can boast. For we are God's workmanship, created in Christ Jesus to do good works, which God prepared in advance for us to do."* [40]

What then must we do to be saved? The fisherman, Peter, an apostle of Jesus, gave the answer some 2000 years ago, and it is still the same today: *"Repent and be baptized, every one of you, in the name of Jesus Christ for the forgiveness of your sins. And you will receive the gift of the Holy Spirit. The promise is for you and your children and for all who are far off—for all whom the Lord our God will call."* [41]

Even as Adam and Eve confirmed the destiny of the will of their hearts by the physical action of eating the forbidden fruit, so must each one of us, by faith, implement the will of our hearts by the physical actions of our mouths. Thus, *"if you confess with your mouth, 'Jesus Christ is Lord,' and believe in your heart that God has raised him from the dead, you will be saved. For it is with your heart that you believe and are justified, and it is with you mouth that you confess and are saved."* [42]

God knows your heart and is not as concerned with your words as He is with the attitude of your heart. The following is a suggested prayer:

> Lord Jesus, I want to know You personally. Thank You for dying
> on the cross for my sins. I open the door of my life and receive

You as my Savior and Lord. Thank You for forgiving me of my sins and giving me eternal life. Take control of the throne of my life. Make me the kind of person You want me to be.[43]

You are now a spiritually rejuvenated human being and a celestial citizen, for *"those he justified, he also glorified."* [45] Now you have been *"born again, not of perishable seed, but of imperishable, through the living and enduring word of God."* [46] By the grace and mercy of God, we are able to fulfill the two greatest commandments, to *"Love the Lord your God with all your heart and with all your soul and with all your mind and with all your strength. The second is this: 'Love your neighbor as yourself.'"* [47]

> **LOVE**
>
> *"Since God so loved us, we also ought to love one another. No one has ever seen God; but if we love one another, God lives in us and his love is made complete in us."* [44]

NOTES:

[1] Lemonick, Michael D., Andrea Dorfman, "One Giant Step for Mankind," *TIME*, July 23, 2001

[2] McGrew, Professor Miami University, Ohio, <www.BBC.co.uk, Friday 10, August 2001>

[3] Small, Meredith F., "Do Animals Have Culture?" Book Review *The Ape and the Sushi Master: Cultural Reflections of a Primatologist*, *Scientific American*, April 2001, pp. 104–105

[4] Small, Ibid. pp. 104–105

[5] Mayer, Ernst, "Darwin's Influence on Modern Thought," *Scientific American*, July 2000, p. 81

[6] Small, Meredith, "Sigma Chi Chimpy," *Scientific American*, July 2001, p. 26

[7] Wright, Robert, "Our Cheating Hearts," *TIME*, August 15, 1994, p. 30

[8] John 4:23–24

[9] Barovick, Harriet, "Drumming Circles," *TIME*, May 7, 2001, p. 17

[10] 2 Corinthians 6:18; Galatians 4:4–7

[11] Schaeffer, Dr. Francis A., *True Spirituality*, Tyndale House Publishers 1971, p. 89

[12] Revelation 12:4

[13] Hebrews 9:27

[14] Romans 3:22–26

[15] Genesis 1:26

[16] Psalm 8:5

[17] John 1:1–5

[18] Rodes, John, *Dragons of the Apocalypse*, <reptoids.com>

[19] Pember, G. H., M.A., *Earth's Earliest Ages*, 1876, New Edition Kregel Publications 1979, pp. 140–141

[20] 2 Thessalonians 2:9–12

[21] Deuteronomy 6:4–5

[22] Matthew 22:37–40

[23] Pember, Ibid. p. 38

[24] Isaiah 24:21

[25] Galatians 3:6–9, 26–29

[26] Hebrews 11:10

[27] Hebrews 11:16

[28] Philippians 3:20

[29] 1 Thessalonians 4:16–17

[30] John 14:1–3

[31] Revelation 21:1

[32] Isaiah 26:19–21

[33] 1 Peter 3:22

[34] Revelation 3:21

[35] Revelation 2:26

[36] 1 Corinthians 6:2–3

37 Schaeffer, Dr. Francis A., *True Spirituality*, Tyndale House Publishers, 1971, p. 3

38 John 3:16

39 Romans 3:23–24

40 Ephesians 2:8–10

41 Acts 2:38–39

42 Romans 10:9–10

43 Bright, Bill, *Would You Like to Know God Personally?* Campus Crusade New Life Publications, p. 10

44 1 John 4:11–12

45 Romans 8:30

46 1 Peter 1:23

47 Mark 12:30–31

Divine Romance

he mystical day seems as if it is set in Paradise. The sky is so blue it sparkles like the crystalline depth of sapphire. The great garden with its majestic trees and ornate foliage of all colors seems to stretch forever, and yet, there is no distance between here and there. Melodious laughter dances with sweet scents from the rainbow of flowers, like soft caresses of tropical air. He stands in the garden watching as she walks slowly towards Him. It has been so long—His heart that had ached within now bursts with a love even the whole universe could not contain. His strong countenance seems to radiate life like an invisible light, as if through Him all that is has been made and has it's being in Him.

She walks slowly towards Him, her eyes filling with joyous tears, oblivious to the friends of the bridegroom and the glittering opalescent city He has built for her. She can only look into His face, a strong determined face, a face radiating with compassionate love, the face of a King who has conquered dominions, powers and principalities. His right hand rests on the handle of a double-edged sword slung from a wide jeweled belt around His waist. Propped at His left side is a solid, ivory-like shield reflecting the sun like burnished bronze. A cloak of many colors is draped over His shoulders, partially covering a jeweled breast-plate that flashes like dancing rainbows at each breath.

Each step she takes along the golden cobblestone path seems to take a thousand years. She is so beautiful; her gleaming white dress ripples with effervescent light at each graceful movement. Her long hair shimmers as soft wisps of scented air caress her checks. That life when she was but a dream in His heart is so far away. Behind Him now are those battles in the dark world of chaos, the kingdom of the great red dragon. He has ransomed her at the cost of His life. His heart quickens with the swirl of memories, tears of joy well up in His eyes. Oh, how He loves her!

His eyes hold the depths of the universe as they reflect her image back to her. His beard, so harshly plucked out, is now thick and trimmed, yet it can not cover the scars where He was beaten, nor can the soft textured hair or the golden crown cover the scars from the thorn punctures that had seeped salty blood down His face. A victory scar on His wrist reminds her of the iron nails and the wooden cross that held His bruised and beaten body. He had done all this for her; she glows with the radiance of His love. Her shoulders shudder as a flood of joyous tears, sparkling like diamonds, well up in her eyes; He did all this for her. She is forever His bride—His wife; eternity is theirs to blossom and grow in joyous love.

Their hands touch. A shout of acclamation from friends, saints of all ages of history and of all dominions, powers and principalities of the universe rumbles through the cosmos and dimensions of dimensions like a massive peal of thunder. The wedding feast will begin.[1]

NATURALISTIC LOVE

The philosophy of naturalism has so bankrupted the concepts of God, love, bride, virgin, wedding, father-husband, mother-wife, marriage, family, son, daughter, good, evil, the uniqueness of being a human and the emotions attached to all these things, that higher-order spiritual principles become difficult to communicate. The concept of a man and a woman coming chaste into a marriage is a joke to modern society. God does not try us out to see if we perform well and then dump us. Entering multiple failed marriages in a white gown has destroyed the image of virgin purity. If your father is a self-ish, abusive person who was always critical of you and abandoned your mother for another woman, you will have little appreciation for the concept of God as a loving heavenly Father. Likewise, if your mother is a shallow flippant person with a penchant for sexual affairs, then neither will you understand the concept of high monogamy—compassionate love in a marriage. Love becomes defined by sexual attributes as glorified in the romance magazines, and

> **THE BRIDE**
>
> Christian men should not be uncomfortable with the imagery of the Church as a bride. The imagery is to reflect the high order spiritual love of God and incite an emotional response of the heart. The strong biological love between a man and his wife should give growth to a powerful sentient-being-to-sentient-being love. Women have a natural comfort with this image as they give of themselves as brides—person to person. As Christians, we should see ourselves dressed in shining white robes of righteousness, faces lit with glorious anticipation as we stand hands raised in praise awaiting our Lord.

marriage becomes a relationship of selfish sexual convenience rather than a bonding experience of sentient being to sentient being. If your family is always fighting, bickering or caustic to each other, or doesn't really care for you, it will be difficult to understand the concept of being part of the family of God.

AMBASSADORS

Contrary to this "naturalistic love" is the deep love of giving one's life for that of another, as did heroes of the New York Trade Towers bombing. Even though they had a job to do, they did not run from adversity but struggled to rescue lives. This is the kind of compassionate love a husband and wife should have for each other and for their children. The children, in turn, should love and honor their parents. In this war of the cosmos, Jesus Christ, in deep compassionate love, died to redeem our corrupted race.

It is only on the basis of this deep compassionate love, and the spiritual uniqueness of our being created in the image of God, that we can understand the supernatural aspects of our relationship

> **JEWISH FEASTS**
>
> Jesus was killed on the Feast of Passover as the Passover Lamb. He arose from the dead three days later on the Feast of First Fruits. The Feast of Pentecost is fifty days after Passover.

with God; therefore, the picture of Jesus as the bridegroom and His Church as His future heavenly Bride,[2] has depth of meaning. His followers on Earth are described as "His Church" or "the Body of believers" of whom He is the head.[3] This commenced at Pentecost, shortly after Jesus ascended into Heaven[4] when the Holy Spirit descended "like tongues of fire" upon a gathering of believers.

The Old Testament prophets and scholars did not foresee this unique period in our space-time history. Paul writes: *"In reading this, then, you will be able to understand my insight into the mystery of Christ, which was not made known to men in other generations as it has now been revealed by the Holy Spirit to God's holy apostles and prophets. This is the mystery that through the gospel the Gentiles are heirs together with Israel, members of one body, and sharers together in the promise of Christ Jesus."* [5] The Church, as a celestial citizen, is to be espoused to one husband, Christ, as a pure virgin.[6] Our response is to act as faithful servants,[7] yet God, the Lord Almighty says: *"I will be a Father to you, and you will be my sons and daughters."* [8]

Because of God's mercy, we are a people called out of the evil darkness of the world into His light of truth. We have become *"a chosen people, a royal priesthood, a holy nation, a people belonging to God."* [9] We are to declare praises to God and to bring others to Him.[10] *"If anyone is in Christ, he is a new creation; the old has gone, the new has come!"* [11] We are to spread the good news of *"God reconciling the world to himself in Christ;"* therefore, we are *"Christ's ambassadors"* [12] to this dark world, which is ruled by the Prince of Darkness and his Legions of Doom.

THE WORK OF THE HOLY SPIRIT

The step of faith taken by each of us to believe in Jesus has an impact on the supernatural world and on the spiritual conflict underway. When we ask Jesus into our lives, the Holy Spirit comes and sits in the regal chair in our inner throne room. In this way, we become temples of the living God as depicted by the symbolism of the Shekinah glory in the most Holy of Holies of the temple. The Scriptures record: *"Having believed, you were marked in him with a seal, the promised Holy Spirit, who is a deposit guaranteeing our inheritance until the redemption of those who are God's possession—to the praise of his glory."* [13] *"For we were all baptized by one Spirit into one body—whether Jews or Greeks, slave or free—and we were all given one Spirit to drink."* [14]

The step of baptism, by immersion under water and coming up again, symbolizes to the world the death and resurrection of Jesus in our lives. *"We were therefore buried with him through baptism into death in order that, just as Christ was raised from the dead through the glory of the Father, we too may live a new life."* [15] The sealing by the Holy Spirit is the guarantee that, at the resurrection, whether dead or alive, we will be elevated to eternal life, into

Heaven as celestial citizens. Through this action of believing by faith in the mercy and grace of God and receiving the Holy Spirit, you have literally become a child of God. Dr. John White explains this supernatural event:

> Your justification is both a heavenly event and a time space event. It is a heavenly event insofar as Jesus is at this moment on the right hand of God's throne acting as your personal guarantor and representative. It is a heavenly event, too, in that your name is now recorded in the "not guilty" annals of heaven. It is an earthly event since you, a creature of time and space, may boldly step into the presence of the God of eternity and hold a conversation with him. Indeed, you are encouraged to do so. Notice, you are not given permission to crawl into God's presence but to approach him with your head held high.
>
> A second event that took place in your body is what is known as regeneration or new birth. By this event, eternity invaded space and re-established permanent links between your personality and the Eternal. Again, you may have experienced little or nothing when this most profound event occurred. By a miracle of divine grace, a nonbiological life was implanted in you. It is a form of life that will enable you one day to inhabit eternity just as your biological life now enables you to live in time-space.[16]

Satan is also acutely aware of your change of citizenship. You are now a defined foe of the Legions of Doom. However, they fear the Holy Spirit within you, since Jesus defeated them at the cross of Calvary. Jesus prayed for each one of us: *"I have given them [us] the glory that you gave me, that they may*

RESISTANCE IS NOT FUTILE

"Resist the devil, and he will flee from you. Come near to God and he will come near to you."[17]

be one as we are one: I in them and you in me. May they be brought to complete unity to let the world know that you sent me and have loved them even as you have loved me." [18] You are important to God but not to Satan. He will only try to get back at God by tempting and deceiving you through your natural bodily desires.

Since the Church is a living dynamic organism of the Body of Jesus Christ, of which He is the head and each member is a temple of the Holy Spirit, we should go out into the world and live a supernatural life of faith. Dr. Francis Schaeffer comments:

> According to the Bible, we are to be living a supernatural life now, in this present existence, in a way we shall never be able to do again through all eternity. We are called upon to live a supernatural life now, by faith. Eternity will be wonderful, but there is one thing heaven will not contain, and that is the call, the possibility, and the privilege of living a supernatural life here and now by faith before we see Jesus face to face. [19]

The reality, however, is that we live in a closed space-time world and do not see the interdimensional conflicts occurring between angelic forces. Angels of Glory encamp [20] around believers who fear the Lord, while the Legions of Doom are out to defeat us. When bad things happen to the good, and good things happen to the bad, those who are Christ's must believe that He who is outside of our space-time world will work things out for His purposes such that we will be glorified in Heaven even as He is glorified. In our daily routine, the twisted arts and sciences are like dancing shadows being cast upon our perceptions of reality as we struggle to live a life of faith.

ETHEREAL WARFARE ON AMERICA

A very unusual event with no scientific explanation took place over the course of several days as the September 11, 2001 tragedy in New York was unfolding. The noosphere group at Princeton University is looking for evidence that reality can be affected by a possible shift in collective human consciousness. The project is titled the Global Consciousness Project (GCP).[21] Even though the researchers believe in evolution, they are searching for "something more" to their being. Following established scientific principles, the group connected thirty-eight computers around the world to a central computer. Each computer generates a random number once a second and sends it by Internet to a central processor. The major assumption being if something was to impinge upon reality, it would somehow affect the computers and the randomness of the numbers would decrease. Yet there is no logical reason why these specific computers should be affected and not every computer in the world!

Remarkably, on September 11, 2001, a statistically unusual event was recorded which formed a double peak at 9:10 and 10:18 a.m. New York time. Even more startling is a data review from each computer shows the randomness of the number differences decreasing the closer one gets to New York. Therefore, the focus point of decreased randomness pinpointed that city.

GCP DATA

"Based upon an analysis of 3 months of GCP data, I conclude that a statistical anomaly occurred that was associated with the date, time and general location of the terrorist attacks of September 11, 2001. There is also evidence that the anomaly began to appear a few hours before the widely visible events unfolded" (Dean Radin, Institute of Noetic Sciences).[22]

The noosphere group, according to their philosophical premise, cautiously interpreted the data as "mass-mind" affecting the physical world.[23] The decreasing randomness can be attributed to only two causes: physical human scamming or supernatural influences. Since the Princeton group could not anticipate such a horrific human tragedy, nor accede to such a diabolical scheme, the former is improbable. Next the question becomes, is there a Scriptural basis or any evidence that a cautious interpretation could be made in favor of the latter?

The scientific "odds against chance graph" for the period September 3 to 14, 2001 shows some intriguing data (remember, this information is being provided every second giving a high order of certainty). The decrease in randomness started on September 10 forming an elevated shoulder. Around midnight, it started to increase steadily until approximately 6 a.m. on September 11 when it then increased rapidly forming a peak at 9:10 a.m. It then decreased rapidly (the numbers become more chaotic, i.e. normal) to around 9:30 a.m. when the graph again turns and ascends rapidly to form another peak at 10:18 a.m. equal to the first one. The noosphere group calculated the odds against chance of this happening at 29 billion to one. After this, the GCP data formed a shoulder through to the 13th of approximately the same height as that on the 10th. On the 13th, it forms a moderate well-defined high from noon to midnight with a peak around 6:00 p.m. On the 14th, the graph descended rapidly to strongly chaotic numbers (became normal) as if the manipulative force was removed.

When we review the chart in detail, it is apparent the Global Consciousness interpretation has its problems. Any "mass-mind" effect should come several hours after the tragedy when the human psyche of the nation and the world was overwhelmed with the scope of the terror—not **starting before**—on September 10th and strongly at 6 a.m. on the

TIME OF EVENTS[24]

8:45—North Tower hit

9:03—South Tower hit

9:43—Pentagon hit

9:58—South Tower collapses

10:28—North Tower collapses

11th. The charts clearly show that the effect is somehow linked to the terror and the supernatural forces causing its precipitation. To suggest it was "mind-mass" effect of people in Eastern America would imply that the citizens of New York willfully brought disaster upon themselves. Before a possible interpretation is given, let us examine the spiritual fabric of the United States of America since any supernatural influences involves Satan and his Legions of Doom who are in conflict against God and the Angels of Glory.

America's motto is, "In God we trust." God is the monotheistic God of the Jews, Christians and Muslims. The United States has a large population of believers—whether Protestant, Catholic or Messianic Jews—who believe that Jesus Christ, evidenced by His death and resurrection, is God's only provision of salvation to the world. No other nation has sent such a large contingent of missionaries around the world. No other nation contributes in such a large way to world aid, or tries to help and bring peace and prosperity to others. Yet within are forces of evil that malign the goodness of God and deny His existence; such was Jesus's parable of the field of mixed wheat and weeds. Many citizens of America are choosing new gods, as did the ancient nation of Israel in the time of the Judges: *"when they chose new gods, war came to the city gates."* [25]

WHEAT AND WEEDS

Jesus, in Matthew 13, explains to His disciples: *"The one who sowed the good seed is the Son of Man. The field is the world, and the good seed stands for the sons of the kingdom. The weeds are the sons of the evil one, and the enemy who sows them is the devil. The harvest is the end of the age, and harvesters are the angels"* (vv. 37–39). Much to Satan's dismay, this spiritual kingdom was established on planet Earth at the Jewish feast of Pentecost by the power of the Holy Spirit.

McCandlish Philips comments:

New gods are swarming into the American culture. Gods that were never heretofore present in the nation are coming in. For that reason there is spiritual warfare at the gates of the nation and the destiny of the United States will depend on whether the people choose to honor God or to honor the gods. There is no true god but the God of Israel, the God of the Bible. Each of the 'gods' is a demon spirit.[26]

Philips relates the episode of the presentation of a young Hindu, Jiddu Krishnamurti, by the Theosophical Society to America in the 1920s. In 1911 in India, "a great coronet of shimmering blue appeared above his head." Spiritualists believed that through him the great "World Teacher would again speak to mankind." The young Hindu had success in India and Europe; however, upon entering New York harbor, he began to complain of "bad atmospheric conditions" and was unable to use any mystical powers while in America.

Much has changed since then. America has drifted into a Godless secular society wherein many citizens feel that they do not need God or His protection. Their thinking will be come twisted as they serve other gods. Jesus prophesied *a time is coming when anyone who kills you will think that he is offering a service to God."* [27]

God created and sustains the universe. He does not manipulate events but may permit the consequence of spiritual attitudes and physical acts to unfold in our space-time world. Moreover, because "God is good and His love endures forever," He will bring goodness from events perpetrated by the forces of evil.

God may hold back His judgment for a time, allowing evil tyrants to have their day, upsetting people's well-ordered lives and presenting them with dilemmas beyond their understanding. Evil brings pain, but it is the genius of God to bring good out of evil (Rom. 8:28).[28]

Now, let us again look at the charts but take into account the spiritual "war of the cosmos." Satan desires to be as God and is capable of manipulating computer electronics as well as the spiritual wills of humans who belong to him. This manipulation was done to convince people that global consciousness exists. Thus, the illusion of "mass-mind" is only a deception that mankind can be "as gods." Based on the GCP graphs, the Legions of Doom concentrated spiritual energy into the Eastern United States on September 10, mobilizing their terrorist human minions. If the terrorists were following the prayer rules of Islam, though they are a deceived cult, they would have prayed five times daily and likely in the early morning as they headed for the airport. The build-up of demonic energy began to increase dramatically around 6 a.m. as the demons made sure their minions were spiritually prepared to fly the planes into the Towers. A second surge of demonic energy may have aided the collapse of the Towers in an attempt to trap as many human victims as possible, or they were just filled with malevolent glee.

> **UFOs**
>
> UFOs are reported to affect the electronics of cars, pursing aircraft and electric power grids.[29]

At the same time, the Angels of Glory were busy—many people were late for work or did not make appointments. Others escaped by miraculous means. Estimates indicate over 50,000 people could have been in the Twin Towers when the terrorists struck, yet over 90 percent of these escaped. The alternate mass-mind theory of dying souls affecting the computers is not valid because the rapid ascension of the graph began early in the morning. Moreover, by the time the second tower collapsed, some 90 percent of the occupants had escaped. One does not want to make too much of it, but reportedly an evil face appeared in the smoke of one of the towers.[30] Yes, the billowing smoke likely caused it; nevertheless, the face is readily discernable.

By midnight of the 13th, the Church of Jesus Christ around the world gathered in intercessory prayer for the American people. On the 14th, concerned Americans gathered to pray. Startlingly evident on the GCP graph, beginning at midnight of the 13th through September 14th, there is a rapid increase to strongly chaotic numbers (becoming normal). Since "free will" thought is a function of the quantum state of chaos, it might be inferred that something spiritual destabilized the unnatural forced order of the numbers. Could intercessory prayer—by the Body of Christ to the throne of God—be that spiritual power?[31]

There is also a deeper symbolism: the day of prayer took place on the third day after the terror, paralleling the resurrection of Jesus from the dead.

Since September 11, there has been a tremendous resurgence in spiritual interest in America, more so than in other parts of the world. America is a cosmopolitan nation similar to the peoples of the Church; could this be a sign that the hearts of those in the Church need to be refreshed? Should you be looking for a sign? A sign may very well have been given. Call out to Jesus and be saved for the hour of the Beast may be at hand.

THE MYSTERY OF THE CHURCH

The Church, as a community of believers, is the supernatural Body of Jesus active in the world. Charles Colson, in his book, *The Body*, writes:

> Hundreds, then thousands, then millions of believers became part of that body. Generations of Christians, gifted in a thousand different ways and empowered by the same Holy 'Spirit, invaded every arena of human life, every country, every field of endeavor, bringing the truth to bear on their surroundings.
>
> In His earthly ministry, Jesus was limited to one human body; now the body of Christ is made up of millions and millions

of human bodies stamped with His image—His followers. That includes you and me, for Jesus prayed for us that last evening, not just for the disciples who were with Him. "My prayer is not for them alone," He told His Father. "I pray also for those who will believe in me through their message. What an astounding thought! Jesus ascended. But His Spirit descended to empower His body—the Church—to do more than He could accomplish as one Person.

In light of this awesome truth, it is scandalous that so many believers today have such a low view of the Church. They see their Christian lives as a solitary exercise—Jesus and me—or they treat the church as a building or a social center. They flit from congregation to congregation—or they don't associate with any church at all. That the Church is held in such low esteem reflects not only the depths of our biblical ignorance, but the alarming extent to which we have succumbed to the obsessive individualism of modern culture.[32]

The greatest mission the Church has is to bring love to a sin-sick, rebellious world in accordance to the commandment of God. The apostle Paul writes: *"If I speak in the tongues of men and of angels, but have not love, I am only a resounding gong or a clanging cymbal."* We can have many positive attributes, make exceptional sacrifices, be educated and give to the poor, but if we do not love from the depths of our hearts, we are as nothing. *"Love is patient, love is kind. It does not envy, it does not boast, it is not proud. It is not rude, it is not self-seeking, it is not easily angered, it keeps no record of wrongs. Love does not delight in evil but rejoices with truth. It always protects, always trusts, always hopes, always perseveres."* [33]

The mystery of the Church being betrothed to Jesus during this age of grace and mercy is like a golden thread weaving its way back through the ages, through space-time to the depths of eternity and the Holy Trinity of God. Before "in the beginning," there was love and communication within the community of the Trinity. Mankind is created in the image of God; thus, there is to be love and communication vertically to God and horizontally between man and wife. Love is the foundation of the family, and the Church. *"Dear friends,"* writes the apostle John, *"let us love one another, for love comes from God. Everyone who loves has been born of God and knows God. Whoever does not love does not know God, because God is love."* [34] That does not mean that God is somehow mystically created by the emotions of loving

> **THE MILLENNIAL KINGDOM**
>
> This is a literal 1,000-year period when Satan is locked in the Abyss and cannot deceive the nations (Rev. 20:3). It is a time of peace when weapons will be made into farming equipment (Isa. 2:4).

someone, but that love is the epitome of the essence of God.

In the course of history, Israel was depicted as the wife of Jehovah.[35] She was to love God with her heart, her soul and her mind. Instead, she disobeyed His laws, committing adultery with other "gods." She will be restored at the time of the millennial kingdom; she will be the light for God and chief of the nations.[36]

The nation Israel and the Church are two distinct identities. Jesus illustrates this in His parables of the hidden treasure and the pearl of great value.[37] Israel is God's treasured possession[38] and was hidden in the field of nations. She was purchased by Jesus at the cross but remains hidden until the fullness of the Church is completed. The Church is the pearl of great value bought with everything He had; she is not hidden in the world but is comprised of people from all nations.

ADMINISTRATIONS OF HEAVEN AND EARTH

There are those who confuse the destiny of Israel with the Church, not recognizing that Israel is a national administration for

Earth while the Church, as the future wife of the King, is a heavenly administration. She is made up of individuals from every tribe and nation and is presented to Christ as a virgin. Though the kingdom of God is at work on Earth, the Church is never described as a kingdom; she is not to be a theocratic state on Earth with rules, rituals and a divine figurehead leader. Clarence Larkin writes:

> The great mistake the Church has made is appropriating to herself, in this Dispensation, the promises of earthly conquest and glory, which belong exclusively to Israel in the Millennial, or "Kingdom Age." As soon as the Church enters into an "Alliance with the World," and seeks the help of Parliaments, Congresses, Legislatures, Federations and Reform Societies, largely made up of ungodly men and women, she loses her spiritual power and becomes helpless as a redeeming force.[39]

She is a result of God's divine program wherein He is calling out a celestial people for Himself.[40] She is to bring the good news of salvation to the world, though the entire world will not be saved. Jesus said: *"The kingdom of God is within you."* [41] Each one in the Body of Christ is indwelt by the Godhead; the kingdom of God, in this present time on Earth, is a spiritual kingdom of which we will be future, physically resurrected, celestial citizens.

It is through Israel that the promised "Seed" came to redeem the world. Jesus is of the royal lineage of King[42] David of the tribe of Judah. Jesus is the nobleman farmer who has gone into a far country to receive His kingdom and be made king. The book of Revelation describes the warfare that takes place when He deposes Satan, the usurper ruler of planet Earth. In the kingdom administration of the world, He will rule all of the Heavens and the Earth as King of Kings and Lord of Lords. His wife, the Church, will rule with Him from the celestial opalescent city, the New Jerusalem, as the heavenly administration. King David will be resurrected[43] and rule Israel from the refurbished earthly Jerusalem and its magnificent temple to be built by Jesus.

The earthly administration of Israel came through the promises of God to Abraham and was prepared *"since the creation of the world."* [44] Whereas, Jesus was chosen as a lamb without blemish *"before the creation of the world,"* [45] God the Father *"chose us in him before the creation of the world to be holy and blameless in his sight."* [46] No greater love story could ever be conceived than the Holy Trinity bringing a Bride into being for the Son, the second person of the Godhead, as the ransom for His life.

Before the creation of the first Adam, the second Adam—Jesus, as God incarnate in man—was already conceived in the heart of God. When we examine the creation of Eve in detail, we see the Bible's supernatural uniqueness because the creation of Eve from Adam's rib, in the Old Testament, foreshadows the creation of the Bride of the King in the New Testament. Adam received his wife not from the dust of the earth, as did the animals, but from living matter taken from his own body. The Lord God caused a deep sleep to come upon Adam and removed a rib. Then, closing up Adam's side, He "made" Eve from the rib.[47] She was of the same breath of life as Adam. Therefore, Adam could say, she *"is bone of my bones and flesh of my flesh... for she was taken out of man."* [48] The Hebrew word for "made" is *banah*, meaning "to build," giving meaning to the verse: *"And in him you too are being built together to become a dwelling in which God lives by his Spirit."* [49] The Bride is being "built" as a spiritual dwelling for the second Adam—Jesus.

MARRIAGE—A DIVINE ORDINATION

God presents Eve to Adam as his helpmate, to be his wife in a high monogamy marriage, a one-husband-one-wife relationship. This word in Hebrew is *ezar*, meaning "to aid." She is not presented to Adam as his wife in some subservient capacity; she is to be his aid in the administration of the Earth. Likewise, the Church as wife of the great King will be His helpmate or aid in His heavenly administration.

In a parallel sense of God taking the rib from Adam's side and creating Eve, the Bride of Jesus came from His side. As Jesus hung on the cross in the sleep of death, a soldier pierced His side with a sword; from it flowed blood and water.[50] It is through the blood and the water that God is building the Bride for His Son. For *"with your blood you purchased men for God from every tribe and language and people and nation."* [51] The water represents the Holy Spirit. Jesus states: *"Whoever drinks the water I give him will never thirst. Indeed, the water I give him*

> **HIGH MONOGAMY**
>
> This term refers to a marriage where man and wife love each other as individuals and live for each other throughout their lives in a joyful relationship.

will become in him a spring of water welling up to eternal life." [52] God is presenting us to Christ as members of the Bride; for *"no one,"* said Jesus *"can come to me unless the Father who sent me draws him."* [53]

Marriage is divinely ordained, for as Eve came from the body of Adam, so will a man *"leave his father and mother and be united to his wife, and the two shall become one flesh."* [54] Likewise, we are members of the Body of Christ. The marital relationship between man and wife is to symbolize the profound relationship between Jesus and His Church. A man is to love his wife as his own body. *"He who loves his wife loves himself. After all, no one ever hated his own body, but he feeds and cares for it, just as Christ does the Church." "Wives, submit to your husband as to the Lord. For the husband is the head of the wife as Christ is the head of the Church, his Body, of which he is the Savior."* [55] The wife is not in some subservient relationship to be lorded over by her husband but is an aid, a helpmate. Both are to love each other, sentient being to sentient being, in compassionate, sacrificial love even as Jesus gave His life for us.

God says, *"I hate divorce."* [56] Marriage within God's chosen people was to be a beautiful loving symbolism to the surrounding nations of the love of God, the husband, to Israel, the wife. In Christendom, marriage is to symbolize Christ's compassionate, sacrificial love for the world in the way the husband and wife love each other, and, within the Body of the Church, how we love each other. When asked about divorce, Jesus told the Pharisees: *"Moses permitted you to divorce your wives because your hearts were hard. But it was not this way from the beginning. I tell you that anyone who divorces his wife, except for marital unfaithfulness, and marries another woman commits adultery."* [57]

In light of the attitudes of secular society towards sex, marriage and the breakdown of the family unit, is it any wonder the world does not understand the betrothal concept of the Church to Jesus Christ? When so-called professing Christian couples divorce, it adds further stigma to the Church as the Bride of Christ. We are called by Jesus to be a people, pure and holy, to be in the world but not of the world. The Bride returns with the Lord to the Earth wearing *"fine linen, bright and clean…. Fine linen stands for the righteous acts of the saints."* [58] Just as extramarital flirtations can lead to adultery, so can flirtations with worldly concepts and values lead to spiritual adultery and unrighteousness.

In order to be "of the something more," we have to come to the knowledge that there is something more. Selfish, "free love" sex encounters seem thrilling for the moment but only lead to meaningless despair, so naturalism is not the solution. This question was raised in an earlier chapter: if God wanted to create free will, sentient, eternal beings of a higher order, how could He accomplish it? It is readily apparent, from the evidence of the war of the cosmos, it does not happen with a divine hand wave; there have to be free will choices with eternal consequences. God is allowing Satan, the rebel, and his Legions of Doom to be free will counterpoints to accepting the ransoming sacrificial death of the Second Person of the Trinity, the God-man, Jesus Christ. His death on the hill of Calvary, outside of His beloved city, Jerusalem, and resurrection three days later from the garden tomb, is the crossroads to eternity: eternal life with God, or death—an eternal separation from the love of God. God is slowly unfolding the future that will one day explode into a universe filled with love and creativity.

Therefore, marital love and paternal love are to reflect, but dimly, the love and communication within the Trinity and Their love for us that we should become children of God. In all this, Satan will try to inflate man's selfish nature of covetousness, lust and passions such that we are blinded to God's grace and mercy. Satan's program of twisted arts, sciences and the delusion we shall be evolutionary gods only leads to the gates of Hell.

MARRIAGE AND THE BRIDE OF CHRIST

Marriage is to be a beautiful symbolic relationship of Christ and His Bride, so let's explore the exciting details and see if they can help us in our marriages and family relationships and with caring for others in the Church. Wedding details, preparations and arrival of guests for the ceremony is stressful yet joyously exciting; then the moment comes.

Weddings have various formats. Besides a bride and

BRIDEGROOMS WAIT

Jesus waits, and symbolically human bridegrooms wait. It was 2 p.m. and then the Church door opened. Gracefully she slowly walked down the isle, the most beautiful woman in the whole world; each step seemed an eternity. Now, at the touch of her lips, it seems as if it were yesterday!

bridegroom there are usually rings, an engagement or betrothal period, shower gifts, attendants, a church, guests, a marriage ceremony and a wedding meal. Needless to say, the marriage of Christ and His Bride is patterned after the Jewish customs. Dr. John Walvoord explains:

> Though marriage customs varied in the ancient world, usually there were three major aspects:
>
> (1) The marriage contract was often consummated by the parents when the parties to the marriage were still children and not ready to assume adult responsibility. The payment of a suitable dowry was often a feature of the contract. When consummated, the contract meant that the couple were legally married.
>
> (2) At a later time when a couple had reached a suitable age, the second step in the wedding took place. This was a ceremony in which the bridegroom accompanied by his friends would go to the house of the bride and escort her to his home. This is the background of the parable of the virgins in Matthew 25:1–13.
>
> (3) Then the bridegroom would bring his bride to his home and the marriage supper, to which guests were invited, would take place. It was such a wedding feast that Christ attended at Cana as recorded in John 2:1–12.[59]

The Church, now in the world, is in the first stage. Jesus has given His life as a dowry for us so we can legally belong to Him by asking Him into our lives.

In the second stage, at some unknown time, the Lord will come suddenly for His Bride: *"For the Lord himself will come down from heaven, with a loud command, with the voice of the archangel and with the trumpet call of God, and the dead in Christ will rise first. After that, we who are still alive and are left will be caught up together with them in the clouds to meet the Lord in the air. And so we will be with the Lord forever."* [60]

The third stage takes place in Heaven with the celebration of rewards and a great wedding supper.

Contrary to having our future in our "own evolved hands," our spiritual destinies are either with God or Satan. Just as God told Eve—*"Your desire will be for your husband, and he will rule over you"* (Gen. 3:16)—we have a God-consciousness that will either be filled by God or by Satan, the false lover. This also applies to the Church as Satan tries to get her to commit adultery with worldly gods just as Israel did.

THE LANGUAGE OF LOVE

God ordained the sexual love relationship between husband and wife. He made them male and female and blessed them, saying: *"Be fruitful and increase in number; fill the earth and subdue it. …God saw all that he had made, and it was very good."* [61] *"The man and his wife were naked and they felt no shame."* [62] The physical union of man and wife as "one flesh" is a deep chemical and emotional language of love that cannot be expressed by words or any other act. Marriage counselor Anne Kristin Carroll, in her book, *Together Forever*, writes:

> The part of us which was created in God's image is invisible and intangible. But God gave us a tangible, visible way of manifesting what is a reality in the soul, and this is done through the body.[63]

In this same way, the love of Jesus Christ becomes tangible to the world as He works through His Body, the Church.

The beautiful symbolism of the Church as a bride begins with the betrothal of accepting Jesus as Lord and Savior.[64] The engagement ring is the indwelling of the Holy Spirit in our hearts *"as a deposit guaranteeing what is to come."* [65] Bridal shower gifts are given though the Holy Spirit. According to His determination, some are given wisdom, knowledge, faith, healings, miraculous powers, prophecy, discernment of spirits and the speaking and interpretation of tongues (languages).[66] In all this, we are clothed with the *"garments of salvation and arrayed in a robe of righteousness… as a bride adorns herself with jewels."* [67] We are to clothe ourselves *"with compassion, kindness, humility, gentleness and patience. Bear with each other and forgive whatever grievance you may have against one another. Forgive as the Lord forgave you. And over all these virtues put on love, which binds them all together in perfect unity."* [68]

The Church is to glow with the radiance of peace and gratitude to God, to make joyful music and encourage one another as she waits for the sudden appearing of the bridegroom to take her to her heavenly home and the great wedding feast that is being prepared. However, what the Church is supposed to be as she lives in the world and what she actually is, is played out in the battleground of spiritual forces, of good and evil, hope and despair. The philosophy of naturalism, our animal nature, our bent self-taking spirit and the powerful dissonance of spiritual deception by Satan and his Legions of Doom, despoil the Bride such that Jesus would say, *"when the Son of Man comes, will he find faith on the earth?"* [69]

Rest assured, Jesus will come for His own because He said to His disciples: *"I tell you, I will not drink of the fruit of the vine from now on until that day when I drink it anew with you in my Father's kingdom."* [70]

NOTES:

[1] Revelation 19:7–10

[2] Revelation 19:7

[3] Ephesians 1:22

[4] Acts 2:1–4

[5] Ephesians 3:4–6

[6] 2 Corinthians 11:2

[7] 2 Corinthians 6:4

[8] 2 Corinthians 6:18

[9] 1 Peter 2:9–10

[10] Romans 7:4

[11] 2 Corinthians 5:17

[12] 2 Corinthians 5:19–20

[13] Ephesians 1:13–14

[14] 1 Corinthians 12:13

[15] Romans 6:4

[16] White, Dr. John, *The Fight*, Intervarsity Press 1976, pp. 12–13

[17] James 4:7

[18] John 17:22–23

[19] Schaeffer, Dr. Francis A., *True Spirituality*, Tyndale House Publishers 1971, p. 72

[20] Psalm 34:7

[21] Web address:

[22] <noosphere.princeton.edu/boundaryanalysis.html>

[23] <noosphere.princeton.edu/terror.html>

[24] *The Day that Changed America*, Vol. II. No. 3, AMI Specials, American Media Specials Inc., September 2001

[25] Judges 5:8

[26] Philips, McCandlish, *The Spirit World*, Victor Books 1972, p. 19

[27] John 16:2

[28] Roper, David R., "Making the Most of Time," *Our Daily Bread*, October 16, 2001, RBC Ministries

[29] Weldon, John Levitt Zola, *UFOs: What on Earth is Happening?*, Harvest House Publishers, 1975, pp. 10, 36

[30] "Satanic Face Appears For Some in Twin Towers Photo," Web: <100megsfree4.com/farshores/psatin.htm>

[31] 1 Corinthians 12:27

[32] Colson, Charles, *The Body*, Word Publishing, 1992, p. 276

[33] 1 Corinthians 13:1–7

[34] 1 John 4:7

[35] Isaiah 54:1–8

[36] Deuteronomy 28:13; Isaiah 60:12; Ezekiel 37:27; Zechariah 8:20–23

[37] Matthew 13:44–46

[38] Psalm 135:4; Exodus 19:5

[39] Larkin, Clarence, *Dispensational Truth*, 1918, Publishers Rev. Clarence Larkin Est., p. 78

[40] Acts 15:13–18

[41] Luke 17:21

[42] Luke 19:11–27

[43] Jeremiah 30:9; Ezekiel 37:24–25

[44] Matthew 25:34

[45] 1Peter 1:20

[46] Ephesians 1:4

[47] Genesis 2:22

[48] Genesis 2:23

[49] Ephesians 2:22

[50] 1 John 5:6–7

[51] Revelation 5:9

[52] John 4:14

[53] John 6:44

[54] Genesis 2:24

[55] Ephesians 5:22–33

[56] Malachi 2:16

[57] Matthew 19:8

[58] Revelation 19:8

[59] Walvoord, John F., *The Revelation of Jesus Christ*, Moody Press, 1966, p. 271

[60] 1 Thessalonians 4:16–17

[61] Genesis 1:27–31

[62] Genesis 2:25

[63] Carroll, Anne Kristin, *Together Forever*, Zondervan Publishing House, 1982, p. 140

[64] Romans 10:8–11

[65] 2 Corinthians 1:22

[66] 1 Corinthians 12:7–11

[67] Isaiah 61:10

[68] Colossians 3:12–14

[69] Luke 18:8

[70] Matthew 26:29

Freedom

he sound of river water lapping against the piling drifts up the pier to where she is standing. She rests her elbows on the rails and gazes across the rippling river to where it meets the incoming tide. Midnight summer breezes wisp through her long hair causing it to shimmer in the moonlight. Titan presses closer, his arm against hers. Taking a deep breath, she subconsciously smoothes her silky dress downward. Titan had smiled very warmly at her over dinner. "Maybe my dress neckline is a little too low," she thinks uncertainly.

The silvery moon hangs low in the horizon, sending dancing moonbeams across the water. As she tilts her head from side to side, flickering beams dance back and forth between her and Titan. Looking across the water to where the river presses against the incoming ocean tide, even the glowing wave crests seem to struggle against each other. Her right hand slowly twists her engagement ring. "Let's have dinner tonight for old times' sake," he had said. Dinner, at the Pier Restaurant, was cloaked in an ambiance of warm and friendly memories. His appearance was always so handsome and charming, but she knows of his dark side. They had once been sweethearts.

"Why did I say yes to dinner?" she questions herself. Joshua is away; time seems to last forever. "After all, we can just be friends," said Titan, but in her heart, she knows better. She can sense the radiation of his manhood beside her. Just then, a moonbeam flashes from a dancing wave, and Joshua enters her heart. He is different—strong with a loving compassionate strength. She can almost feel his comforting arms around her and see his eyes shine with a faithfulness that will last forever. She laughs and gives Titan a quick, friendly punch on his arm to break up any ideas he might have. "Let's head back," she hears herself say. "It has been fun, but I have a hard day at work tomorrow."

She gently closes the convertible door, tucks her pearl embroidered purse under her arm and waves goodbye. "Remember, if you want a great time, I'm available," are his laughing words as the car accelerates, the taillights twinkling into the distance. She resolves to tell Joshua about this evening and ask for forgiveness, not that he wouldn't understand, but what would others think of Joshua if they saw her with her old boyfriend? Her heart skips one of those happy beats as she walks up the sidewalk—Joshua is returning soon. There is freedom and trust within his love, but she is to be faithful even as he is faithful.

Love is the foundation of marriage and the Church: *"since God so loved us, we also ought to love one another."* [1] Even as a marriage is to bring forth happy, well-adjusted children (and that, we know as parents, is not easy), so is the Church to go in love *"and make disciples of all nations, baptizing them in the name of the Father and of the Son and of the Holy Spirit."* [2] Jesus uses the dynamics of marriage, through the writings of Paul the apostle, to bring the Church to a higher order of understanding of our celestial destiny.

While serving as a deacon and teaching adult Sunday school classes, it became apparent that poor marriage relationships reflect back into poor congregational attitudes affecting the heartbeat and image of the Church. Marriages are intense interpersonal relationships with similar problems to dysfunctional spiritual heart attitudes of the Church. Anne Kristin Carroll's marriage-counseling book, *Together Forever*, proved to be an excellent basis for teaching a Sunday school class on the "Bride of Christ." In understanding and dealing with marriage conflicts, we can improve our marriages and relationships within the Body of believers. Moreover, whether single or married, we need to know who we are as individuals. Positive servant attitudes enhance the image of the Bride of Christ to the watching world.

Church groups wonder why spiritually seeking individuals seldom come into their churches. Maybe they should see themselves as others see them. Once, on a business trip to a rural area, this type of problem was dramatically played out. An evangelical Christian group dominated the town and surrounding villages. The Church was well bound with rules and regulations and of sufficient wealth to meddle in the local politics. Our business group met at a local coffee shop; the hot coffee had barely settled in my cup when someone commented on a recent adulterous relationship of a Sunday school teacher. Various comments continued regarding other improprieties and self-righteous unforgiving attitudes. Yet the people could be seen walking to church, Bibles in hand, in their nice suites and dresses. One of my contacts was questioning who Jesus Christ really is; a number of enjoyable conversations ensued. However, because of the hypocrisy and lack of evidence for fruits of the Spirit, compassion, peace, joy and love, there is no way he will visit one of these churches.

When people visit a church service, will they encounter preconceived ideas that drive them away? A small, dynamic church, led by an inspiring, caring pastor, had just completed an expansion-building program. One sunny Sunday morning, a poorly dressed man and woman came into the church each holding a little kitten. They sat down in the back of the church with happy smiles on their faces. Maybe, being mentally handicapped, it was the love they felt for the kittens that brought them to seek the love of God. However, it was not long before a well-dressed usher had them take their kittens outside. They slowly wandered away as if they had lost something. Within a number of years there were rumblings; the pastor's sermons weren't inspiring enough, this or that person wasn't really walking with God, and so it went until the Bride of Christ was wearing a soiled dress.

"My brothers," said James, brother of Jesus, *"as believers in our glorious Lord Jesus Christ, don't show favoritism. Suppose a man comes into your meeting wearing a gold ring and fine clothes, and a poor man in shabby clothes also comes in. If you show special attention to the man wearing fine clothes and say, 'Here's a good seat for you,' but say to the poor man, 'You stand there' or 'Sit on the floor by my feet,' have you not discriminated among yourselves and become judges with evil thoughts?"* [3]

LOVE BRINGS FREEDOM

Both in marriages and in the Church, what begins as relational outlines for harmonious freedom in living soon become entrenched as documented guidelines and then as rules and regulations. How many times have you questioned something only to be informed, "That's just not the way it's done," and no explanation can be given as to why? Usually these dead guidelines have become a basis for authority and control; institutional walls are built until the once-beautiful cottage is an ugly monstrosity. In the first few centuries after Christ, the simple power of the gospel of freedom changed lives and nations by the blood of its martyrs, but as the Church was impregnated with rules of sanctification, it degenerated into a religious prison for the soul. Glorious cathedrals full of pomp and ceremony gave people a feeling of spiritual appeasement. What was lost was the transforming message of the gospel and the freedom to live as future celestial citizens? Martin Luther rebelled against the regulations of religious power in the Catholic Church only to have the Protestant Churches of the reformation succumb to the same affliction.

RULES AND REGULATIONS

Temptation began in the Garden of Eden; Eve saw, she wanted, she took. Pride and selfishness are the two faithful bulldogs of covetousness. The innate programming of our animal natures also subverts our higher spiritual aspirations. Natural animal instincts are to outline a territory for survival, to protect the territory, to take a livelihood from it and then to form family groups for the continuation of the species. Only humanity has the higher instinct to seek God or willfully deny His existence. Self-directed natural tendencies in our personal lives, our marriages and our spiritual pursuits will alienate one from another, resulting in distrust. Subsequently, in the name of freedom and security, we create power structures with rules and regulations.

When we become believers by the transforming message of the gospel (meaning "good news"), the redeeming work of Jesus sets us free from the slavery of our self-taking natures. He states: *"If you hold to my teaching, you are my disciples. Then you will know the truth and the truth will set you free. …So if the Son sets you free you are free indeed,"* [4] and: *"Now the Lord is the Spirit, and where the Spirit of the Lord is, there is freedom. And we, who with unveiled faces all reflect the Lord's glory, are being transformed into his likeness with ever increasing glory, which comes from the Lord, who is the Spirit."* [5] Rules and regulations of religious systems do not give freedom; it is through the love of God we love, and *"do to one another what you would have them do to you"* (Matt. 7:12) brings freedom.

"It is for freedom that Christ has set us free. Stand firm, then, and do not let yourselves be burdened again by a yoke of slavery." The

apostle Paul, in writing these words, is addressing the God-given laws of Moses versus the contrived laws of the Jewish religious system (this applies equally to the religious Church systems of modern Christendom). He adds, *"You who are trying to be justified by the law have been alienated from Christ; you have fallen away from grace."* 6 One of the paradoxical mysteries of Christendom is that to be free, we are to live as servants. The apostle Peter writes: *"Live as free men, but do not use your freedom as a cover-up for evil; live as servants of God. Show proper respect to everyone; Love the brotherhood of believers, fear God, honor the king."* 7

CHURCH LEADERSHIP

The Church is to have leaders and councils just as James, the brother of Jesus, Peter and Paul were leaders meeting in council to pray about and decide upon the questions of laws and regulations affecting the newly born fellowship of believers. The underlying principle of the Church should be: *"Do nothing out of selfish ambition or vain conceit, but in humility consider others better than yourselves. Each of you should look not only to your own interest, but also to the interest of others."* 8 Jesus made the following comment regarding the attitudes of leadership: *"You know that the rulers of the Gentiles lord it over them, and their high officials exercise authority over them. Not so with you. Instead, whoever wants to become great among you must be your servant, and whoever wants to be first must be your slave—just as the Son of Man did not come to be served, but to serve, and to give his life as a ransom for many."* 9

Charles Swindoll, a well-known author on Christian living, talks about servanthood in his book, *Improving Your Serve*:

When people follow image-conscious leaders, the leader is exalted. He is placed on a pedestal and ultimately takes the place of the Head of the Church. When people follow leaders with servant hearts, the Lord God is exalted. Those people speak of

God's person, God's power, God's work, God's name, God's Word… all for God's glory. Let me suggest a couple of revealing tests of humility:

1. An undefensive spirit when confronted. This reveals a willingness to be accountable. Genuine humility operates on a rather simple philosophy: Nothing to prove Nothing to lose.

2. An authentic desire to help others. I'm referring to a sensitive, spontaneous awareness of needs. A true servant stays in touch with the struggles others experience. There is that humility of mind that continually looks for ways to serve and to give.[10]

Neither in a marriage nor in the Bride of Christ is one to be enslaved by, or hidden behind, imagined rules. New believers may find that some Christian groups lay out a whole series of "do and do nots" according to their system of religious superiority (pride). Don't be enslaved by people's concepts; the love Jesus brings into our lives gives freedom. It is readily apparent one must not murder, lie, cheat, steal, commit adultery or fornicate. However, to be adamant about the type of clothes you wear, the beat of your Christian music, what you eat or drink, the length of your hair—the list goes on and on—creates an enclave of fear and selfishness which perpetrates legalism.

"What about the spiked colored hair, the baggy pants the bare midriff, the earrings?" you might say? So what? Christ died for each one of us as unique individuals. The Church is not a Western institution; it is made up of people of all tribes and nations. There are cultures with bare-breasted women and men with all

> **SERVANTS**
>
> Remember when government public servants were to assist and help? Now derogatorily referred to as "bureaucrats," they are highly paid, self-perpetuating and exist on a myriad of rules and regulations.

sorts of bangles and beads who worship God with different musical rhythms and instruments. In warm countries, in the years of strict legalistic missionaries, women missionaries preferred an open, square-cut neckline. When tribal women became believers, the image of the square-cut dress became a requirement of being Christian. How much better would it have been if the missionaries had lived their Christian ideals within the tribal culture such that the love of Christ was exhibited instead of creating a confusion between the Church and westernization?

Whether within the local Church or a multicultural Church, Jesus said it is by their fruit[11] you can discern if they are ferocious wolves in sheep's clothing. *"The fruit of the Spirit is love, joy, peace, patience, kindness, goodness, faithfulness, gentleness and self-control. Against such things, there is no law. Those who belong to Christ Jesus have crucified the sinful nature with its passions and desires."*[12] *"I am the vine;"* said Jesus, *"you are the branches. If a man remains in me and I in him, he will bear much fruit; apart from me you can do nothing."*[13]

Magnificent architectural and scientific discoveries enhance civilization such that the pursuit of wealth and technological achievements lessen the hardships of humanity. However, we are not to love the world; we are to be in it, but not of it. *"For everything in the world—the cravings of sinful man, the lust of his eyes and the boasting of what he has and does—comes not from the Father but from the world,"*[14] which is the empire of Satan and his Legions of Doom. *"For where your treasure is,"* said Jesus, *"there your heart will be also."*[15]

THE WALK OF FAITH

Just before Jesus took Peter, James and John up a high mountain to give them a glimpse of the "something more" by being transformed in glory before them, He told them that being one of His disciples would be difficult, that there will be trials, tests and hardships, but not to be bewitched by the glitter of the world for *"what good will it be for a man if he gains the whole world, yet forfeits his soul? For the Son of Man is going to come in his Father's glory with his angels, and then he will reward each person according to what he has done."* [16] Yet, in our struggles to "walk the talk," many times a silence of spiritual deadness bodes upon our souls, and the possibility of a transforming glory is a distant haze.

The intellect begins to question, "Am I really saved? Does God really love me? Do I have any purpose? Why do I keep thinking bad thoughts?" Then the darkness of guilt slowly snuffs out the light of hope allowing the chill of despair to put its icy hand around our hearts of love. When this starts to happen, remember: *"God is faithful; he will not let you be tempted beyond what you can bear. But when you are tempted, he will also provide a way out so that you can stand up under it."* [17] These trials come *"so that your faith—of greater worth than gold… may be proved genuine and may result in praise, glory and honor when Jesus Christ is revealed."* [18] *"Blessed is the man who perseveres under trial, because when he has stood the test, he will receive the crown of life that God has promised to those who love him."* [19] The battle of the cosmos becomes personal since, through our wills, we allow the Holy Spirit of the kingdom of light to battle the foes of darkness plundering Earth's civilization.

A walk of faith through the non-evasive guidance of the Holy Spirit is the substance of Christianity, not transcendental experiences. Some churches in Christendom, becoming tired of a walk of faith, are being deceived by pseudo-spiritual experiences through their emotions. These are taking place through laughing sessions[20] or being tossed around and knocked over by some sort of "spirit." The forces of darkness can give counterfeit experiences like this in times of true spiritual revival. Participants of counterfeit experiences become tired and spiritually disillusioned. Yes, the Holy Spirit does give glorious moments of transcendental affirmation but only in ways that will honor and glorify Jesus Christ.

Our brains are complex memory banks storing sights, sounds and sensual experiences, all of which at sundry

A GOOD LAUGH

"A cheerful heart is good medicine," and has nothing to do with spiritualism.[21]

times can flash from the subconscious to the conscious mind. God, upon renewing our spirits by His Holy Spirit at our by "faith" conversion, does not press a computer's "delete" key and erase all the bad or disturbing memories—we are stuck with them! It is the spontaneous popping up of these memories, the surging of lusts, passions and desires of the natural body that apostle Paul refers to as the flesh, or carnal mind, which wars against our desire for spiritual purity. These unruly thoughts may be aided and abetted by temptations from the Legions of Darkness; however, it is usually our own fallen nature that betrays us.

By our wills we allow God to transform our minds, so we *"will be able to test and approve what God's will is—his good, pleasing and perfect will."* [22] The dubious activity of our fallen nature causes doubt; we may say, "Maybe I am not good enough for God; perhaps I have not completed enough good works," or maybe, and this is the deep black hole, "Was I really saved?" Then guilt, like slimy black oil, oozes into our soul; despair darkens the sunshine of love. Yet none are *"righteous, not even one."* [23] It is through the righteousness of Jesus Christ, our redeemer, that we are saved, not of our own works lest we become filled with pride.[24] *"This righteousness from God comes through faith in Jesus Christ to all who believe."* [25] God states emphatically: *"I, even I, am he who blots our your transgressions, for my own sake, and remembers your sins no more."* [26] This is the miracle of salvation; your debt has been paid, your sins are gone, gone, gone and forgotten by God! However, the consequences for these actions will continue in our space-time world.

OUR RELATIONSHIP TO GOD

The following is a diagram which illustrates our relationship to God.[27]

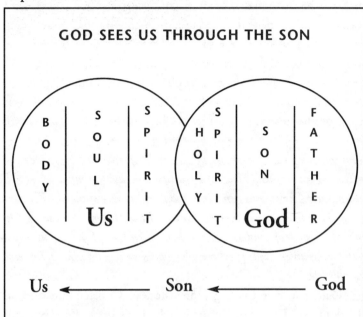

GOD SEES US THROUGH THE SON

Us ← Son ← God

This diagram shows that the Father sees us through the completed work of salvation by the Son; our sins are forgiven and forgotten. Our spirits are empowered by the Holy Spirit Who operates through the God-consciousness of our soul to the renewing of our mind, which is our body. God does not see what we were or what we think we are but sees us justified and glorified through the redeeming work of the Son, Jesus Christ.[28]

FIGURE 1   Diagram courtesy Chet McArther

When we look towards the Father, we are empowered by the Holy Spirit, through our spirits, to worship and adore the Son, through whom we know and worship the Father. This diagram makes clear that what is of most concern to us, our bodies, is of least concern to the Father because, through salvation, we are being conformed into the image of Jesus Christ, the Son, through the working of the Holy Spirit.

By the will of your mind, rebuke thoughts of doubt, guilt and despair, turn and look towards the Father and fix the will of your mind on the steadfast love of Jesus Christ. *"May the God of hope fill you with all joy and peace as you trust in him, so that you may overflow with hope by the power of the Holy Spirit."* [29] Therefore, the apostle Paul wrote: *"Here is a trustworthy saying that deserves full acceptance: Christ Jesus came into the world to save sinners—of whom I am the worst. But for that very reason I was shown mercy so that in me, the worst of sinners, Christ Jesus might display his unlimited patience as an example for those who would believe on him and receive eternal life."* [30]

Cults and rule-creating propagators of Christendom feed on the doubt of the mind. Unfortunately, Jesus has some very harsh words for these regulated power-hungry Churches, whether rich or poor: *"I know your deeds, that you are neither cold nor hot. I wish you were either one or the other! So, because you are lukewarm—neither hot nor cold—I am about to spit you out of my mouth. You say, 'I am rich: I have acquired wealth and do not need a thing.' But you do not realize that you are wretched, pitiful, poor blind and naked. I counsel you to buy from me gold refined in the fire, so you can become rich; and white clothes to wear, so you can cover your shameful nakedness; and salve to put on your eyes, so you can see.*

"Those whom I love I rebuke and discipline. So be earnest, and repent. Here I am! I stand at the door and knock. If anyone hears my voice and opens the door, I will come in and eat with him, and he with me.

"To him who overcomes, I will give the right to sit with me on my throne, just as I overcame and sat down with my Father on his throne. He who has an ear, let him hear what the Spirit says to the churches." [31]

LOVE IN MARRIAGE

Love and freedom go hand in hand, for love requires risk, and freedom in marriage survives on the communication of love. Other than what the movies try to make you believe is love, a man responds to a woman in the realm of the sensual, her movements, her looks, her perfume and her touch, while her heart quickens more to his actions and words than physique. Look at Adam. It took Satan six verses to deceive Eve while all she did was give Adam some fruit and he ate it. She must have been something else! We men are in trouble right from the start. I read on the Internet somewhere, recent brain research on men has shown that the sight of a beautiful face across a room instantly kick-starts a sensual response.

In whatever magic moment the "I-will-love-you-forever-I-can't-live-without-you" kind of love begins, it needs to grow roots and deepen into a "until-death-does-part" kind of love—sentient being to sentient being. In the same way, the excitement of being forgiven by God and entering into the freedom of His love, needs to grow in spiritual depth and wisdom. Someone wise in the ways of marriage told me, just after I was married, to be sure to pour love into my bride as if she were a beautiful vase and that, later in life, the love poured in would multiply and still be flowing out. Because God has so ordained that, in a man-woman relationship, the woman seeks after the man, a newly married husband unwittingly holds his future relationship in his inexperienced hands. Likewise, says the book of Proverbs: *"The wise woman builds her house, but with her own hands the foolish one tears hers down."* [32]

The secular world has so glamorized the female body that women, consciously or subconsciously, work to be sensual packages,

193

yet their inner desire is to be loved for who they are—a person. Men are more sensually responsive and find themselves bombarded with sensory overload. Intense youthful desires can lead to premarital relationships where she thinks she is being loved as a person. These breakups are damaging to a women's psyche because it affects who she is as a person. The world of free love says, "have fun, keep on breeding," while her heart feels cheated of a deeper "something more." Her lover, tired of her outbursts of inner turmoil and unfulfilled sensual feelings, leaves because he has made no deep soul-to-soul commitment. He will drift from one shallow sensual relationship to another.

If a marriage has degenerated into a robot situation functioning on sex hormones, it will likely blow apart by the time you are in your thirties. A woman will put her children first, focusing on them; he will immerse himself in his job. A deep soul-to-soul love relationship "of the something more" requires commitment, a strong self-image and communication which involve the secret of learning how to listen. Anne Carrol writes about the Other Man Syndrome and the Other Woman Syndrome:

> Most starved housewives run into an appreciative man accidentally—perhaps the insurance agent who drops by with the new policy, the tennis or golf pro she is taking lessons from. But sooner or later, if she is hungry to feel feminine, and you aren't fulfilling your God-given position to "Love, cherish, and make her happy," then some man is going to pick up the signals. It had better be you!
>
> What she is looking for, what most women are looking for in the way of satisfaction, is appreciation, a reaffirmation of herself as a woman, not as the children's mother, but as your woman, personally, as a living, breathing female. If she isn't reassured verbally and nonverbally, she will find that in time appreciative looks from other men become more and more appealing.

She may try to shake the feeling off, but if she is continually ignored, if her feminine needs for appreciation, affection, romance, quiet talks, aren't met, she may in time secretly turn to that man who has noticed her as a woman, who has reminded her that she is attractive, who perhaps flirts with her, letting her forget for time that her teenage years are long past.[33]

"...Far from being the sexy blonde he met at last year's convention," the other woman is usually knowledgeable in his field of interest, either because she happens to work in the same field, or because she wanted your man enough to learn what he cared about, enough to discuss it intelligently; and beyond that, she has learned the secret of communication—she has learned how to listen, she's taken the time to hear what he says verbally and nonverbally.

There is one aspect of men few wives seem to realize, and that is the difference between the man he is and the one he wishes to be, or in some cases imagines himself to be. He likes to think of himself as the world's greatest lover, a success in business, a fascinating conversationalist, the lighthearted, unrestricted young man you probably met

> ## FRIDAY NIGHT
>
> It happened to me. I had to realize my wife was my bride, my friend, my lover; she is the most beautiful woman in my whole world! That meant if there was only enough money for a Friday night coffee, we went, I listened and admired her for who she is and, yes, appreciated her sensually, verbally and nonverbally as in the exciting discovery days of our youth.

ten or twenty years ago. In most instances, we women fail to recognize this. We let him know exactly what he is, we ignore him instead of giving him the attention he so dearly needs and seeks; we fail to praise him in the lovemaking category. All he either wishes to be, or thinks he is, is crushed the moment he looks at us.[34]

LOVE IN THE CHURCH

Just like newlyweds, the exciting first love of coming to know Jesus as Lord and Savior can grow and blossom in the fellowship of the Church Body. However, like the problems affecting marriage, church fellowship can become mechanical and stale. Jesus said: *"I know your deeds, your hard work and your perseverance. I know that you cannot tolerate wicked men, that you have tested those who claim to be apostles but are not, and have found them false. You have persevered and have endured hardships for my name, and have not grown weary. Yet I hold this against you: You have forsaken your first love. Remember the height from which you have fallen! Repent and do the things you did at first."* [35]

HOW MUCH?

Feminists get riled at Ephesians 5:22–27, saying, "No man is going to tell me what to do," while some religions of Christendom manipulate its meaning to authenticate their views of male domination. Put your biases aside and read what I am trying to write: we are equal sentient beings before God. Study the life of Jesus and note that He never, in any way, treated women with an attitude of superiority. Each of us should ask ourselves, "Do I love my wife enough to die for her?" "Do I love my husband enough to live for him?"

Just as Christ is the head of the Church, His Body, so is the husband the head of his wife. She is to submit to him and respect him as "to the Lord." The husband has an immense responsibility. He is to love his wife *"just as Christ loved the Church and gave himself up for her to make her holy, cleansing her by the washing with water through the word, and to present her to himself as a radiant Church, without blemish, but holy and blameless. In this way, husbands ought to love their wives as their own bodies."* [36]

By the "vertical" love of husband and wife to Christ, and the "horizontal" love for each other, their children and the watching world can see God as a loving Father. Even as husband and wife respect each other "as to the Lord," the children will see and obey their parents "as to the Lord." *"Children, obey your parents in the Lord, for this is right. 'Honor your father and mother'—which is the first commandment with a promise—'that it might go well with you and that you may enjoy long life on the earth.' Fathers [parents], do not exasperate your children, instead, bring them up in the training and instruction of the Lord."*[37] Self-centered exasperating parents do not reflect the patient love God has for us, His sons and daughters; attitudes of dissidence will quickly invade their household. Are you lonely, single or have you lost your husband or wife in some way? Don't despair. If you are a believer, you are part of God's family. God is *"a father to the fatherless, a defender of widows."* He *"sets the lonely in families."*[38]

In Christendom, the Church practices "high monogamy" even as Jesus has only one Bride, His Church/Body of believers. A man is to be the husband of one wife and is to be respected by his children, particularly in Church leadership. He is to be *"self-controlled, respectable, hospitable, able to teach, not given to drunkenness, not violent but gentle, not quarrelsome, not a lover of money. He must manage his own family well and see that his children obey him with proper respect. …In the same way, their wives are to be women worthy of respect, not malicious talkers but temperate and trustworthy in everything."*[39] The veteran missionary, Paul of Tarsus, wrote these words of instruction to Timothy, a young pastor. In our modern world, his words to Timothy regarding women appear legalistic. In using the words "I say," they are his opinion and reflect personal experience. He is instructing Timothy concerning churches struggling spiritually in a culture of pagan goddess worship involving sexual rites and orgies.[40]

Marriage conflicts and interpersonal relationships within the Bride of Christ usually begin with self-doubt. Self-doubt is driven by a poor self-image that lies like a latent virus in all of us. The joy of becoming a new Christian, or the excitement of romance and marriage, may suppress doubt, but self-pity works hard to resuscitate it. Furthermore, when family, church, personal, financial or health problems seem overwhelming, we build a prison made of walls of attitude, wants and rights, then furnish it with self-pity and despair.

There is little or no joy in a marriage, no spiritual life of worship and prayer in this situation. A man builds walls, a woman nags and the Bride of Christ starts to bicker. Then rationalization starts: "if things could only have been different—if I had only" and out comes the jealousy of a past boyfriend, girlfriend or some past conflict. "After all, we did it this way in the church we used to go to." "You never talk to me—you never say anything nice to me anymore." "I didn't get anything out of the pastor's message." "Did you see what those teenagers were doing?" So the big "I" raises its snake-like head and hisses at everyone and everything.

Have you ever noticed couples or families become unhappy because they focus on each other's faults rather than on their positive aspects? Some mates start on a quiet firm campaign to change the other one. Then walls of super organization and cleanliness (or complete disaster) get built, or rules of law and order get so instituted that children and mate are afraid to move. The martyr complex usually follows—everything is done grudgingly. Laughter, joy and the freedom of being are now hiding in the garage. The Church suffers from the same ailment of faultfinding or a superworker joins the Church and it is their way or the highway.

INNER TREASURES

So what do we do? Start again? The wedding bells are still ringing! Yes, Jesus has forgiven all your sins. Yes, your sweetheart loves you for who you are. Yes, Jesus loves you for who you are. He created you to be a joyous celestial citizen forever. As we give Him our lives and submit to each other as husband and wife, Jesus works to conform us into His image, full of love, joy and compassion. After all, you married your mate for who they are; it is only God who knows what each one of us can be. To not grow stale in your marriage; take time to be sweethearts. This builds a foundation of love and memories which will carry you into a contented tomorrow; such is the joy of a "high monogamy" marriage. *"May you rejoice in the wife of your youth. A loving doe, a graceful deer—may her breasts satisfy you always, may you ever be captivated by her love."* [41]

Family picnics, holidays, just quietly putting arms around each other in a circle of love creates unspoken unity and bonding. Likewise, within the Church family, events, picnics, choir, plays and times of helping others in the community form a bond of love that will last into eternity. Love the singles in your Church. You are their family. We will know each other in Heaven and continue our relationships in perfect harmony. In the meantime, to create harmony we need to communicate to each other with a heart of love and servanthood. We need to encourage each other: do not be judgmental, do not pretend, forgive and above all, love each other as Christ loves us.

Begin by evaluating and adjusting your own self-worth; this begins with vertical praise and worship to Jesus. A new refreshed attitude will transfer horizontally to your mate, children, friends and Church relationships. "But," you say, "you don't understand. I...." Okay, let's start at the beginning. Find somewhere quiet, sit down, close your eyes and

MOOD DISORDERS

That is, assuming your moods of despair are normal daily feelings of uselessness that affect us all, not a chemically related mood disorder.

willfully push self-pity and doubt out of your mind. The way do to this is to create what I call my "little golden cube" which I step into. First, I focus on one thought that I know: Jesus loves me as I am and has totally forgiven me. I quote a positive verse of Scripture to myself: *"Praise the LORD Almighty, for the LORD is good; his love endures forever."* [42] Now, because I know God created me and loves me for who I am, I bring in a positive thought of self-worth about who I think I am. Next, because I am to love my wife as myself, I think something positive about her and of what she thinks about me. If you are not married, it can be a parent, a sibling or a friend. If you are really down, it might be the barest scrap of a thought, but search until you find one.

In this way, you have hidden the Word of the Lord in your heart—which is vertical communication—and established a back and forth horizontal link with your sweetheart or fellow human being. These are the treasures you have willfully created—your secrets—and are kept in a special place within your heart. As you focus on these treasures, with praise and thanksgiving, the love flowing from Jesus into your heart will increase flowing horizontally into life's daily relationships. From this foundation you can enhance the effectiveness of your vertical relationship to the Creator-Redeemer and your horizontal interpersonal relationships.

COMMUNICATION THROUGH LOVE

Love and communication are the foundation of the Trinity. Likewise, they should be the foundation of our marriages, our worldly relationships and to those within the Bride of Christ. Love is communicated by actions, words and deeds, verbally and non-verbally. Communication is a fundamental principle upon which love is manifested, from our inner world of being into our outer world of living. *"The tongue,"* said King Solomon, *"has the power of life and death, and those who love it will eat its fruit."* [43] Therefore, with our tongue we sow the seeds of good or evil. *"The tongue that brings healing is a tree of life, but a deceitful tongue crushes the spir-*

it."44 "*A wise man's* [person's] *heart guides his mouth, and his lips promote instruction. Pleasant words are a honeycomb, sweet to the soul and healing to the bones.*" 45

Communication begins in the morning—"vertically" to God and "horizontally" to your loved one, family and friends. Just as you are start to awaken, whisper a "thank you" prayer to Jesus for whatever comes to mind, even if your husband or wife is snoring and has pulled all the covers to their side. Most times, in those semi-waking moments, the anxious thoughts of the world have not yet crowded in. You may drift back to sleep, but when you do awake, it is easier to tell your mate you love them. Start each day with a spiritual devotion to the Lord: *"for in all your ways acknowledge him and he will make your paths straight."* 46 How you willful-

WHO STARTED IT?

The anecdote is told of a husband who snarls at his wife while leaving for work. She harps at her daughter who hits her younger brother who whacks the family dog. In turn, the dog annoys the pet cat all day. When husband returns home after work, the cat scratches his master's leg as he walks by king cat's favorite chair. Now, Mr. Leader of the Household, you have an empathetic decision to make. You can smack the cat and start the circle running backwards, or you can pet kitty; then, having cleverly figured out the problem, you can, with a quiet demeanor, walk into the kitchen and apologize for your actions. Take your sweetheart-lover-friend in your arms and tell her she means the whole world to you! But, just remember, she may very well be angry inside (and the kids are fighting) so you are going to have to be man enough to accept what you started. *"Humble yourself before the Lord and he will lift you up."*48 Your wife and children will see your sincere quiet strength and love you. This is how your family will grow in the ways of the Lord.

ly start the day has a direct bearing on other people (particularly if you are the husband since you are to be the spiritual umbrella for your family).[47]

Communication, contrary to popular opinion, is not about talking, it is about actions and listening. *"My dear brothers"* (and sisters of course), says James, *"take note of this: Everyone should be quick to listen, slow to speak and slow to become angry, for man's anger does not bring about the righteous life that God desires."* [49] Practice the old saying, "God gave us two ears and one mouth, they should be used in that proportion." Anger should never be allowed to simmer overnight. An unforgiving attitude can lead to sin and marital dissension. *"Do not let the sun go down while you are still angry, and do not give the devil a foothold."* [50] Moreover, *"he who guards his mouth and his tongue keeps himself from calamity."* [51]

Communication is a complex relationship of words, body language and other people's perception of themselves at any given moment. You may walk into your church preoccupied with minor details, maybe even with an, "I'm thinking" frown on your face. Unwittingly, you walk by someone you would normally speak to. It so happens they are a little down this morning and, because of your negative body language and their private pity-party, they get the feeling you have something against them. So the next time you go to talk to them, you get a brush-off. So what do you do? Give them the silent treatment and really open the breach or recognize you need to communicate your love to them?

Communication is looking and listening. Look at the person. They have just communicated a deep inner spiritual need. Have you really looked into their eyes before? Are they walking a road of difficulties that you can't even begin to relate to? Speak softly, relax, smile and maybe say, "Are you okay?" Then listen. If someone unintentionally comes to break the conversation, you can say a friendly, "Hi, just a minute" along with a touch of your hand, but try not to lose eye contact with your friend in need. The eye is the gateway to the soul; through it, you transmit love and compassion. We all have a need to express ourselves with words, but the power, or inner effect of the spoken word has meaning only in the way that the listener absorbs it.

Marriages lose vitality because words become meaningless sound, and in our stress-filled world, usually with both spouses working, it takes effort to communicate love to each other. Husbands, listen to your wife. Her drama with work, children, friends, traffic, shopping and a host of other events are as meaningful to her as your job-related problems are to you. Don't dump insecurities on her the minute you walk in the door; she already has her world of problems. Money and job-related problems only give her more insecurity as they affect her children-protection home-making instincts. If you are both working, share home responsibilities; home life is a full-time job. Wives, listen to your husband. Don't hit him with all the domestic problems the minute he walks in the door or you both get home from work. Take time to have supper, tell him you love him and reintroduce him to your world. If he understands who he is and who you are, he will listen. Each of you will feel rewarded because your words have taken on expression and meaning.

Communication is encouragement. Encouragement from your heart to others is an affirmation of who they are and an inner confirmation of who you are. You are a child of the King; you are part of a royal priesthood, an ambassador for Jesus Christ. If someone encourages you, say "thank you"; it reaffirms him or her. Words of "I don't think so… do you really think so" are usually indications of self-centeredness. Some people are so filled with vanity and pride (usually not in the Church) they gobble up encouragement as self-adoration. In all this, we are to love with a gentle kindness of compassion, concern and empathy. Do not fall into the "but I" syndrome. In a marriage, this innocent statement can leave a feeling of emptiness, a why-bother attitude which can start a day out all wrong. "Honey, you look nice this morning!" "But I don't…" and on it goes. My experience as a husband of a wonderful wife, and father of four beautiful daughters, is that a woman's self-awareness, more so than a man's, is dictated by commercialism which creates self-criticism in order to sell product. If complimented, my daughters knew to respond with, "Thanks, Dad. I'm glad you appreciate me."

Communication is a forgiving spirit. Recognize that "being right" is often a self-directed perception of a given circumstance. If you feel you have been wronged, *"Do not say, 'I'll pay you back for this wrong!' Wait for the LORD, and he will deliver you."* [52] *"Therefore, as God's chosen people, holy and dearly loved, clothe yourselves with compassion, kindness, humility, gentleness and patience. Bear with each other and forgive whatever grievances you may have against one another. Forgive as the Lord forgave you. And over all these virtues put on love, which binds them all together in perfect unity."* [53] To be in perfect unity means to forgive, forget and not, for the sake of self-pity or pride, dig up that which was forgiven. *"He who covers and forgives an offense seeks love, but he who repeats or harps on a matter separates even close friends."* [54]

Forgiveness from the heart is one of the hardest things to do in your spiritual walk. Our carnal self-taking attitudes war against it, yet to be bitter in spirit is destructive to the body and a prison for the soul. To make matters worse, the grievance may be one of perceived circumstance, and the supposed offender isn't even aware of what has happened or has totally forgotten it. The apostle Paul poses the question: *"Why not rather be wronged? Why not rather be cheated? Instead, you yourselves cheat and do wrong, and you do this to your brothers."* [55]

Forgive, because forgiveness brings freedom to the soul and a joy of spirit. Forgiveness does not mean "reunion," particularly if there has been no restitution or forgiveness by the offender.[56] Even

if there has been forgiveness
and restitution by both parties, particularly in marriages
or business deals, reunion is an
option of freedom in Christ

BE FREE

Don't create walls of hate—
communicate!

Jesus, not a law, rule or regulation. In particular, women who have
suffered marriage abuse, have divorced, left or are contemplating
leaving, and have, through the love of Jesus Christ, forgiven their
spouse from their hearts removing the prison of bitterness from
their souls, do not have to bow to those of twisted legalistic thinking in Christendom and re-enter or stay in the abusive situation.

Communication is being non judgmental. *"Do not judge, or
you too will be judged. For in
the same way you judge others,
you will be judged, and with
the measure you use, it will be
measured to you."* [57] We have
to take the "plank" out of our
own eye before we take the

ROSES

A forgiving nature is like a bouquet of roses, sweet to the scent,
a delight to the eye and warm
to the heart.

"speck of dust" out of another's eye. The judgments of gossip, crit-
icism and contrived regulations are a reflection of a poor self-image
and have no place in the Bride of Christ. Do not try to build up
your self-image by criticizing others—be an encourager. Appreciate
others as unique individuals. The clothes they wear, the foods they
eat and drink, the beat of their music and when and how they worship have no bearing on their salvation. *"For the kingdom of God is
not a matter of eating and drinking, but of righteousness, peace and joy
in the Holy Spirit, because anyone who serves Christ in this way is
pleasing to God and approved by men."* [58]

Communication is love and trust. Jealousy is the dark side of a
despairing self-image. It destroys freedom in a marriage and ruins
friendships. Have you poured enough love into your mate such

that they reflect it in an attitude of self-confidence? If your loved one happens to be physically handsome or beautiful, this confidence will attract others of the opposite sex who are having relationship problems. Normally that intense conversation that took place across the room (typically at a party) between your mate and a handsome or beautiful him/her was one of trying to solve their relationship problems. He/she was sought after

> **OIL AND VINEGAR**
>
> Judgmental attitudes in a marriage are like olive oil and vinegar; love and sarcasm don't mix. Just as a mixture of oil and vinegar separate, so will a critical attitude divide your higher order, sentient-being-to-sentient-being relationship.

because of the positive attitude of trust and love demonstrated in your mate's relationship. In the Bride of Christ, we are to show love and trust between each other, *"because the one who trusts in him will never be put to shame."* [59]

To trust is to not worry. Our lives are filled with daily uncertainties, many of which relate to finances. "If there were only more money in our bank account" is the cry of our society. Assuming you are doing your best in all of life's circumstances, we Christians are to be content and trust in the Lord for His provisions. *"Keep your lives free from the love of money and be content with what you have, because God has said, 'Never will I leave you; never will I forsake you.'"* [60] Abuse of credit cards creates adversity, for: *"The*

> **AN ENCOURAGER**
>
> "I try to emulate a man I respect. If a group of people were standing around running a person down, he would always have something good to say about them. I knew because of his attitude he would not be slaying my character behind my back." [69] (Robert Smith).

rich rule over the poor and the borrower is servant to the lender." [61] Do we have confidence in the Lord's provision, or are we distraught with worry the same as our worldly friends? Reflect on the immense complexity of creation and realize that, even though you're like a small microdot on planet Earth, He loves you so much, He died to redeem you.

Sort your needs from your wants. God assures us He feeds the birds and creates the beautiful lilies. Therefore, we should not worry about our daily needs. *"If that is how God clothes the grass of the field, which is here today and tomorrow is thrown into the fire, will he not much more clothe you, O you of little faith? So do not worry, saying, 'What shall we eat?' or 'What shall we drink?' or 'What shall we wear?' For the pagans run after all these things, and your heavenly Father knows that you need them. But seek first his kingdom and his righteousness, and all these things will be given to you as well. Therefore, do not worry about tomorrow, for tomorrow will worry about itself. Each day has enough trouble of its own."* [62]

Communication is praise and thanksgiving. Praise is about who someone is, and thanksgiving is about what they have done for you. Throw away the list of all the things your mate isn't and what they didn't do. Replace it with a list of praise and thanksgiving, and see the difference it makes to your soul-to-soul relationship. Worshiping God is done through praise and thanksgiving. "God dwells on the praises of His people," was my mother's favorite saying. *"Enter his gates with thanksgiving and his courts with praise; give thanks to him and praise his name. For the LORD is good and his love endures forever; his faithfulness continues through all generations."* [63] Therefore, when we have needs: *"Do not be anxious about anything, but in everything, by prayer and petition, with thanksgiving, present your requests to God. And the peace of God, which transcends all understanding, will guard your hearts and your minds in Christ Jesus."* [64]

Worshiping God, through praise and thanksgiving, empowers us to witness to others through the Holy Spirit. It is also effective warfare against our spiritual adversary, Satan and his Legions of Doom. We are to give thanks in all circumstances[65] and to offer up to God a sacrifice of praise. *"And do not forget to do good and to share with others, for with such sacrifices God is pleased."* [66]

Have you heard the amazing news? The Angels of Glory are excited, and the Legions of Doom are becoming agitated because the Bridegroom is going with His friends to bring His Bride to her new home. You haven't heard? Well, I'm telling you now! *"Listen, I tell you a mystery: We will not all sleep, but we will all be changed—in a flash, in the twinkling of an eye, at the last trumpet."* [67]

GOD IS GOOD

Yes, clap your hands, or raise them high, or dance and sing, for soon you may be proclaiming "Hallelujah!" to Jesus Christ our Bridegroom, our Lord and King!

"For the Lord himself will come down from heaven, with a loud command, with the voice of the archangel and with the trumpet call of God, and the dead in Christ will rise first. After that, we who are still alive and are left will be caught up together with them in the clouds to meet the Lord in the air. And so we will be with the Lord forever. Therefore encourage each other with these words." [68]

It was then, in that instant, in the twinkling of an eye, she found herself walking down the golden cobblestones leading towards two magnificently flowered trees to where He stood waiting. No words can describe the radiance of His smile. She is His triumph. Soon He will retake His rightful dominion, but now is the time for her rewards of victory.

NOTES:

1. 1 John 4:11
2. Matthew 28:19
3. James 2:1–4
4. John 8:31–36
5. 2 Corinthians 3:17–18
6. Galatians 5:1, 4
7. 1 Peter 2:16–17
8. Philippians 2:3–4
9. Matthew 20:25–28
10. Swindoll, R. Charles, *Improving Your Serve*, Word Books 1982, p. 25
11. Matthew 7:16
12. Galatians 5:22–24
13. John 15:5
14. 1 John 2:16
15. Matthew 6:21
16. Matthew 16:26–27
17. 1 Corinthians 10:13
18. 1 Peter 1:7
19. James 1:12
20. Ostling, Richard, "Laughing for the Lord," *TIME*, August 15, 1994
21. Proverbs 17:22
22. Romans 12:2
23. Romans 3:10
24. Ephesians 2:8–9
25. Romans 3:22
26. Isaiah 43:25
27. McArther, Chet, 100 Mile Baptist Church, B.C., Canada
28. Romams 8:30
29. Romans 15:13

[30] 1 Timothy 1:15

[31] Revelation 3:15–22

[32] Proverbs 14:1

[33] Carroll, Anne Kristin, *Together Forever*, Zondervan Publishing House 1982, p. 93

[34] Carroll, Ibid. p. 91

[35] Revelation 2:2–5

[36] Ephesians 5:25–33

[37] Ephesians 6:1–3

[38] Psalm 68:5–6

[39] 1 Timothy 3:2–4, 11–13

[40] Bilezikian, Dr. Gilbert, Willow Creek Leadership Conference, Kelowna, B.C., April 20–21, 2001

[41] Proverbs 5:18–19

[42] Jeremiah 33:11

[43] Proverbs 18:21

[44] Proverbs 15:4

[45] Proverbs 16:23–24

[46] Proverbs 3:6

[47] Gothard, Bill, Institute in Basic Youth Conflicts, Basic Seminar Textbook, 1979, p. 20

[48] James 4:10

[49] James 1:19

[50] Ephesians 4:26–27

[51] Proverbs 21:23

[52] Proverbs 20:22

[53] Colossians 3:12–14

[54] Proverbs 17:9 (Amplified Bible, Zondervan 1964)

[55] 1 Corinthians 6:7–8

[56] McArther, Ibid.

[57] Matthew 7:1–2

58 Romans 14:17–18

59 Romans 9:33

60 Hebrews 13:5

61 Proverbs 22:7

62 Matthew 6:30–34

63 Psalm 100:4–5

64 Philippians 4:6–7

65 1 Thessalonians 5:18

66 Hebrews 13:15–16

67 1 Corinthians 15:51–52a

68 1 Thessalonians 4:16–18

69 Smith, Robert, editor *Of the Something More*, Vernon, BC

The Whole Heaven

he beautiful Bride of the Lamb[1] has just entered Heaven clothed in garments of salvation and righteousness. Awaiting her are friends of the Bridegroom[2] which includes all pre-Church saints, the prisoners of hope[3] who were freed from Hades[4] when the compartment of Paradise (Abraham's Bosom) was transferred to Heaven.[5]

The apostle Matthew indicates some of them, as first fruits, may have already received their resurrection bodies at the resurrection of their redeemer, Jesus Christ. "Many holy people" were seen for a short period in Jerusalem.[6] Once the *Bema* (victory) rewards have been given to His Bride in heaven, King Jesus will execute the "wrath of the Lamb" on rebellious Earth. Martyrs (killed by the evil world ruler) coming out of this time of wrath, or great tribulation,[7] will be the last group to join this realm of celestial citizens.

Heaven is not an old-age rest home for resurrected humanity. It is a divine administrative concept involving our space-time universe and all the dimensions of God's creation. It began with the Lamb chosen **before** the creation of the world. The prophet Daniel was given a momentous holographic capsule vision of this future administration of the cosmos. *"I looked, and there before me was one like a son of man* [Jesus Christ], *coming with the clouds* [deity] *of heaven. He approached the Ancient of Days* [God the Father] *and was led into his presence. He was given authority, glory and sovereign power; all peoples, nations and men of every language worshiped him. ... Then the sovereignty, power and greatness of the kingdoms under the whole Heaven will be handed over to the saints, the people of the Most High. His kingdom will be an everlasting kingdom, and all rulers will worship and obey him."* [8]

The people of the Most High are the Church, a body comprising people of all tribes, nations and languages, a hidden mystery[9] at the time of Daniel. The words **whole Heaven** signify our local sky and all heavens, both space-time and celestial.

The philosophy of naturalism teaches that Earth is ancient, yet mankind, even by evolutionary standards, is very recent. Just as many scientists stick to their monkey-to-man dogma, others recognize the shortfalls and are advocating a panspermia origin of life or paranormal intelligent design (ID) by some unknown super alien. In contrast, regardless of theological time differences of "In the beginning God created," fundamental believers in Christendom recognize the sudden appearance of man upon the Earth as a divine creation. The viewpoint of the Holy Scriptures is that God is at the "beginning" of His plan for flesh and blood mankind in the space-time universe, and therefore at the "beginning" of creating an eternal heavenly administration of celestial citizens of human origin.

After the cross of Calvary, when we revisit creation in the book of Genesis and study world history, we see God working patiently to implement His plan. *"For he chose us in him before the creation of the world to be holy and blameless in his sight. … And he made known to us the mystery of his will according to his good pleasure, which he purposed in Christ, to be put into effect when the times will have reached their fulfillment—to bring all things in heaven and on earth together under one head, even Christ."* [10] The words "all things in heaven and on earth" confirm the rule of Christ and His Bride over all "dominions, powers and authorities" in Heaven and on Earth.

Because naturalism makes us feel nothing is really happening and God is not making Himself known in any obvious transcendental ways, we may believe nothing cosmologically is about to happen. God warns us of this modern attitude of apathy. The apostle Peter writes: *"First of all, you must understand that in the last days scoffers will come, scoffing and following their own evil desires. They will say, 'Where is this "coming" he promised? Ever since our fathers died, everything goes on as it has since the beginning of creation.'"* [11] The Bible declares: *"for you know very well that the day of the Lord will come like a thief in the night. While people are saying 'Peace and safety,' destruction will come on them suddenly, as labor pains on a pregnant woman, and they will not escape."* [12] The unexpected departure (rapture) of the Bride to her new heavenly home would certainly cause chaos in societies where she now dwells.

CONCEPTS OF HEAVEN

Fantasies of an idyllic Paradise, floating on clouds playing harps, or of a merging into nothingness, or of everlasting self-indulgence, is not the Heaven of Christendom. We know that it is being specially prepared for us. For *"no eye has seen, nor ear has heard, no mind has conceived what God has prepared for those who love him."* [13] Heaven is not about us; it is about God as Jesus Christ our redeemer. We were created to bring Him glory through our "free will" adoration and worship. Thus, the **whole Heaven** is not a disjointed, after-the-cross-of-Calvary idea; it began "before creation." When God created our space-time universe, He said that it was "very good." We do not know if biological life forms were patterned after things in heaven, but we do know God had an awesome concept to elevate a creature made of dust, that He created in His image, into a heavenly being a little lower than Himself. We do not know when, but we do know the peace of the spiritual dimension was shattered with a rebellion that impinged upon our universe.

Modern Christendom, in their pursuit of peace and prosperity, has lost their excitement about heaven; it has become an escape hatch for the despairing, the sick and the old. Oh yes, lip service is given by the young, happy and healthy that Heaven is a glorious place to go to, but, "I just got engaged," or, "it is my son's or daughter's birthday tomorrow," are the true desires of our carnal nature. No, we do not want the dragon of death to take us individually from the joys of living, but are we ecstatic that Jesus could come suddenly for

SPACESHIPS IN HEAVEN?

The Psalms recorded: *"The chariots of God are tens of thousands and thousands of thousands."*[14] Somehow, angelic travel can involve wheels turning within wheels that *"sparkled like chrysolite."* The prophet Ezekiel heard them being referred to as *"the whirling wheels."*[15] The prophet Elijah was transported to heaven in a chariot. Zechariah saw[16] riders on horses traversing the Earth in the spirit dimension.[17] Elisha saw chariots and horses surrounding him and his servant.[18] In the book of Revelation, the apostle John describes a temple in heaven after which the one in Jerusalem was patterned.[19] He is also shown a huge 1500-mile by 1500-mile by 1500-mile city containing a river and fruit trees.[20] Manna that the Israelites ate in the wilderness is the food of angels, "grain from heaven."[21]

His Bride at anytime? Are we watching and waiting with joyous anticipation? If life is good, the answer is usually no; we're really looking forward to… whatever it may be, and there is a tinge of regret at the thought of a possible cosmic interruption.

Each one of us has something in our lives, usually as children, unfortunately, that we were so excited about, it was all we thought about for days. If this is not your concept of heaven, you have only a dim vision of what God has prepared for those who love Him. The sort of Heaven most Christians have is that of a fuzzy glow where there is no more sickness, pain or tears, where there is happiness and laughter with loved ones—but you have to sing and go to church every day. Maybe there is golf, skiing, swimming or whatever you like, but the thought of doing it forever seems purposeless and your thoughts of Heaven stagnate. No more family challenges, no more big business deals, no more of life's intrigues, no more fighting in hockey, no more cops and robbers or war and destruction and so we create feelings of anticipated boredom. That's because we have not really understood Heaven.

We view the concept of Heaven through the eyes of our fallen human nature. Somehow, we conceive Heaven as being so different that our earthly pleasures will not extend into the era of eternal life. Nowhere does the Bible say we will not be in familiar settings. I have often wondered, because scientists cannot find the "missing mass" in our universe,[22] if God has maybe created a parallel anti-

A PICNIC IN HEAVEN

What would happen if the Sunday school picnic scheduled for tomorrow were postponed temporarily while we were resurrected and then took place in heaven? There you would be a dynamic glorified perfect human being, picnicking with others who have been so transformed in a garden setting of magnificent luxurious beauty.

matter universe that is separated from ours by an energy barrier. This would explain the tunnels traversed in NDE and OBE experiences. Possibly this anti-matter world is a mirror image of this one but is perfect and cannot be entered by flesh and blood humanity under God's curse against the disease of sin. If this is the case, it may be the home of all departed redeemed spirits awaiting the resurrection. Then, after the great White Throne judgment when Earth is transformed by fire, it is the replacing of our matter space-time universe with the anti-matter one that causes the melting of the atoms referred to by the apostle Peter. *"But the day of the Lord will come like a thief. The heavens will disappear with a roar; the elements will be destroyed by fire, and the earth and everything in it will be laid bare"* (some manuscripts say "burned up").[23]

Adam and Eve were intellectually brilliant, biologically perfect humans. Their spirits were sustained by the energizing link of the Holy Spirit. When this link was broken, they were dismissed from the Garden of Eden. It is then that they and their progeny built highly technical civilizations which were later destroyed. The concept of evolution blinds our thinking to this possibility and causes scientists to deny evidences of mysterious ancient sophisticated technology. That post-Eden civilization did not need to build a vast manufacturing base to conquer space and live comfortably because the mysterious *"sons of God"* [24] quickly invaded it.

Heaven is for the fulfillment of all the human attributes of Adam and Eve by redeemed humanity. There, all those redeemed by the blood of the Lamb live as perfected humanity, molded in His divine image with resurrection bodies created of heavenly substance. Paul writes: *"We have a building* [body] *from God, an eternal house in heaven, not built by human hands. ...For while we are in this tent, we groan and are burdened, because we do not wish to be unclothed but to be clothed with our heavenly dwelling, so that what is mortal may be swallowed up by life."* [25] How great will be that life as we rule with

THE WHOLE HEAVEN

The term "whole heaven" also encompasses the earthly administration of humanity through the Millennium into the "Ages of
Ages" and the heavenly administration of the celestial citizens
with Christ over all kings, rulers, powers, dominions and authorities for all eternity. The details of these administrations become
clear when we follow God's actions from the beginning of the
Schism of the Cosmos to its unification at the Ages of Ages. They
are rooted in "forever" promises made to Abraham, Isaac, Jacob,
Moses and David. God said: " *I will open my mouth in parables, I
will utter hidden things, things from of old,*"[26] which means these
administrations were part of a predestined plan. Jesus describes
them in parable form to His disciples.[28] God also promised that
Ishmael, because he was the son of Abraham through Sarah's
Egyptian handmaiden, Hagar, would be made into a great nation.

Christ in the **whole heaven**. Even as the Holy Spirit now only dimly
sustains us and we inadequately praise and *"pray continually; give
thanks in all circumstances,"* [27] then we will walk in the abundance
of the sustaining power of the Holy Spirit in perfect fellowship of
love and communication, horizontally with each other and vertically giving praise and worship to the Father and Son.

THE LAND OF EDEN

Because of Jesus being chosen as the sacrificial Lamb before
creation, we know God knew that Adam and Eve would not withstand the contest of wills between them and Lucifer, the rebellious
Angel of Light. In the land of Eden, He prepared a garden in which
he placed Adam and fashioned Eve. It was as if a spot in this garden was to be of eternal significance to show His justice, mercy and
grace to the *"rulers and authorities in the heavenly realms."* [29] After

the fall, cherubim guarded the Garden of Eden with flaming swords to protect the Tree of Life. Subsequently, to prevent attempted access by the fallen "sons of God," it must have been removed from our terrestrial dimension.

The flood of Noah would have altered the local physiography, but geographically it would be **the land** promised to Abraham "forever." It is very likely that the local city of Jerusalem parallels the heavenly city of Zion,[30] and the local Hill of Calvary is the spot where Adam and Eve forfeited the dominion of planet Earth. From Satan's perspective, he would be killing the innocent sinless second Adam (Jesus) at the same place as he defeated the first Adam by deception. For the second person of the Trinity, incarnated as the God-man, Jesus Christ, it would

> ### NO CONTINUUM
>
> History is made by moment-by-moment decisions of the will; there is no sci-fi time continuum whereby wrongs can be adjusted by time travel.

cost Him His life to defeat Satan. Thus, the cross and the resurrection are the crossroads to life, or death, for eternity.

THE ABRAHAMIC COVENANT

The land is not mentioned again until long after Noah's flood when God makes an unconditional covenant to give title to **the land** to a man He calls His friend. This man was Abram, later to be renamed Abraham. He was a Chaldean from Ur, an ancient city in what is now modern Iraq, which lay between Babylon and the Persian Gulf. God tells Abram: *"Leave your country, your people and your father's household and go to* **the land*** *I will show you. I will make you into a great nation and I will bless you; I will make your name great, and you will be a blessing. I will bless those who bless you, and whoever curses you I will curse; and all peoples on earth will be blessed through you"* (*emphasis mine).[31]

God ratified this covenant unconditionally in the Chaldean tradition of law by walking between the halves of butchered animals laying opposite each other.[32] Normally both parties would walk hand in hand between the halves signifying the contract between them. In this case, only God walked between the halves because only God could keep this covenant. Abraham was given **the land** as a gift. Even though Abraham was 100 years old and Sarah his wife ninety, God assured him: *"your wife Sarah will bear you a son, and you will call him Isaac. I will establish my covenant with him as an everlasting covenant for his descendants after him."*[33]

Abraham was indeed blessed and became father of many nations, both physically and through faith. Modern Islam claims Ishmael as their father. God gave "the promise of Ishmael" when He said to Abraham: *"And as for Ishmael, I have heard you: I will surely bless him; I will make him fruitful and will greatly increase his numbers. He will be the father of twelve rulers, and I will make him into a great nation."*[34]

"But my covenant," said God, *"I will establish with Isaac, whom Sarah will bear to you by this time next year."*[35] God later confirmed this covenant with Isaac,[36] his son Jacob[37] and then to Moses[38] when he led the Hebrew slaves out of Egypt.

Salvation for the world was to come through Isaac. Paul explains: *"The promises were spoken to Abraham and to his seed. The Scripture does not say 'and to seeds,' meaning many people, but 'and to your seed,' meaning one person, who is Christ."*[39] Jesus Christ came through the lineage of King David of the tribe of Judah, the son of Jacob, the son of Isaac the son of Abraham. God gave King David a national promise for the nation Israel when He said: *"Your house and your kingdom will endure forever before me; you throne will be established forever."*[40] This promise is referred to as the "Davidic covenant."

The "children of faith" also come from Abraham. *"Consider Abraham: 'He believed God, and it was credited to him as righ-*

teousness.' ... The Scripture foresaw that God would justify the Gentiles by faith, and announced the gospel in advance to Abraham: 'All nations will be blessed through you.' So those who have faith are blessed along with Abraham the man of faith," and *"if you belong to Christ, then you are Abraham's seed, and heirs according to the promise."* [41] *"This mystery is that through the gospel the Gentiles are heirs together... of one body, and sharers together in the promise in Christ Jesus."* [42] This means that those of the Bride of Christ are the children of Abraham through personal faith in the sacrificial work of Christ.

Some believe the Church has supplanted all the promises to Israel. This is not so; Israel is the prophetic time clock of history. At present, the Church, through the power of the Holy Spirit, is being made up of all tribes, nations and languages whether Jew or Gentile. Paul writes: *"I do not want you to be ignorant of this mystery, brothers, so that you may not be conceited: Israel has experienced a hardening in part until the full number of the Gentiles has come in. And so all Israel will be saved, as it is written: 'The deliverer will come from Zion; he will turn godlessness away from Jacob. And this is my covenant with them when I take away their sins.'"* [43] Israel rejected

A MIRACLE?

No other ethnic group has ever re-established themselves as a nation including language, law and worship.

Jesus and the kingdom; therefore, as prophesied by the prophet Hosea, Jesus said: *"I will go back to my place until they admit their guilt. And they will seek my face; in their misery they will earnestly seek me."* [44] This powerful and amazing event will take place over Jerusalem as described by Zechariah: *"They will look on me, the one they have pierced, and they will mourn for him as one mourns for an only child, and grieve bitterly for him as one grieves for a firstborn son."* [45]

Dr. Charles Ryrie, who studied the relationship of the Church to the fulfillment of God's promises in the Abrahamic and Davidic covenants, writes:

> In no case are the national promises to Israel destroyed. By these three contrasts, natural Israel and the Gentiles, natural Israel and the Church, spiritual Israel and the Church, it is clear that the Church in its entirety is never designated Israel in Scripture. Thus there is no basis for transferring to the Church the promises which belong to Israel. Since the Church does not fulfill the promises of the Abrahamic covenant, Israel herself must fulfill them at a future date.[46]

The formation of Israel in 1948, after being dispersed amongst the nations for over 1,900 years, is a fulfillment of prophecy; it also gives meaning to the prophetic future earthly administration of Israel during the period of the Millennium and the Ages of Ages. Now let's look in more detail at the promises to Ishmael and then at the fulfillment of the Davidic covenant.

WILL ISLAM INHERIT THE PROMISES TO ISHMAEL?

Only Jews, Muslims and Christians worship God as the monotheistic God, creator of the universe. In these days of heightened concern, when Satan and his evil forces are trying to polarize the Muslim world against Israel and Christendom, we must recognize that he is agitating the carnal nature of humanity against the fundamental attributes of God—love, grace and mercy. Of course, not all those who bear the name of Judaism, Christianity or Islam, are true followers of God. God declares: *"These people come near to me with their mouth and honor me with their lips, but their hearts are far from me. Their worship of me is made up of rules taught by men."*[47]

Syrian Christians, in the fifth century AD, would retreat to caves for spiritual meditation which influenced other spiritually seeking

4

Arabs.[50] The prophet Muhammed records that the angel Gabriel, sometime around 600 AD, visited him while he was meditating in a cave located on Mount Hira near Mecca. Here the Qur'an (recitations) in a series of Suras (revelations) descended upon him. "In addition to the Qur'an, Muslims rely on the Hadith, or tradition. The traditions form a vast library of recollections about what Muhammed (or his companions) said and did. Some of the material also comes from Jewish and Christian tradition."[51] Not all of these traditions are accepted. The famous authority Al-Bukhari chose only 7,000 of the 600,000 apocryphal sayings in circulation.[52]

> **QUR'AN**
>
> In 670 A.D., there were multiple confusing handwritten verbal transmissions. One official version was compiled and approved; all the rest were condemned and burned.[48]

The teachings of the Qur'an are about entering Paradise through self-accomplishing works of faith and righteousness. "Those who reject Faith, and die rejecting—on them is Allah's curse."[53] "But those of Faith are overflowing in their love for Allah. If only the unrighteous could see, behold, they would see the Punishment."[54] "But it is righteousness to believe in Allah."[55] "And follow not the footsteps of the Evil One; for he is to you an avowed enemy."[56]

After the death of the prophet, power struggles took place within Islam. Members

> **ALLAH**
>
> "Allah is simply the Arabic word for God; it is used by Arabic speaking Christians as well as by Muslims. ...It is important to remember that the Muslim conception of God differs from that of the Bible at several major points. ...Allah means the God. The doctrine of the unity and oneness of God is the most fundamental aspect of Islamic faith."[49]

of Muhammed's own family were killed.[59] Various factions sought to interpret the Suras and Hadith in their own way to gain power and control, creating Islamic wolves and Islamic lambs similar to what was happening in Roman Christendom. Comparable to the interpretations of papal power in Rome involving the creation of rules, regulations and systems of worship, Islam developed their own factions as they struggled with what was secular.[60] The modern Taliban in Afghanistan are a classic example of individual interpretation of rules and regulations in an attempt to gain religious power and superiority under the guise of a "pure Islamic" belief.

Matters of food and dress do not change the lusts of the heart. What is required is a spiritual change of heart, to love each other and produce the fruits of the Holy Spirit rather than enforced regulation. Not being able to forgive[61] one another is self-centered pride (as shown by Iblis [Satan]—Surah 7:13), which will create a wall against humility, faith and righteousness.

The Qur'an recognizes that there is a Beast to come

MUHAMMED PROTECTS JEWS AND CHRISTIANS

The Roman emperor Theodosia commanded all his subjects become orthodox Christians, resulting in power-hungry Christian wolves persecuting fellow Christian lambs. Fleeing Christians were accused of being spies for Rome. In Persia, the "Zoroastrian priests often broke out into violent persecutions of Christians. In this way hundreds of thousands of Christians were martyred." Yet, in this time[57] of power struggles, the prophet Muhammed protected the Jews under the Constitution of Madina and the Christians by the Najar'n document.[58]

in the last days. "And when the Word is fulfilled against them (the unjust), we shall produce from the earth a Beast to (face) them, for that mankind did not believe with assurance in our Signs,"[62] and

225

OF THE SOMETHING MORE

"The Beast will be one of the Signs of the Last Days to come, before the present World passes away and the new World is brought into being. In symbolic language, it would represent gross Materialism. It will be the embodiment of fat worldly triumph, which will appeal to a misguided and degenerate world, because such a corrupt world will have no assured belief in the Signs of Allah or in spiritual light."[63]

This is the schism within Islam: "what level of materialism makes one secular?" rather than "what does it mean to be spiritual within the attitudes of the heart?"

The book of Revelation confirms that the Beast will come and dictate economic prosperity in that no man will be able to buy or sell without a number.[64] The Beast is a man rather than a concept. He will then claim to be God (or Allah) in the temple in Jerusalem, which is idolatry to the Jew, the Christian and the Muslim. All who will not bow and worship him will be killed. Just as the Bible records in Isaiah 24:21: *"In that day the LORD will punish the powers in the heavens above and the kings on the earth below,"* the Qur'an states in Surah 27:87: "And the Day that the Trumpet will be sounded—then will be smitten with terror those who are in the heavens, and those who are on the earth."

GROSS MATERIALISM

Osama bin Laden and many other Islamic zealots, even as they are supported by materialism, have made their own interpretation of gross materialism. To them the United States is symbolic of the Beast of gross materialism in Western civilization.

The old terminology Jesus was "begotten" is a language misunderstanding as it implies sexual intercourse. Jesus as God was the "Word" implanted by the Holy Spirit of God in the Virgin Mary. To worship Jesus is not idolatry, as He is God, the Word, who took on the form of man. Evildoers asked Muhammed a tricky question

226

trying to discredit him: "Did God die on the cross?" He answered correctly, "God cannot die." Because Jesus the God-man was both biological and spiritual, it was the biological "dwelling" that died while God, the Son, taking all

NOT BEGOTTEN

"Say: He is Allah, The One and Only; Allah, the Eternal, Absolute; He begetteth not, nor is He begotten; And there is none Like unto Him" (Surah 112:1–4).

our sins upon Himself, went into Hades to herald the event to the world of the departed spirits.[65] He then rose again from the dead,[66] showing that He was indeed God. Both Jew and Muslim have to come to terms with the Trinity in the way God has revealed Himself in the Torah as Elohim,[67] "Us," and in the Qur'an as "We,"[68] yet God is One.[69] Christianity believes God is "One," yet, subsists as three individual personalities: Father, Son and Holy Spirit,[70] an unfathomable mystery of the Godhead.

There are three avenues of belief extending from Abraham: the children of faith, the line of Isaac and the line of Ishmael. When we examine the lines of belief in God extending from Abraham, Israel is bound with the laws of Moses, the required sacrifices and additional self-proclaimed rules and regulations to be righteous. Islam is bound with the revelations of the Suras on the self-achievement of faith and righteousness and the additional rules and regulations of the Hadith. The Christian stands by faith on the completed act of redeeming sacrifice by the God-man, Jesus Christ.

The law given to Moses shows us who we are with respect to the holiness of God. The law brings spiritual death because no man, by his own works, can achieve the self-righteousness required by God. If you have any doubts about whether or not your faith and righteousness will get you to Paradise, get excited: God found a way to bring mankind to Himself! Paul explains: *"Therefore, there is now no condemnation for those who are in Christ Jesus, because through Christ Jesus the law of the Spirit of life set me free from the law of sin and death. For what the law was powerless to do in that it was weakened by the sinful nature, God did by sending his own Son in the likeness of sinful man to be a sin offering. And so he condemned sin in sinful man, in order that the righteousness requirements of the law might be fully met in us, who do not live according to the sinful nature but according to the Spirit."* [71]

Abdiyah Akbar Abdul-Haqq, who spent many years as an evangelist for the Billy Graham organization and whose father was a convert from Islam, writes:

> In short, Jesus Christ, the son of Mary, was sent by God to publish the Good News of salvation to all mankind which was made available in history by Him and in Him. In this remarkable way He was given the Gospel to proclaim which Gospel He himself was. God does not hesitate to use weak and inadequate human languages like Arabic or Hebrew in order to establish contact with fallen man, did not abhor a virgin's womb to accomplish the redemption of mankind. This is the Injil (the Gospel) of our Lord Jesus Christ, the Word of God (John 1:4; Sura 4:171), who came from God the Father (John 3:16, 17; Sura 57:27) and was strengthened by God the Holy Spirit (John 1:32–34; Sura 2:87, 253). [72]

Jesus Christ is not a Western concept. He is God born to a Jewish virgin. He wore Eastern clothes and was likely olive-skinned with a beard and shoulder-length hair.

National traditions, dress and culture have no bearing on salvation; each will be like the many different types of beautiful flowers in the Paradise to come. Just as many Messianic Jews, having researched the Trinity and the God-man, Jesus Christ, have accepted Him as their Messiah and worship Him in Jewish culture, so are some Muslims realizing that Jesus is the fulfillment of their search for righteousness. They, too, by willfully asking Him into their lives, can worship God in their national traditions and culture and be sustained by the Holy Spirit of God. Religious wolves with a bouquet of rules and regulations, however, always attack freedom of worship.

In all this there is an interesting coincidence not valid 100 years ago and which will not be valid 100 years hence. For close to 600 years from Abraham to Moses, the family lines of Isaac and Ishmael could follow the example of their patriarchal father and worship God by faith and sacrifice. From Moses to Jesus Christ, who came to fulfill the law, law bound the Jews for approximately 1400 years while the sons of Ishmael stood outside the law for those 1400 years. Close to 600 years after the accomplishment of Christ on the cross of Calvary, that freed Jew and Gentile (including Ishmaelites) from the chains of the law, the sons of Ishmael took on the laws of Islam and have now labored under them for almost 1400 years. Six hundred years plus 1400 years is 2000 years, or two prophetic days. Christianity has been in existence for almost 2000 years. The years 2000 to 2030 will be the beginnings of the third day when we may see the fulfillment of biblical prophesy of the return of Jesus Christ.[73] Meanwhile, at any time in this period, Jew, Muslim or Gentile could have drunk, and still can drink, from the fountain of living water[74] (Holy Spirit) Jesus has provided.

In symbolic fashion, the laws given to Moses pointed towards the cross—showing that neither the law nor animal sacrifice was sufficient for salvation. The rules and regulations of Islam point backwards to the cross—showing that salvation is not obtained by self-works of faith and righteousness. Of course, a follower of Islam believes self-works of faith and righteousness are another way to God, or Allah. However, Jesus Christ, the sinless second Adam, fulfilled all the requirements of God's laws with their rules and regulations and became the perfect sacrifice to appease the justice of

God. It is by willfully accepting the grace and mercy of God, because of Christ's sacrificial death, that salvation is obtained.

Unbelievable as it is at this junction of history, Arabs in the millennium, as a result of the promise God gave to Abraham for Ishmael, will be aligned with Israel in their worship of God, bringing gold, incense and sacrifice offerings into the glorious millennial temple.[75] *"In that day there will be a highway from Egypt to Assyria. The Assyrians will go to Egypt and the Egyptians to Assyria. The Egyptians and Assyrians will worship together. In that day Israel will be the third, along with Egypt and Assyria, a blessing on the earth. The LORD Almighty will bless them, saying, 'Blessed be Egypt my people, Assyria my handiwork, and Israel my inheritance.'"* [76] In this way, God's promises for Ishmael are fulfilled.

THE DAVIDIC COVENANT

It is the Davidic covenant that gives the fulfillment of the cosmological significance to **the land**. While the rulers and authorities in Heaven are watching, God has redeemed mankind in the great "Schism of the Cosmos." He has elevated the Bride to be celestial citizens to rule with Him. **The land** is the link between the earthly administration and the heavenly administration. The Lord states: *"Heaven is my throne, and the earth my footstool. Where is the house you will build for me? Where will my resting place be? Has not my hand made all these things, and so they came into being?"* [77] The prophet Ezekiel is given a holographic futuristic vision of the incredible temple to be built in **the land** by the Messiah in the opening years of the millennium. The Lord answers: *"I will glorify the place of my feet,"*[78] and *"this is the place of my throne and the place for the soles of my feet. This is where I will live among the Israelites forever."* [79] Now let's see how this comes to be fulfilled.

The Davidic covenant is the promises God made to King David through the prophet Nathan regarding the nation Israel.

They involve the building of the temple and the succession of the throne through the lineage of David. God's words are recorded in 2 Samuel 7:9–17: *"Now I will make your name great, like the names of the greatest men of the earth. And I will provide a place for my people Israel* [**the land**] *and will plant them so that they can have a home of their own and no longer be disturbed.*

"…I will raise up your offspring to succeed you, who will come from your own body, and I will establish his kingdom. He is the one who will build a house for my Name, and I will establish the throne of his kingdom forever.

"…Your house and your kingdom will endure forever before me; your throne will be established forever."

In fulfillment of this declaration by God, King Solomon, David's son, built the magnificent first temple, one of the wonders of the world in that era. Subsequently, the nation declined as they sought after "other gods" and were taken into captivity. The prophet Jeremiah was reassured by God in Jeremiah 23:5–6: *"'The days are coming,' declares the LORD, 'when I will raise up to David a righteous Branch, a King who will reign wisely and do what is just and right in* **the land**.* In his days Judah will be saved and Israel will live in safety. This is the name by which he will be called: The Lord Our Righteousness'"* (*emphasis mine).

The prophet Isaiah was told by God who this righteous Branch would be. Isaiah 9:6–7: *"For to us a child is born, to us a son is given, and the government will be on his shoulders. And he will be called Wonderful Counselor, Mighty God, Everlasting Father, Prince of Peace. Of the increase of his government and peace there will be no end. He will rule on David's throne and over his kingdom, establishing and upholding it with justice and righteousness from that time on and forever. The zeal of the Lord Almighty shall accomplish this."*

And how he would be born. Isaiah 7:13–14: *"Hear now, you house of David! Is it not enough to try the patience of men? Will you try the patience of God also? Therefore the Lord himself will give you a sign: The virgin will be with child and will give birth to a son, and will call him Immanuel* [Immanuel means "God with us"].

The angel Gabriel, speaking to the Virgin Mary, verifies that the birth of Jesus of Nazareth through her is the fulfillment of this prophecy in Luke 1:30–33: *"Do not be afraid, Mary, you have found favor with God. You will be with child and give birth to a son, and you are to give him the name Jesus. He will be great and will be called the Son of the Most High. The Lord God will give him the throne of his father David, and he will reign over the house of Jacob forever; his kingdom will never end."*

Moreover, in God's cosmologically dealing with **the land**, King David will be resurrected and serve as king-prince of **the land** under the Kingship of Jesus Christ. The Lord states: *"I will return to Zion and dwell in Jerusalem. Then Jerusalem will be called the City of Truth, and the mountain of the LORD Almighty will be called the Holy Mountain."* [80] God informs the prophet Ezekiel of these matters in Ezekiel 37:24–28: *"My servant David will be king over them, and they will all have one shepherd. They will follow my laws and be careful to keep my decrees. They will live in **the land*** I gave to my servant Jacob, the land where your fathers lived. They and their children and their children's children will live there forever, and David my servant will be their prince forever. I will make a covenant of peace with them; it will be an everlasting covenant. I will establish them and increase their numbers, and I will put my sanctuary among them forever. My dwelling place will be with them; I will be their God, and they will be my people. Then the nations will know that I the LORD make Israel holy, when my sanctuary is among them forever"* (*emphasis mine).

In the future, Jacob, a term meaning the unified twelve tribes, will occupy **the land** in safety as the kingdom of Israel. It is a literal kingdom on Earth ruled "forever" by the God-man, Jesus Christ,

King of Kings and Lord of Lords, and His resurrected servant King David. Dr. Ryrie writes:

> If Christ is the Man who is fulfilling Jeremiah's statement, (of the Lord Our Righteousness) then He is certainly not now fulfilling the Davidic covenant, for not one New Testament reference can be found which teaches that the Lord Jesus Christ is now on the throne of David, and His present relation to the Church certainly has no equivalence to the throne of the house of Israel. Twenty-one times in the New Testament Christ's present position is described by the phrase, "at the right hand" of God, or of the Majesty on High, etc., and this location is expressly defined as the throne of the Father, (Revelation 3:21; 12:5). It then follows that if Christ is not now fulfilling the Davidic covenant, there must be a future fulfillment.[81]

However, for Israel to be set "high above all the nations on earth,"[82] as the head of nations rather than the tail, she must be holy and follow all of God's commandments, which **she has not done**. The angel Gabriel informs the prophet Daniel that Israel has been given a prophetic time period of seventy weeks of years for this to be accomplished. *"Seventy 'sevens' are decreed for your people and your holy city to finish transgression, to put an end to sin, to atone for wickedness, to bring in everlasting righteousness, to seal up vision and prophecy and to anoint the most holy"*[83] ("Seventy sevens" is seventy weeks of years, for a total of 490 years).

God Himself will accomplish this. He came at the end of sixty-nine weeks (483 years) as the God-man to atone for wickedness, not only for Israel, but also for all peoples when He died on the cross of Calvary. The last prophetic week has been held in abeyance while the mystery "Bride of Christ" is called out of the nations of the world. The last week is thought to begin when the Bride is called to Heaven to receive her rewards. Israel, to fulfill the conditions given by God, will take up where John the Baptist and Jesus left off and proclaim the coming Messianic kingdom. In this last week of years (seven years yet to come from our viewpoint), God will appoint 144,000 Jewish preachers[84] to herald the gospel of the coming literal-physical kingdom to the entire world. It will be the time of Jacob's (Israel's) trouble, after which God says:

> **MODERN ISRAEL**
>
> Modern Israel is not loved by God for what she does, or any sanctimonious rules or regulations she may keep, but because He chooses to love her because of His friend Abraham.

"They will serve the Lord their God and David their king, whom I will raise up for them." [85] Zechariah describes this great scene of holy purification for Israel, when God says: *"they shall look on me the one they have pierced."* [86] In this way, the nation will be made holy in fulfillment of the conditions God gave to Moses. The millennial kingdom begins at this point in time when the twelve tribes of Israel will be in **the land** as head of nations as God's inheritance through His covenant with Abraham. King Jesus, Wonderful Counselor, Mighty God, Everlasting Father, Prince of Peace will be on the throne of David "forever" in fulfillment of the Davidic covenant. After 1,000 years have passed, the Ages of Ages will commence.

GOD DWELLS WITH MEN

At the beginning of the Ages of Ages, in the complete unification of the cosmos, the holy celestial city, the New Jerusalem, throne of the Bridegroom and home of His celestial Bride, comes to Earth. *"And I heard a loud voice from the throne saying, 'Now the dwelling of God is with men, and he will live with them. They will be his people, and God himself will be with them and be their God.'"* [87] Here Christ is head of all Heaven and Earth and so completes that which was declared to Isaiah the prophet: *"Heaven is my throne, and the Earth is my footstool"* (66:1). Redeemed mankind from the millennial kingdom will now populate the universe under the rule of Christ and His Bride.

Joseph A. Seiss, a deeply God-fearing theologian of the 19th century, writes:

> There is not a word which asserts any purpose of God to terminate the perpetuity of humanity as an ever expanding race. It was constituted and given command for unending perpetuity before sin touched it. If it fails to go on forever, it can only be in consequence of the introduction of sin. But there has been promised and constituted a Redeemer to ransom it from all captivity to sin and corruption. And if his redemption does not go far enough to exempt the ongoing race from being finally extinguished, then it is not redemption, and the Destroyer beats out the Almighty Redeemer.
>
> There is no escape from this alternative if we do not allow that the race of man as a race continues in the new earth, and there realizes its complete and final recovery from all the effects and ill consequences of the fall. Ransomed nations in the flesh are therefore among the occupants of the new earth, and the blessed and happy dwellers in it, as Adam and Eve dwelt in Paradise. The Sitter on the throne saith, "Behold, new I make everything." That everything includes heaven, earth, and sea and by necessary implication, had we no other proofs, the race of humanity is also included as a subject of the great **Re-Genesis*** (*emphasis mine).[88]

Though we cannot know all God has prepared for those who love Him, we can see that, as celestial citizens, eternal life will be a tremendous time of fulfillment in the administrations of Heaven and Earth under the *whole heaven.*

Now that the Bride has entered her eternal home and is walking down the golden cobblestones towards her lover, the Great King, let's examine what will take place next.

CROWNS FOR THE BRIDE

The jubilation in Heaven will be like nothing we can even begin to imagine, for it is the wedding of the Great King. She who was betrothed to the Messiah has been brought to her wedding chamber. These events are remarkably fulfilled in the intimate details of the Jewish betrothal and wedding customs. The cup of wine shared between Jesus and His disciples on the night of His betrayal is the cup of betrothal wine. The Bridegroom will not drink[89] of it again until He brings His Bride to the wedding chamber He goes to prepare.[90] She is to partake continually as a reminder of her betrothal.[91] The newly married couple spends

HEAVENLY EXCITEMENT

Can you imagine the excitement? Your faithful believing relatives and friends are there. You are in your new imperishable, non-destructible, immortal "heavenly dwelling"—the forever youthful unique individual God planned you to be. Surrounding you are the celebrating children who died before the age of accountability, including those aborted spontaneously due to genetic incompatibilities and those of selfish motives. We will know even as we are known.[92] Those of the ages with their own incredible stories to tell will be there; you will have the opportunity to meet them. Your unfulfilled dreams will be there to complete and possibly your favorite pets if you so wish them. Teaching, exploring, building, creating or any other talents, or undeveloped talents, will be given opportunity to unfold. First, though, we will receive our crowns and rewards.

seven days in intimate communion in the wedding chamber where He gives her gifts and the marriage is consummated.

The seven days likely prefigure the last week (seven years) of Daniel's prophecy when there is great tribulation on Earth. The apostle John is given a vision of the Bride returning in triumph with the Great King[93] at the end of this seven-year period. Some Bible scholars believe that this seven-year period is also the time of the coronation of the Great King.[94] There is no way we can begin to imagine the exaltation and celebration that will take place in Heaven at the coronation and wedding of the Great King! Certainly, it is the period when He crowns His Bride and gives her rewards of authority in preparation for her rule with Him. The wedding feast would then occur at the beginning of the millennium, after He has subdued the cosmic rebellion and taken claim of planet Earth.

In 2 Corinthians 5, the apostle Paul talks about our heavenly rewards. He writes: *"For we must all appear before the judgment seat of Christ, that each one may receive what is due him for the things done while in the body, whether good or bad"* (v.10). This statement is further illuminated in his comments in 1 Corinthians 3:11–15. He pens: *"For no one can lay any foundation other than the one already laid, which is Jesus Christ. If any man builds on this foundation using gold, silver, costly stones, wood, hay or straw, his work will be shown for what it is, because the Day will bring it to light. It will be revealed by fire, and the fire will test the quality of each man's work. If what he has built survives, he will receive his reward. If it is burned up, he will suffer loss; he himself will be saved, but only as one escaping through the flames."* Paul is talking about our relationship with our Lord and Savior, "our work" that is done in His name. We are to build, in humility, on the foundation of salvation that He has provided, by living the fruits of the Holy Spirit—faith, hope, love, charity, peace and forgiveness—rather than on works of self-glorification for the church which are wood and straw. Based on the statement of Jesus: *"There is nothing concealed that will not be disclosed, or hidden that will not be made known,"*[95] there are those who believe this judgment is a revealing of all past sins as one stands on the victory podium. Applying this saying to the victory podium is not correct; Satan and evil people were the subject of Jesus's conversation. This statement applies to God's law of retribution to unrepentant sinful people on Earth, and though the evil they did while on Earth may have been successfully hidden, it will be fully exposed at the White Throne judgment of the lost, of men and angels.[96]

God deals with people in three ways: as sinners, as His children and as servants. In the first case, *"if we confess our sins, he is faithful and just and will forgive us our sins and purify us from all unrighteousness."*[97] These sins He has forgiven and remembers no more.[98] They are gone: *"For you died, and your life is now hidden with Christ in God."*[99] *"Who is a God like you, who pardons sin and forgives the transgression… you will tread our sins underfoot and hurl all our iniquities into the depths of the sea."*[100] *"For as high as the heavens are above the earth, so great is his love for those who fear him; as far as the east is from the west, so far has he removed our transgressions from us."*[101]

As His children, we are to *"run with perseverance the race marked out for us… because the Lord disciplines those he loves, and punishes everyone he accepts as a son."*[102] We may have made mistakes in life, but do not dwell on them. Don't look back and hinder your race. Paul writes: *"But one thing I do: Forgetting what is behind and straining toward what is ahead, I press toward the goal to win the prize for which God has called me heavenward in Christ Jesus,"*[103] and, *"if we judged ourselves, we would not come under judgment. When we are judged by the Lord, we are being disciplined so that we will not be condemned with the world."*[104] Then, as we stumble along in this world filled with its hopelessness and despair, if we do sin: *"we have one who speaks to the Father in our defense—Jesus Christ, the Righteous One."*[105]

It is as a servant that we, as the Bride, receive our crowns and rewards in Heaven. The "judgment seat of Christ" is one of celebration; it is one of great victory where we will receive our crowns. The Greek word for this judgment seat is *Bema*; it is the "**victory podium**" where the tribunal gives out the victory laurels to the winners. *"Do you not know that in a race all the runners run, but only one gets the prize? Run in such a way to get the prize. Everyone who competes in the games goes into strict training. They do it to get a crown that will not last; but we do it to get a crown that will last forever."* [106] Here the Greek word for crown is *stephanos*, which is a badge of "royalty." Therefore, we are presented to the Great King as His Royal Bride, adorned in gold of Ophir.[107]

At the judgment seat of the Great King, we are given the five crowns of His grace.

1: THE CROWN OF LIFE

"Blessed is the man who perseveres under trial, because when he has stood the test, he will receive the crown of life that God has promised to those who love him" (Jas. 1:12).

"Be faithful even to the point of death, and I will give you the crown of life" (Rev. 2:10).

USING OUR TALENTS

Jesus taught parables about how we are to use our talents and deal with responsibilities that we are given here on Earth. These teach that some will rule many cites and others none in the ages to come. In the same way, God desires Admirals, Generals and committed soldiers of faith. Earth is the training and testing ground for a heavenly administration of celestial citizens. If you whimper and moan in the corner after having gone through minor testing, Satan is delighted that you were an easily defeated saint. On the other hand, the greater is your desire to serve the Lord, the greater your trials.[117]

"Consider it pure joy my brothers, whenever you face trials of many kinds, because you know that the testing of your faith develops perseverance." [108]

"These have come so that your faith—of greater worth than gold, which perishes even though refined by fire—may be proved genuine and may result in praise, glory and honor when Jesus Christ is revealed." [109]

Trials are anything that can affect your moral principles and your attitude of trust and faith that *"the LORD is good; his love endures forever."* [110] A trial may be something that seems so insignificant yet can have huge heavenly consequences in the way that it affects others. Even in this so-called modern "age of enlightenment," Christians are being martyred for their beliefs.

Be encouraged that *"the Lord knows how to rescue godly men from trials and to hold the unrighteous for the day of judgment."* [111] On the other hand, trials may come upon us as discipline from a loving Father to correct a shifting morality. *"God disciplines us for our good, that we may share in his holiness. No discipline seems pleasant at the time, but painful. Later on, however, it produces a harvest of righteousness and peace for those who have been trained by it."* [112] In either case, may we say with Job: *"He knows the way that I take; when he has tested me, I will come forth as gold."* [113]

2: THE CROWN OF REJOICING

"For what is our hope, our joy, or the crown in which we will glory in the presence of our Lord Jesus when he comes? Is it not you? Indeed, you are our glory and joy" (1 Thess. 2:19).

"Therefore, my brothers, you whom I love and long for, my joy and crown, that is how you should stand firm in the Lord, dear friends" (Phil. 4:1).

Do you think of yourself as a jewel? God sees you as one. He says: *"And they shall be Mine says the Lord of hosts, in that day when I publicly recognize and openly declare them to be My Jewels—My spe-*

Tasteless Saints

C. S. Lewis, in his book, *The Screwtape Letters*, has a senior devil instructing a junior devil on the art of temptation. He complains that both sinners and saints are getting to be tasteless meals.

Oh to get one's teeth again into a Farinata, a Henry VIII or even a Hitler! There was a real crackling there; something to crunch; a rage, an egotism, a cruelty only just less robust than our own. It put up a delicious resistance to being devoured. It warmed your innards when you'd got it down. The great (and toothsome) sinners are made out of the very same material as those horrible phenomena the great Saints. The virtual disappearance of such material may mean insipid meals for us. But is it not utter frustration and famine for the Enemy? He did not create the humans—He did not become one of them and die among them by torture—in order to produce candidates for Limbo, "failed" humans. He wanted to make Saints; gods; things like Himself.

Is the dullness of your present fare not a very small price to pay for the delicious knowledge that His whole great experiment is petering out? But not only that, as the great sinners grow fewer, and the majority lose all individuality, the great sinners become far more effective agents for us. Every dictator or even demagogue—of almost every film star or crooner—can now draw tens of thousands of the human sheep with him. They give themselves (what there is of them) to him; in him to us. There may come a time when we shall have no need to bother about individual tempta-tion at all, except for the few. Catch the bellwether, and his whole flock comes after him.[116]

241

cial possession, My peculiar treasure." [114] The prophet Isaiah writes that even as the Bride is clothed in garments of salvation and arrayed in a robe of righteousness, she adorns herself with jewels.[115] Jewels of saints may not be what Isaiah meant, but it certainly illustrates the function of the Bride on Earth: that she is to win others to the Lord and therefore receive a crown of rejoicing. Hold fast to your faith in your times of trials; how you face them is a witness to others. You may be young, old or handicapped, but even a smile or a word of encouragement will be a witness to your eternal hope. You may be surprised how many jewels are credited to you in heaven! Your crown may be sparkling with brilliant colors.

3: THE CROWN OF RIGHTEOUSNESS

"I have fought the good (worthy, honorable and noble) fight; I have finished the race; I have kept (firmly held) the faith. (As to what remains,) henceforth there is laid up for me the (victor's) crown of righteousness— for being right with God and doing right—which the Lord, the righteous Judge, will award to me and recompense me on that (great) day; and not to me only but also to all those who have loved and yearned for and welcomed His appearing (His return)" (2 Tim. 4:7–8, Amplified Bible).

Shouts of jubilation ring through the magnificent heavenly wedding chamber as each of the members of the Bride receive their crowns of righteousness. In the meantime, this joyous event is yet to come, so fix your eyes on the author of your salvation, Jesus Christ. Seek the sustaining power of the Holy Spirit to withstand the worldly temptations of the Legions of Doom, who would so quickly seek to despoil you in this kingdom of darkness.

4: THE CROWN "INCORRUPTIBLE"

"Everyone who competes in the games goes into strict training. They do it to get a crown that will not last; but we do it to get a crown that will last forever" (1 Cor. 9:25).

"When Christ appears, then you also will appear with him in glory. Put to death, therefore, whatever belongs to your earthly nature: sexual immorality, impurity, lust evil desires and greed, which is idolatry" (Col. 3:4–5).

In contrast to the perishable crown of laurels, our new resurrected bodies will never have the desire or ability to think or act in sinful ways. As celestial children of God, we will have no inclination for an illicit love affair with a mortal. It will be incomprehensible, even as it is now to the Angels of Glory. On Earth, our carnal nature raises havoc with our spirituality every day as it besieges us with negative words, sights and feelings like fragments of sound tapes and filmstrips—all this will be gone.

The Legions of Doom hate Christian music of worship and praise to God;[118] they flee in fear because they know their day of judgment is coming, so here on Earth, in our trials and tribulations, we are encouraged to *"speak to one another with psalms, hymns and spiritual songs. Sing and make music in your heart to the Lord, always giving thanks to God the Father for everything, in the name of our Lord Jesus Christ."* [119] If you are young and like music with a zesty beat, make the words inspirational. If you are a country and western fan, praise the Lord in all things. If you are a crooner, may your words be of thanksgiving and encouragement. However, as the apostle Paul would say, in this sense we of the Church have no rules and regulations; just make a joyful noise unto the Lord and worship Him from your innermost being.

5: THE CROWN OF GLORY

"To the elders among you, I appeal as a fellow elder, a witness of Christ's sufferings and one who also will share in the glory to be revealed: Be shepherds of God's flock that is under your care, serving as overseers—not because you must, but because you are willing, as God wants you to be; not greedy for money, but eager to serve; not lording it

over those entrusted to you, but being examples to the flock. And when the Chief Shepherd appears, you will receive the grown of glory that will never fade away" (1 Pet. 5:1–4).

The importance of godly leaders witnessing by example cannot be overstated. They will receive this crown of glory. Godly leaders are so important to the Body of believers that Jesus refers to them as "angels" of the churches.[120] Yet some church leaders build great edifices with multiple services and never shepherd their flock. Their church organizations become social religious systems of Christendom having form but really being whitewashed tombs.[121] Jesus says that He stands outside and knocks[122] trying to gain entrance. The quiet, unassuming elders who know their flocks and shepherd them one by one may very well have the largest crowns of glory.

We do not often think of it this way, but it would appear that, at the fall of Adam and Eve, the forward movement of God's active creation stopped. *"The creation waits in eager expectation for the sons of God to be revealed. For the creation was subjected to frustration, not by its own choice, but by the will of the one who subjected it, in hope that the creation itself will be liberated from its bondage to decay and brought into the glorious freedom of the children of God."* [123] This answers the question of what we will we be doing in the whole Heaven. If creation was stopped at the rebellion of Adam and Eve, then, by implication, it will start up once again when the "Glorified Sons of God" are revealed. The book of Job tells us that the *"angels shouted for joy"* [124] when God started the stupendous creation event. How much greater will the excitement be when the heavenly hosts see Jesus with His Bride, ready to rule the whole heavens, and the Father starts to create once again?

As celestial beings, we go far beyond that of angels. We are individuals, yet we are indwelt by God: *"for in him we live and move and have our being."* [125] Our self-taking wills are gone, and our will is of

God. Thus the words of Jesus are fulfilled: *"On that day you will realize that I am in my Father, and you are in me, and I am in you."* [126] Can you imagine the heavenly choirs serenading on planets inhabited by purified humanity, or the inter-planet sports competitions?

Maybe celestial engineers will move Venus, which is almost the same size as Earth, into Earth's orbit but in a stable position on the opposite side of the sun. Then move Europa, with its ocean of ice-water, around Venus. Its orbit would be positioned to create seasons. The water would be discharged onto Venus, and the core of Europa would become the moon of Venus. Next, it would need a biological system. All this would be done through the love, wisdom and power of God, the Father through His Sons. And so, the twin sisters of Sol would orbit the heavens.

> **FOREVER YOUNG**
>
> Do you remember the crazy excitement of youth? I can remember driving in my little Hillman car. The side window would be open, fresh air flowing in, and I would be yelling for the sheer joy of it—something like the young animals as they run and kick their hooves into the air or tussle with each other. You will have that youthful spontaneous joy.

Whatever your view of Heaven is, it has to encompass the **whole Heaven**, for God has created us to be "of the something more." Even though the world is dimly aware something is happening, the signs of the times of the coming "Day of the Lord" are all around us.

NOTES:

[1] 1 Thessalonians 4:16–18

[2] John 3:29

[3] Zechariah 9:11; Isaiah 48:9; Isaiah 61:1

4 Note: Hades is not the Lake of Fire which is Hell proper. Confusion exists because Hades is commonly referred to as Hell. Yes, it is Hell, but it is only a prelude to Hell proper which was prepared for the devil and his angels. When Jesus told the history of the poor man and Lazarus, Hades contained the compartments of Torments and Paradise (also called Abraham's Bosom). Jesus said to the thief on the cross *"today you will be with me in Paradise"* (Luke 23:43), which is where the eternal Spirit of Jesus went to herald His victory on the cross to all the lost sinners of the ages including the imprisoned angels mentioned by Peter (2 Pet. 2:4–6). Revelation 19:20 informs us that the antichrist and the false prophet are the first two beings to be cast into the Lake of Eternal Fire. The rest of the damned of men and angels await the Great White Throne judgment (Rev. 20:11–15) when they, death and Hades (which only contains the compartment of Torments) are cast into the Lake of Fire which is Hell proper.

5 Upon the resurrection of Jesus, all the prisoners of hope are released and go up into what Paul calls the "third heaven" (2 Cor. 12:2). Paul was taken up to the third heaven in contrast to Jesus and the repentant thief who went down before the resurrection.

6 Matthew 27:52–53

7 Revelation 20:4

8 Daniel 7:13–14, 27

9 Ephesians 3:6

10 Ephesians 1:4, 9–10

11 2 Peter 3:3–4

12 1 Thessalonians 5:2–3

13 1 Corinthians 2:9

14 Psalm 68:17

15 Ezekiel 10:9–14

16 2 Kings 2:11

17 Zechariah 6:1

18 2 Kings 6:17

19 Exodus 25:9—The tabernacle formed the inner design of the temple surrounding the Holy of Holies which held the ark of the covenant (Rev. 11:19, 14:5).

[20] Revelation 21:16; note 1400–1500 miles depending on the length of the cubit

[21] Psalm 78:25

[22] Lemonick, Michael D., Madeleine Nash, "Unraveling Universe," *TIME*, March 6, 1995, p. 42

[23] 2 Peter 3:10

[24] Genesis 6:1–4

[25] 2 Corinthians 5:1, 4

[26] Psalm 78:2

[27] 1 Thessalonians 5:17–18

[28] Matthew 13; Luke 8, 13, 14

[29] Ephesians 3:10

[30] Hebrews 12:22, 11:16

[31] Genesis 12:1–3

[32] Genesis 15:9–21

[33] Genesis 17:19

[34] Genesis 17:20

[35] Genesis 17:21

[36] Genesis 26:2–4

[37] Genesis 28:13–15

[38] Exodus 3:8; Deuteronomy 29:12–13

[39] Galatians 3:16

[40] 2 Samuel 7:16

[41] Galatians 3:6, 8–9, 29

[42] Ephesians 3:6

[43] Romans 11:25–27

[44] Hosea 5:15

[45] Zechariah 12:10

[46] Ryrie, Dr. C. Charles, *The Basis of the Premillennial Faith*, Loizeaux Brothers, Neptune, New Jersey, 1953, p. 70

[47] Isaiah 29:13

48 Saal, William J., *Reaching Muslims for Christ*, Moody Press, 1991, p. 29

49 Saal, Ibid, p.33

50 Abdul-Haqq, Abdiyah Akbar, *Sharing Your Faith with a Muslim*, Bethany House Publishers, 1980, p. 16

51 Saal, Ibid pp. 29,31

52 Abdul-Hagg, Ibid p. 45

53 Surah 2:161, *The Holy Qur'an*, Abdullah Yusuf Ali New Edition with Revised Translation and Commentary, Amana Corporation, 1991

54 Surah 2:165

55 Surah 2:177

56 Surah 2:208

57 Abdul-Haqq, Ibid. p. 18

58 Zakaria, Dr. Rafiq, *The Struggle Within Islam*, Penguin Books, 1989, p. 30

59 Zakaria, Ibid p.57

60 Zakaria, Ibid pp. 43–59

61 Surah 4:17; 1:109: commentary 110, "as Allah does to our sins with His grace"

62 Surah 27:82

63 3313 commentary on Surah 27:82

64 Revelation 13:16–18

65 1 Peter 3:18

66 John 10:18

67 Genesis 1:26, 3:22, 11:7; Isaiah 6:8

68 Surah 7:10–11

69 Deuteronomy 6:4

70 Isaiah 48:16; Matthew 28:19

71 Romans 8:1–4

72 Abdul-Haqq, Ibid. p. 61

73 Exodus 19:10–11; Hosea 6:2

[74] John 4:10

[75] Isaiah 60:6–7

[76] Isaiah 19:23–25

[77] Isaiah 66:1

[78] Isaiah 60:13

[79] Ezekiel 43:7

[80] Zechariah 7:3

[81] Ryrie, Ibid. p. 81

[82] Deuteronomy 28:1–2

[83] Daniel 9:24

[84] Revelation 7:1–8, 14:1

[85] Jeremiah 30:9

[86] Zechariah 12:10

[87] Revelation 21:3

[88] Seiss, Augustus Joseph, *The Apocalypse Lectures on the Book of Revelation*, 1900, Zondervan Press, 1993, p. 492

[89] Luke 22:18

[90] John 14:1

[91] 1 Corinthians 11:25

[92] 1 Corinthians 13:12

[93] Revelation 19:1–16

[94] Luke 19:15, Matthew 25:34

[95] Matthew 10:26

[96] Revelation 20:11–15

[97] 1 John 1:9

[98] Hebrews 8:12

[99] Colossians 3:3

[100] Micah 7:18–19

[101] Psalm 103:11–12

[102] Hebrews 12:1, 6

[103] Philippians 3:13–14

[104] 1 Corinthians 11:31–32

[105] 1 John 2:1

[106] 1 Corinthians 9:24–25

[107] Psalm 45:9

[108] James 1:2

[109] 1 Peter 1:7

[110] Jeremiah 33:11

[111] 2 Peter 2:9

[112] Hebrews 12:10–11

[113] Job 23:10

[114] Malachi 3:17 (The Amplified Bible, Zondervan)

[115] Isaiah 61:10

[116] Lewis, C.S., *The Screwtape Letters*, Macmillan Publishing Co. Inc., reprint 1961, pp. 154, 158

[117] Luke 19:11–27; Matthew 25:14–30

[118] Strauss, Helmut, Pastor, 100 Mile Baptist Church, August 2001, 100 Mile, B.C.

[119] Ephesians 5:19–20

[120] Revelation 1:20

[121] Matthew 23:27

[122] Revelation 3:20

[123] Romans 8:19–21

[124] Job 38:7

[125] Acts 17:28

[126] John 14:20

Signs of the Times

"For you know very well that the day of the Lord will come like a thief in the night. ...But you, brothers, are not in darkness so that this day should surprise you like a thief. You are all sons of light and sons of the day." [1]

Movies of magic and starship space exploration are psychologically preparing our modern civilization to meet the alien. The idea that these aliens are our creators attacks the science of evolution and opens the door to mysticism and psychics. Is it a step into light or is it a regression into darkness?

Evolution, psychics and God are incompatible. Prayers to God on the crisis of September 11, 2001 can only be considered an emotional placebo by an evolutionist. In the reprisal against Osama Bin Laden that followed in Afghanistan, some newspapers reported that psychics were being used to try and pinpoint his location. Once again, an evolutionist can't condone this. If any of those who prayed to God, as Jehovah-God, during this crisis and then participated in the use of spiritualists, they beseeched the enemy of God similar to acts of whoredom that caused God to punish ancient Israel.

Scientists have diligently searched the heavens in the visible light and radio spectrums for any signals of advanced technological civilization. None have been found.[4] From a naturalist's viewpoint, if we evolved from the elements of Earth, we do not have to be anything like an alien species. If evolutionists yield to the hypothesis of panspermia, then advanced aliens should, in general, look like us because we would all originate from a standard set of space-generated, carbon-based molecules. If evolutionists accept the paranormal postulation that genetic manipulation by aliens controlled our evolution, logically we should be in their form

UFOs

From the first, the UFO question has been shrouded in secrecy. Some blame the US government for this, and that isn't wrong. But it is also true that whatever is behind this phenomenon is also extremely secretive and careful. However, a close examination of the phenomenon reveals that there has been a slow, steady process of accumulation of experience in our culture that has led more and more people to believe that UFOs are somehow real.

This belief, which used to mark a person as mentally suspect, is now considered perfectly acceptable and ordinary. At the same time, UFO encounters are becoming more intimate and more complex.[2]

(Whitley Strieber)

and substance. If the principle of evolution—the survival of the fittest—governs the universe, we can expect to be subjugated if we are discovered. Self-incriminating evidence shows that humanity is unfit to inhabit the heavens. Not only are diverse species being eliminated from Earth's biosphere, self-taking humanity continues to slaughter its members.

ALIEN DECEPTION

Prophets of the movie industry predict, by the type of films produced, if human space colonies are established, sooner or later we will start an interplanetary war.

AN ALIEN JOKE?

We may have been built to use as slaves or possibly for cosmic amusement to see how fast we can annihilate ourselves.

Human history indicates that the more advanced the technology, the greater the destruction. The arrival of a galactic starship cruiser in the Star Trek Next Generation format to welcome Earth into the Federation of Galaxies would certainly have the naturalists crying, "I told you so." Nevertheless, how would we know we weren't being duped by the Legions of Doom who already occupy our terrestrial domain? If one accepts that even a small percentage of

THE VISION THING

"Ten years and $20 million later, the Pentagon discovers that psychics are unreliable spies"[3] (Douglas Waller, *TIME*).

the complicated crop circles, UFO sightings and astral-plane meditation transmissions are valid, then aliens are already present, and, according to the biblical account, they have been around for centuries. The concepts of channeler, the force or group consciousness are only modern terms for witchcraft which calls upon self-serving spiritual identities to manifest themselves in our space-time dimension. Satan's ultimate purpose is to deceive mankind of our eternal destiny and to destroy us.

Acts of goodness, peace, joy, love and forgiveness are not concepts of the philosophy of the survival of the fittest. Evolutionists will say they are here because we must have evolved them, which is circular reasoning and is totally different to an absolute moral right or wrong. Only God can be appealed to for such a decision. The laws of Western society, giving individuals uniqueness and value, were formulated under the cloak of Judeo-Christian principles. Naturalism is eroding these values. Under the hypothesis of evolution, there is no moral principle stating it is wrong if a government or a dictator mandates stealing, killing, rape or slavery as being beneficial to the survival of the fittest. Major historical examples of the mentality of mass murder are the totalitarian governments in the early 20th century in Russia and China and the rise of Aryanism in Nazi Germany.

The Bible predicts events to come and defines a purpose for humanity. The philosophy of naturalism has no defined future destiny nor can it ascribe a purpose for history. It teaches that the growth of civilization, culture, knowledge and technology has been linear; that is,

SENSELESS HATE

It is estimated one million people were killed in the Iraq-Iran wars. Next came the Khmer Rouge of Cambodia, the Hutu slaughter of the Tutsi people in Africa, the Serb/Croatian atrocities and the ongoing attacks by Muslims against Christians in Africa and South East Asian countries. The swell of war continues as tribe fights tribe, religion attacks religion escalating to nation against nation and, finally, a great worldwide consummation of ideology against ideology. Islamic terrorist organizations are actively trying to pit the one-billion-five-hundred-million believers of Islam against Christianity, while the hidden agenda of the extreme socialists and totalitarian regimes is to dethrone freedom.

we started with a monkey and, over time, modern man evolved. The ancient Greeks thought that life and civilization went in endless cycles. From the biblical viewpoint, we are in a window of chaos with several cycles of civilization. Modern archaeology is showing this window of chaos has had several cycles of sophisticated human civilization. Therefore, opposite to modern naturalistic wisdom, the Bible and the ancient Greeks, to a lesser degree, are in agreement.

The Bible prophesies Earth is headed for a world government that will implement economic and religious control. The dynamic charisma of this world dictator, who is also endowed with super-natural powers, will convince spiritually deluded humanity that they are finally evolving into new cosmic beings. He will use a religion of mysticism to gain control of the world. The demonic forces of the Legions of Doom will act as spirit guides to empower this New Age religion. All who do not believe will be considered to be hindering this cosmic shift, or new paradigm, and will have to be eliminated. The basis for this reasoning, by followers of this ultimate manifestation of secular humanism, is that if there is no moral wrong in naturalistic evolution, why should there be a moral wrong in weeding out those unfit for spiritual evolution? This will be a pogrom of the kingdom of darkness against the kingdom of God who, through grace and mercy, has sent a Great Light into the world whereby men may be saved.[5]

THE DAYS OF THE GIANTS

Archaeological discoveries have uncovered evidence that ancient human societies used advanced agrarian techniques showing they were more than hunter-gathers. The further back in time human societies and human technology can be traced, the more complicated the evolutionary explanations become. Uniformitarianism has no explanation for gigantism of plants, insects and animals which ended suddenly some 6,000 to 10,000 years ago.

MAN AND DINOSAURS

The Web site omniology.com shows pictures of coincident occurrences of man and dinosaur tracks. Moreover, dinosaurs are depicted in cave and rock paintings.

Meganthropus, the fossil of a giant human, was discovered in Australia. He is estimated to be between ten and fourteen feet tall and used large tools. One tool, a copper axe, weighed thirty-seven pounds.[6] Gigantopithecus was discovered in China. Large skeletons have been found in Europe and North America. Giants may have built the large mysterious underwater platforms with three-foot steps in the ocean off Okinawa Japan.[7]

CONTRARY FINDINGS IGNORED

Reasonable scientific inquiry by Christians and secular scientists is suppressed because contrary findings, such as related man and dinosaur tracks, do not fit evolutionary dogma. If evolution is true, it will stand under critical examination, but if it is false, it is evidence for the agenda of spiritual deception of humanity by the cosmic rebels.

Eight anomalous sites have been found so far. Mysterious statutes have been found in the jungles of Indonesia. It may be speculated that a large area of the South Pacific Ocean around Indonesia may be a lost continent of giants.

Evolutionists ignore the period of gigantism, the finds of human giants in particular, because it defeats the chimp-to-man theory. Yet the Word of God states clearly: *"There were giants on the earth in those days, and also afterward, when the sons of God lived with the daughters of men, and they bore children to them. These were the mighty men who were of old, men of renown."*[10] The word "afterwards" refer to the period after the Noachian flood when alien blood was

GIANT ANGELS

There is no reason to believe angels are all the same size as humans. Author Grant Jeffrey[8] reports a large Angel of Glory protected his wife's family. Pastor Roland Buck describes large angels in his book, *Angels on Assignment.*[9]

once again mixed with human blood. These people were called Rephaites, likely after a fallen angel named Raphel. King Og of Bashan was a Raphite. His bed was over thirteen feet long and six feet wide.[11]

Why did it suddenly end? The Bible records a worldwide flood that destroyed an advanced civilization because they had become thoroughly evil. Could it be Noah's flood brought an end to the world of gigantism? From a naturalist's viewpoint, the extinction of so many species and the diminishing physical attributes of plant, insect and animal fauna suggests we are in a period of retrograde evolution. From the biblical prospective, God stopped creating on the sixth day. Then, upon the rebellion of Adam and Eve, the curse of hardship, death and decay was put into effect.

THE WOLLEMI PINE

A remarkable tree type, the Wollemi Pine, was discovered in Australia in a deep gorge in Wollemi Park, 200 km west of Sidney. According to evolutionists, it grew in the Jurassic age, 150 million years ago. It is impossible for seeds to sprout after 150 million years, so the question needs to be asked: is evolutionary history correct, or is it imagined?

WARS OF THE ANCIENTS

Archeological discoveries reveal that a second period of advanced civilization may have occurred. Fables of the lost continent of Atlantis and its sophisticated civilization appear to be based on fact. Evidence of a civilization that may have been at war with the Atlantians has been uncovered under the desert of the Indus valley in India.[12] At Rajasthan, there is a heavy layer of radioactive ash dated sometime between 2,000 to 8,000 BC. At the buried cities of Harappa and Mohenjo-daro, archaeologists found radioactive skeletons and ancient writing that has not been deciphered.

David Davenport,[13] who studied the site and Hindu scripts for twelve years, came to the conclusion that they were destroyed by a nuclear blast. A suggested date for a war between Atlantis and Rama (the Indus valley civilization) is around 6,500 BC. Researcher D. Hatcher Childress writes:

> The so-called "Rama Empire" of Northern India and Pakistan developed at least fifteen thousand years ago on the Indian sub-continent and was a nation of many large, sophisticated cities, many of which are still to be found in the deserts of Pakistan, northern, and western India. Rama existed, apparently, parallel to the Atlantean civilization in the mid-Atlantic Ocean, and was ruled by "enlightened Priest Kings" who governed the cities. The seven greatest capital cites of Rama were known in classical Hindu texts as "The Seven Rishi Cities."[14]

The Mahabharata ancient writings of India describe the Vimanas, flying machines that could deliver awesome destruction. The hideous war between Atlantis and Rama used weapons of destruction reflecting technology developed in the 20th century. The Mahabharata records the following details:

> Ghurkha, flying a swift and powerful Vimana hurled a single projectile charged with all the power of the universe. An incandescent column of smoke and flame as bright as the thousand suns rose in its entire splendor... a perpendicular explosion with billowing smoke clouds... the cloud of smoke rising after its first explosion formed into expanding round circles like the opening of giant parasols... it was an unknown weapon, an iron thunderbolt, a gigantic messenger of death which reduced to ashes the entire race of the Vrishnis and the Andhakas.... The corpses were so burned as to be unrecognizable. The hair and nails fell out. Pottery broke without apparent cause, and the birds turned white. After a few hours all foodstuffs were infected... to escape

from this fire the soldiers threw themselves in streams to wash themselves and their equipment.[15]

On the South American continent, Lake Titicaca straddles the Peruvian-Bolivian border in a large basin at an altitude of 13,000 feet. It is 150 miles long, 50 miles wide and 500 feet deep. Studies of lake bottom sediments indicate it has been shrinking and expanding over the past 25,000 years.[16] In its depths are the mysterious intricate pre-Inca ruins of Tiahuanaco which archaeologists agree must have been built by a people with sophisticated technological knowledge, some time between 2,000 and 12,000 BC. Marine fossils indicate the lake may have been at sea level at one time, or a gigantic deluge inundated it.[17] The possible antiquity of the ruins and workmanship suggest they may be of the Atlantis era.

Deep underwater sidescan sonar exploration off of Cuba in 2001 found evidence of a huge land plateau with clear images of what appears to be man-made large-size architectural designs partly covered by sand. From above, the shapes resemble pyramids, roads and buildings. These have now been verified by video camera from a remote controlled submersible vehicle.[18] All evidences indicate Atlantis was a real civilization.

In the Middle East, the ancient Sumerian culture made famous by Zecharia Sitchin with his insightful interpretations of cuneiform writing described in his 1985 book, *The Wars of Gods and Men*, came from an even older group of people called the Ubaidians from around 5,000 to 5,500 BC. D. Laing writes:

Another flood was recorded in archaeological evidence in Mesopotamia. In a dig in Ur, layer after layer of artifacts from the ancient Ubadian culture were found in an excavation pit until workers encountered a level that contained only river sediments. This layer proved to be eight feet thick, and beneath it workers began to encounter more artifacts. The river sediments have been interpreted to have resulted from a flood that would have killed thousands in the valley, and from a much earlier period than that which gave rise to the Gilgamesh epic.[19]

In Asia Minor, the Black Sea covers an area of 162,280 square miles and drains into the Mediterranean Sea through the narrow Bosphors Strait. Its southern shores lap onto the country of Turkey. The area is thought to have once been a large basin below sea level. Sonar and video cameras have uncovered an ancient civilization on this basin floor.[20]

It is evident there has been a dramatic change of sea level around the world in recent history. The Atlantis civilization is under at least 2,000 feet of water, while the Tibetan and Bolivian Plateaus have been elevated some 13,000 feet above sea level. Geophysical studies have shown that the world's mountain ranges form a series of arcs,[21] and that many of their steep towering peaks show little erosion which suggests rapid emplacement.

Powerful catastrophic events, such as a close planetary encounter discussed in chapter one, would explain these topographic changes and the destructive demise of these civilizations. Donald Patten, a celestial mechanics specialist, writes:

> There are Alpine-Himalayan Cycle and at least one sector of the Circum-Pacific Cycle. Our theory holds that the Alpine-Himalayan Cycle (12,500 miles long) was uplifted in one day, the day of Noah's Flood when Mars made a flyby between 14,500 and 15,000 miles close. The age of the Alpine-Himalayan Cycle is 2 million minutes (not years). Its swath-like pattern of crustal deformation coincides perfectly with a flyby pattern providing that one understands that a spin axis shift occurred at the height of the flyby.[22]

Naturalists consider these theories outlandish, however they have no explanation for catastrophic events affecting past groups of peoples. In one of these flybys, the Black Sea and Mediterranean basins may have been topographically depressed flooding cities along the Mediterranean Sea coast. A destructive fault zone rupture likely caused the Bosphors Strait, allowing the Mediterranean ocean waters to flood the civilization of the Black Sea basin. Then, as the Tibetan highlands formed, the South Pacific landmass, which formed a land bridge to Australia, plunged beneath the waters of the Pacific Ocean also flooding cities off of the coast of India and China. At the rate the evidence for lost civilizations is being accumulated, it would appear additional profound archaeological discoveries are yet to be made which will further confound the theory of linear evolution.

RETURN OF THE MESSIAH

Our modern civilization may be a third peak of sophisticated advancement on planet Earth. Certainly it now stands at its highest peak of enlightenment—technologically through the advancement of science, and spiritually because the Son of God entered our space-time reality. Based on history and biblical evidence, God has prohibited direct physical interaction by the Legions of Doom into our space-time world for approximately four millennia. Spiritual revelation provided by Scripture, scientific technological achievements of design and astronomical observations place mankind in an elevated position of cosmic awareness such that they now stand intellectually accountable to God. In all this, the Sons of Light have battled the Forces of Darkness to secure the celestial destiny of mankind for those who believe. To whom will they direct their wills—to Satan, the rebel, or Jesus Christ, creator-redeemer?

The plan for the cosmos is unfolding: *"This is the plan determined for the whole world; this is the hand stretched out over all nations. For the LORD Almighty has purposed, and who can thwart him? His hand is stretched out, and who can turn it back?"* [23] Even now, if we listen with the ears of faith, the pounding hoof beats of the four horsemen of the apocalypse can be heard on Earth. God says: *"I will show wonders in the heavens above and signs on the earth below, blood and fire and billows of smoke. The sun will be turned to darkness and the moon to blood before the coming of the great and glorious day of the Lord. And everyone who calls on the name of the Lord will be saved."* [24]

Signs of the times are not about expanding technology but focus on the cosmological conclusion of the window of chaos with the return of the Messiah, the Great King. The nations of the world are now in the correct ethnological alignment of Japheth, Ham and Shem; world power will be shifted to the sons of Shem, as prophesied by Noah.[26] The man, Abraham, is an established historical fact. The nation Israel came into being through the twelve sons of Jacob and established a literal kingdom under King David in the land. Even though there are those who decry the miracles of Jesus of Nazareth, He is an established historical fact. After the

ALIGNMENT OF NATIONS

"May God extend the territory of Japheth; may Japheth live in the tents of Shem, and may Canaan [Ham] be his slave" (Gen. 9:27). The sons of Japheth founded Turkey, Greece, Russia and the European countries. Israel, parts of Iran, Syria and counties of the Persian Gulf are of the linage of Shem. The sons of Ham populated Iraq through the central Arabian Peninsula to North Africa.[25]

destruction of the temple in Jerusalem in 70 AD, Israel was banished into the wilderness of the nations according to prophecy. Then, remarkably, on May 14, 1948, the nation that should never be once more became a nation, fulfilling prophesy.[27]

One of my favorite books, *Armageddon Appointment With Destiny*, by Grant Jeffrey, outlines amazing biblical anniversaries of Israel based on their Appointed Feasts. Moreover, Jeffrey details the factual arrival date when Jesus Christ was presented to Israel as their Messiah. As revealed by the angel Gabriel to the prophet Daniel some 600 years earlier, God had foreordained that the day, known in history as Palm Sunday, would occur during Daniel's "seventy weeks of years" when, as God had predicted, Israel rejected their Messiah.

> **LENGTH OF YEAR CHANGED**
>
> Velikovsky and Patten note that various world cultures record a change in the length of a year around 700 BC from 360 days, which is the length of a Jewish prophetic year, to our calendar year of 365.25 days.

The promised physical kingdom, heralded by John the Baptist and Jesus, is now being held in abeyance until the fullness of the Gentiles is brought into the spiritual kingdom of God. Jeffrey discovered how God had foretold, in a complex way through the prophet Ezekiel, when Israel would once again become a nation. Ezekiel was in captivity in Babylon around 590 BC when God instructed him to give a pictorial example of what would happen. He was told to lay on one side for forty days and on his other side for 390 days as a sign of the length of time for Israel's punishment.[28] The forty plus 390 equals 430 days—a measure of time similar to Daniel's week of years—which means 430 days represents 430 years.

The prophet Jeremiah had prophesied that Israel was to go into captivity for seventy years. Therefore, 430 years minus the seventy years of captivity leaves 360 years. If they did not repent, their punishment would be extended seven times longer.[29] Since there was no repentance and only a partial return to the land in 536 BC, the allotted time was increased to 360 years multiplied by seven which gives 2,520 Jewish prophetic years. Because God is dealing with the Jewish people, the length of this 2,520 Jewish prophetic years needs to be converted to our calendar years. To calculate the possible date when the time of punishment was to end from 536 BC—when the seventy years of captivity ended—multiply 2,520 years by 360 days and divide by 365.25 days. This gives 2,483.8 calendar years. Subtract 536 BC from this number and add one year for the period one BC to one AD (i.e. December 31, 1 BC was one day before January 1, 1 AD because there is no year zero), and one arrives at May 1948,[30] the date Israel was recognized by the United Nations as a nation. One can only conclude that a force extraneous to evolutionary concepts is molding history.

BACK TO THE LAND

Many biblical scholars consider the "times of the Gentiles" to have begun with the fall of Jerusalem in 606 BC and extended into our era. Jesus, who came in this period, told His disciples: *"Jerusalem will be trampled on by the Gentiles until the times of the Gentiles are fulfilled."* [32] This is thought, by biblical scholars over the years,[33] to be a period of 2,520 prophetic Jewish years (360 days times seven years) represented by King Nebuchadnezzar's seven-year period of insanity described in the book of Daniel. His insanity signified the nations of the world would suffer war and turbulence until they *"acknowledge that the Most High is sovereign over the kingdoms of men."* [34] Starting at 606 BC, the fall of Jerusalem, and using the Jewish prophetic time of 2,483.8 calendar years (as described above 2,520 Jewish years converts to 2,483.8 calendar years), brings us to the fall of 1878 AD.

The fall of 1878 AD may be significant in God's plan since it parallels the return of a remnant back to the land. Just as only some of the captives returned to Jerusalem in 536 BC, the first agriculture settlement after approximately 1700 years began in Palestine in 1878 AD. Sir Moses Montifiore and others in Britain, after a number of years trying, managed to purchase land from the government of Turkey in what is now Israel. The Petah Tikva (meaning Gate of Hope) agriculture settlement began in malaria-infested swampland. The land had been devastated by centuries of misuse. There were no forests, no agriculture and no industry. Yet God had foretold that Israel would once again be occupied and farmed.[35] The wandering tribes of Israel would return as one people, no longer divided, Judah (Judah and Benjamin) against Ephraim (the other ten tribes).[36] Israel would have to be back in the land as a nation before all the other "end-time" prophecies could come into alignment. Israel is now a historical fact.

THE FRUIT OF ISRAEL

Israel is largely a secular nation. Her people are back in the land but in unbelief. Even though the Orthodox Rabbis

2,520 CALENDAR YEARS

2,520 calendar years (356.25 days) takes us to 1915. World War I started on August 1, 1914 and may have been the start of the period of which Jesus said: *"Nation will arise against nation, and kingdom against kingdom."*[31] It began a time of intense persecution of the Jews in Russia, Germany and Eastern Europe. This started a movement of the Jewish people back to "the land." Jerusalem, which was under the control of the Ottoman Empire of Turkey, surrendered to General Allenby of Britain in 1917. Britain agreed to facilitate a Jewish national homeland in Palestine in the November 2, 1917 Balfour Declaration.

are struggling to implement religious customs, rules and regulations and bring back the sacrificial worship system, God is an abstract concept to the average citizen. God refers to the nation Israel as a fig tree.[38] When Jesus cursed the fig tree along the road outside of Jerusalem for having no fruit,[39] His disciples knew that he was referring to their nation. *"As he approached Jerusalem and saw the city, he wept over it and said, 'If you, even you, had only known on this day what would bring you peace—but now it is hidden from your eyes. The days will come upon you when your enemies will build an embankment against you and encircle you and hem you in on every side. They will dash you to the ground, you and the children in your walls. They will not leave one stone on another, because you did not recognize the time of God's coming to you.'"* [40] Jesus then told His disciples a parable: *"Look at the fig tree and all the trees. When they sprout leaves, you can see for yourselves and know that summer is near. Even so, when you see these things happening, you know that the kingdom of God is near. I tell you the truth, this generation will certainly not pass away until all these things have happened. Heaven and earth will pass away, but my words never pass away."* [41]

PALESTINE

The term "Palestine" appears to be derived from the Philistines, an Aegean people who, in the 12th century BC, settled along the Mediterranean coastal plain of what is now Israel. In the second century AD (132 CE), the Romans crushed the Jewish revolt. Three years later, in conformity with Roman custom, Jerusalem was "plowed up with a yoke of oxen" and renamed Aelia Capitolina. Judea (the southern portion of what is now called the West Bank) was renamed Palaestina in an attempt to minimize Jewish identification with the land of Israel. [37]

Modern prophetic interpretation has taken these words to mean that the generation which sees Israel become a nation would see the climax of the second coming of Jesus within forty to seventy years. However, Jesus was speaking of the fruit of the fig tree. What was the fruit? Shortly after Jesus' death and resurrection, thousands of Jewish people accepted His atoning work of salvation. [42] Joseph Good writes:

True to both prophesies of the destruction of Israel, forty years later the Roman army of Titus destroyed Jerusalem and dispersed Israel. For 2,000 years the Jewish people have wandered from nation to nation without a homeland as prophesied by

Hosea 6:1–3 and Jeremiah 50:4–8, until 1948 when Israel became a nation once again. As already stated, many people regard this as the fulfillment of the blossoming of Israel.

Is it? The Fig Tree was cursed for not having fruit on it. What was the expected fruit? It was for Israel to receive Yeshua as their Messiah. Therefore, since Israel in 1948 was no closer to having received her Messiah than in 30 C.E., how could this be a fulfillment of Luke Twenty-one?[43]

Mr. Good goes on to note:

On June 7, 1967 (around Shavuoth or Pentecost) during the Six Day War, Israel recaptured Jerusalem from Arab Jordan. True to the prophecy ("Israel has experienced a hardening in part until the full number of the Gentiles has come in." Romans 11:25), blindness is falling off Israel and they are receiving Yeshua as their Messiah. It is believed that more Jews have received Yeshua since 1967 than in the 1900 years since the first century.[44]

The Messianic Jewish movement has swept around the world. It is a remarkable coincidence that the spiritual wailing of the Jews at the Western wall on the feast of Pentecost 1967 parallels that first Pentecost that gave birth to the Bride of Christ around 32 AD.

DO WE HAVE A PROPHETIC WARNING OF END TIMES?

If the spring of 1967 was an important event to God, it should show up in His calendar of events, and it does in an interesting way. The captivity of the Jews began in 606 BC. The temple was ravaged and burnt twenty years later in 586 BC. A remnant returned to **the land** in 536 BC. A rebuilt temple of less grandeur was dedicated in 515 BC, which is a period of twenty-one years. The prophet Daniel did not understand that the first return on 536 BC did not complete the "desolation of Jerusalem and the temple;"[45] this was completed on March 14, 445 BC when the Persian King Artaxerxes Longimanus gave permission to rebuild the "walls" of Jerusalem.[46] This is a period of ninety-one years (536 to 445) or 161 years from 606 BC.

In order to develop an interesting observation that may affect end times prophecy, let's use the calendar year and correct for spring and fall.

SUMMARY OF IMPORTANT DATES:

DATE	SIGNIFICANCE	CORRECTION
Fall of 606 BC	Fall of Jerusalem	606.7 BC
586 BC	Temple sacked and burnt	
539 BC	Fall of Babylon	
Spring of 536 BC	Return to "the land"	536.3 BC
515 BC	Rebuilt temple	
March 14, 445 BC	Decree to rebuild walls	445.3 BC
Fall of 1878 AD	Modern return to "the land"	1878.7 AD
Spring of 1948 AD	Birth of modern Israel	1948.3 AD
1967 AD	Capture of Jerusalem	

The date of 536.3 BC is the anchor date from which we begin our investigation because it is the year a small contingent of Jews returned to the land. Going back to the beginning of the captivity of 606.7 BC and subtracting 536.3 BC, we find the Jews were in captivity for approximately 0.4 of a year too long (606.7 - 636.3 = 70.4). The next important date is 445.3 BC when the command was given to rebuild the "walls" of Jerusalem. This date is ninety-one years from the anchor date of 536.3 BC (536.3 - 445.3 = 91), which is also one year past the period of ninety years which signifies the fullness of judgment. Now as you read this you might think the author is being finicky. You are right, but wait—a principle of "over and under" becomes evident.

We have observed that 1878.7 AD is somehow important to God as it concluded the period of 2,520 Jewish years (2,483.8 calendar years). Israel was reborn at 1948.3 AD. This is 69.6 years from 1878.7 AD (1948.3 - 1878.7 = 69.6). Notice this period of seventy years is significant to God since He has shortened it by the same amount it was

PERFECT NUMBERS

Seven is God's perfect number. Nine is the number of judgment and ten is the number of fullness. Seventy, 7x10, is the period of God's fullness and ninety, 9x10, is the fullness of judgment. Thus, 70 + 90 = 160 years is the perfect fullness of God's judgment.

lengthened (i.e. 70.4 + 69.6 /2 = 70). For some reason, God added back the seventy years of punishment as seventy years of grace. It is also possible, since God had said He would punish Babylon for seventy years,[47] this seventy years needs to be added back to the "times of the Gentiles" to complete the fullness of the Gentile period.

How then does the ninety-one years from 606 BC to 445 BC fit our modern times? We find the 1967 beginning of the Jewish spiritual wakening is approximately eighty-nine years from 1878. The (91 + 89/2 = 90 is exactly the ninety years for fullness of judgment. What are the coincidences of an order being given to rebuild the walls in 445 BC and the modern nation of Israel spiritually seeking God at these same walls at a set prophetic time interval later? The year 1948 AD becomes an anchor year for prophetic interpretation the same as 536 BC and may be the key to "end time" events.

Why would God overdo the seventy and ninety-year periods of judgment in BC by approximately one year and underdo it in AD by the same amount? It appears that where there is a lengthening in BC we are to deduct those years in AD. It took twenty-one years to rebuild the temple—536 to 515 BC—and it took nineteen years—1948 to

1967—to recapture Jerusalem. This follows the same pattern. Based on this information, since 606 BC to 445 BC is 161 years, a date 159 years from 1878 AD would appear to have prophetic significance. This would be the year 2037 AD. In addition, when we examine the period of 161 years from 606 BC to 445 BC, we see that it contains a period of fifty years (586 to 536 BC) which is the length of the time between the God-ordained Jewish Jubilees. This period may have immediate prophetic significance (see Figure 2, p. 272).

WILL WE SEE A SUDDEN CHANGE IN WORLD AFFAIRS?

In 539 BC, a thunderous party was in progress in the magnificent powerful city of Babylon. King Belshazzar felt safe behind massive walls and fortifi-

FULLNESS OF TIME

For those who care about further curiosities, the nineteen years between 1948 and 1967 is one eclipse cycle, which is the time it takes for a full moon (the moon orbits the earth in 29.53059 days) to occur on the same day (the earth orbits the sun in 365.2422 days) within a twelve-hour period. A period of 315 years gives an almost perfect repeat of the time of a full moon to within one hour and forty-eight minutes. This 315-year period multiplied by eight yields 2,520 years. The number eight signifies a new beginning. It is also interesting to note 2,520 is the lowest common multiple of all the digits, one through nine.[48] Nine is the unit of judgment, which supports the 2,520-year periods of judgment to the Jews and the Gentiles.

cations, even though it was under siege by the Medes and Persians (modern Iran). The walls were eighty-seven feet thick, 350 feet high with a circumference of some seventeen miles. Supplies had been laid away for many years. The king, his wives, princes, concubines and thousands of invited lords were feasting and toasting the "gods of gold, of silver, of brass, of iron, of wood and of stone" using all the golden drinking vessels taken from the temple of Jerusalem in an act of blasphemous repudiation of the God of Israel. Suddenly, a hand appeared in the flaming torchlight and wrote in large letters on the plaster wall: *MENE, MENE, TEKEL, PARSIN*. The king's knees shook with fear. Eventually Daniel, now an old man, was called to provide an interpretation. He informs the king. *"This is what these words mean: MENE: God has numbered the days of your reign and brought it to an end. TEKEL: You have been weighed on the scales and found wanting. PERES: Your kingdom is divided, and given to the Medes and Persians."*[49] That night the invading army diverted the river flowing under the massive walls and waded into the unsuspecting city. King Belshazzar was slain.

> ### THE YEAR OF JUBILEE
>
> After forty-nine years (seven sabbaths of years—seven times seven years), on the fiftieth year the Israelites were to sound the trumpet throughout the land. *"Consecrate the fiftieth year and proclaim liberty throughout the land to all its inhabitants. It shall be a jubilee for you; each one of you is to return to his family property and each to his own clan."*[51] God gave instructions on how to equalize inequities that had accumulated over this fifty-year period.

There is tremendous significance to this story as it pertains to the "times of the Gentiles." King Belshazzar was possibly the grandson or great grandson of King Nebuchadnezzar. God had informed the prophet Jeremiah that, when the captivity period for Israel was over, He would punish the Babylonians.[50] It seems God was so angered at Belshazzar's blasphemy, He implemented Babylon's punishment that night. The period 606 to 539 BC is only sixty-seven years, thus there is a divine credit of three years (70 - 67 = 3) because the punishment started three years too soon. These three years are significant in the later years of AD.

The following diagram depicts the two periods, BC and AD, that appear to show the same pattern of dates but in reverse. Does this pattern have prophetic significance for our generation? The BC period has an extra year while the AD period has one year less.

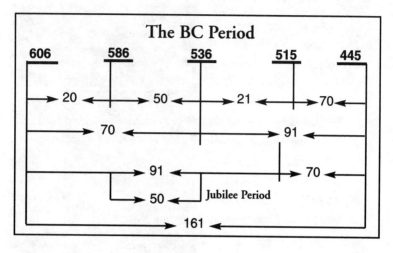

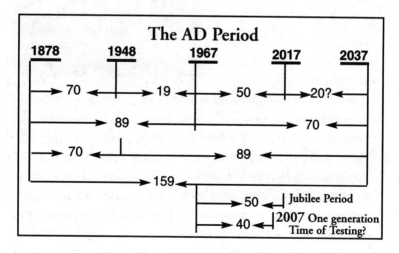

FIGURE 2

The Chaldee words *MENE, TEKEL, PARSIN* are equivalent to the Hebrew words *MENAH, SHEKIEL, PARAS* or *PERES* which are units of weight. One shekel equals twenty gerahs,[52] a smaller unit of weight. One meneh equals sixty shekels of product except gold and silver. One meneh equals fifty shekels of precious metals.[53] Professor Rusk explains the significance:

> At Belshazzar's feast the gold and silver from the temple were being desecrated by the Babylonians, so which scale of measure is going to apply here? Naturally, the one dealing with gold and silver. A meneh of 50 shekels of gold would weigh a total of 1000 gerahs. Let us count the value of the words as follows:
>
> | MENE | Maneh | 1000 gerahs |
> |------|-------|-------------|
> | MENE | Maneh | 1000 gerahs |
> | TEKEL | Shekel | 20 gerahs |
> | PERES | 1/2 Maneh | 500 gerahs |
> | | | 2520 gerahs |
>
> The numerical value of the handwriting on the wall is that wonderful number 2520![54]

The author can find no references to the following numerical disclosure. It is readily apparent from the handwriting on the wall that the "times of the Gentiles" is to be 2,520 Jewish prophetic years. Starting at 539 BC, the year of the sudden demise of the Babylonian empire, and converting the Jewish prophetic years to 2,483.8 calendar years and adding the extra year, we arrive at the year 1945 AD. This is the year the Gentile world desecrated humanity with the atomic explosions of Hiroshima and Nagasaki on August 6 and 9 respectively. Next, when we add back the three years credit for the early demise of Babylon, we arrive at the anchor year of 1948 AD.

The sudden fall of the great city of Babylon may possibly reflect the words of Scripture: *"for you know very well that the day of the Lord will come like a thief in the night. While people are saying, 'Peace and safety,' destruction will come on them suddenly, as labor pains on a pregnant woman, and they will not escape. "* [60] This would suggest that, in a single night, the power structure of the world could suddenly be turned upside down. The Gentile world is pregnant with evil as it desecrates the God of Israel, Jesus our redeemer, the Holy Scriptures, human life and even the denial of biblical history and archaeology discoveries in Israel.

In our calendar study, when we put all these date findings together, we arrive at a pattern of dates that may or may not have any prophetic significance but certainly suggest we may be in the "signs of the times." In particular, the interval of dates from 606 BC to 445 BC are appearing in **reversal** from 1878 AD onwards into our 21st century.

> **TWISTED BELIEFS**
>
> There was no miraculous escape from Egypt.[55] The walls of Jericho never collapsed.[56] Moreover, Jerusalem, King David and King Solomon never existed.[57] The Jewish revolt against Rome around 70 AD at Masada has been questioned[58] and the Dead Sea Scrolls have been interpreted to degrade the Virgin Mary.[59] In modern history, the holocaust of Hitler has been disputed, and, in this 21st century, some Middle East Arabs are even willing to believe the New York Twin Tower catastrophe was caused by Israel even though all were Arab terrorists.

The following diagram, Figure 2, illustrates the interval of years between the significant dates. The BC period depicts the intervals between 606 BC and 445 BC, while the AD period covers the years 1878 to 2037 AD. The years 1878, 1948 and 1967 fit the pattern; only time will tell if the dates 2007, 2017 and 2037 have any prophetic significance.

Events occurring in the interval between the years 1967, 2007 and 2017 AD are possibly reflected by the Jewish feast days and the interval between the resurrection and ascension of Jesus. Jesus came to fulfill the law.[61] He is considered by many to have been born on the feast of Tabernacles in our month of October. He gave His life as a Lamb, without spot or blemish, as the eternal blood sacrifice on Passover, our March/April depending on the day of a full moon. He arose from Hades on the first day of the feast of First Fruits of the Barley Harvest. Fifty days later, on the Feast of Pentecost, the last day of the ingathering of the Wheat Harvest, the Holy Spirit gave birth to the Bride of Christ. This fifty-day interval is known as the Feast of Weeks. During this period, Jesus was seen by His disciples and up to 500 believers at one time[62] over a period of forty days and then ascended into Heaven. In days for years, this period of fifty days may represent the Jubilee interval between 586 BC and 536 BC, which would then be the period between 1967 AD and 2017 AD.

Forty years is God's number of testing and probation. In the days of Noah, it rained for forty days and nights. Israel wandered in the wilderness for forty years. Moses was on Mt. Sinai for forty days. Jesus was tempted for forty days. Jerusalem was destroyed some forty years after His ascension into heaven. If 1967 is the beginning of figs on the fig tree, is forty years from this date (2007) an important milestone? The ascension of Jesus forty days into the Feast of Weeks has no specific feast day. This would imply His return for His Bride could be at any time.

The forty-day period within the fifty-day period seems to give validity to the previously suggested pattern; of course 1967 may or may not be an end time critical date. Whenever these events do take place, it would appear from this pattern of numbers the true temple of the Messiah would be built within a period of fifty years. In an additional twenty years, the great millennial city of Zion would be completed (50 + 20 = 70, reflecting the pattern between 606 to 536 BC).

SIGNS OF THE TIMES

God is sovereign. If there is repentance, then, just as He delayed the flood of Noah and the judgment of the Gentile city of Nineveh, nothing may happen in our lifetime. There is no fixed date for Christ's return, whether it is for the possible rapture of the Bride of Christ or for His return to the Mount of Olives, nor is there a fixed date for the beginning of the last prophetic week of the seventy weeks of Daniel. However, the "signs of the times" suggest the fulfillment of prophecy might be just around the corner.

ARE WE THE GENERATION?

Are we living in this period of testing and probation—the generation that will see these things come to pass? (Luke 21:32). Israel and her cycle of feast days are the time clock of world history. The future dramatic visible return of Jesus with His Bride to the Mount of Olives to rescue Israel at the battle of Armageddon, and their wailing for *"the one they have pierced"* (Zech. 12:10) is likely to be on the Feast of Atonement.

Significant "signs of the times" are eight in number.

1—"I will show wonders in the heavens and on the earth, blood and fire and billows of smoke." [63]

It is a remarkable coincidence that, by three different calculations—Ezekiel laying on his side, the days of madness of king Nebuchadnezzar, and the handwriting on the wall—the year 1948 is important in world history. The atomic blasts of 1945 can easily prefigure blood, fire and billows of smoke as the age of nuclear of warfare. The Hubble telescope is showing wonders of other planets in the heavens. The Cydonia Face on Mars stares silently at the satellites overhead, suggesting the possibility of a long-ago angelic rebellion when a planet disintegrated between Mars and Jupiter. Ancient civilizations not thought possible are being discovered. Unexplainable underwater structures, statues and pyramids in unusual places require a rethinking of world history. Was there atomic warfare between Atlantis and Rama?

Just as the wonders of the heavens are being uncovered, scientists are discovering the wonders of the nano-world which is one billionth of a meter. Single atoms have been manipulated to write the letters IBM. Moreover, the biological complexity of the human cell is not the simple blob of organic matter envisioned by Darwin. In his book, *Darwin's Black Box*, Professor Behe, a molecular biochemist, makes a logical case for the intelligent design of life (ID), though he makes no attempt to identify the designer. He writes:

> **SLOWLY COOKED**
>
> Sometimes we look for dramatic things to happen, but like the story of the frog boiled to death by a very slow increase in water temperature, events leading to the coming of God's wrath are already heating things up.

> Now it's the turn of the fundamental science of life, modern biochemistry, to disturb. The simplicity that was once expected to be the foundation of life has proven to be a phantom; instead, systems of horrendous, irreducible complexity inhabit the cell. The resulting realization that life was designed by an intelligence is a shock to us in the twentieth century who have gotten used to thinking of life as the result of simple natural laws.[64]

Indeed, there are wonders in the heavens above and on the Earth below. However, is the human will so self-centered that the desire to be evolution's "gods" has blinded the intellect to the marvelous biological design and innate programming complexity of form and context of the human being as body, soul and spirit?

2—The Vision of the Lead Basket

Governments of the Western nations are concerned Iraq is harboring chemical or nuclear weapons of mass destruction. Yet, close to 2,520 years ago, God showed the prophet Zechariah a vision of a measuring basket with a lead lid. A lead container usually indicates radioactivity. This basket was a measure of the evil of the people in the land. Zechariah asked the angel who was showing him the vision: *"Where are they taking the basket?"* The angel replied: *"To the country of Babylonia to build a house for it. When it is ready, the basket will be set in place."* [65] Is it any wonder the U.N. inspectors are trying to find the "house" that contains nuclear armaments?

The name Zechariah means "Jehovah remembers." He wrote the prophecy of the basket between the years 520 and 515 BC. Earlier in this chapter, when we used the calendar year of 365.25 days which pertains to the Gentile nations, we discovered that 2,520 years brought us from 606 BC to 1915 the period of World War I. Again using the calendar year of 365.25 days, 2,520 years brings us from 520 and 515 BC to our era of 2001 to 2006 AD which is a remarkable coincidence with respect to the concern that Iraq may be harboring nuclear weapons.

3—The Melting of Flesh From the Bones

Zechariah is shown a scene of nuclear warfare around Jerusalem, possibly a form of neutron bomb or an intense x-ray laser beam which he describes as a plague. He observes what happens to humans and animals: *"Their flesh will rot while they are standing on their feet, their eyes will rot in their sockets, and their tongues will rot in their mouths."* [66] When a massive army invades Israel, the prophet Ezekiel is told that there will be plague (the same as Zechariah saw?) of bloodshed, hailstones and burning sulfur. Intercontinental ballistic missiles will leap into the skies: *"I will send fire on Magog and those who live in safety in the coastlands."* [67]

What Zechariah described in chapter 14 of his book—the melting flesh—may possibly relate to the final battle of Armageddon. The prophecy was written at some unknown period after 515 BC. If this coincidence of dates has any prophetic meaning, it is in our future, after 2006 AD.

The United States and Russia have now cancelled their 1972 ICBM agreement, ostensively to build a better system of anti-missile protection against rogue nations. In the early 1970s, Dr. Charles Taylor, founder of Bible Prophecy Inc., published a book titled, *World War III and the Destiny of America*.

THE BIBLE CODE

Michael Drosnin writes: "The years 2000 and 2006, in the ancient calendar 5760 and 5766, were the only two years in the next hundred that matched both 'atomic holocaust' and 'World War.' All the dangers stated in the code—'the End of days,' 'holocaust of Israel,' even 'great earthquake'—also matched in 5766.'" He concludes, "In the end, what we do determines the outcome, so we are left where we have always been, with one big difference—we now know that we are not alone."[68]

In it, he quotes a man he calls the evangelist. In 1954, this man had a supernatural vision while visiting the viewing area at the top of the Empire State building. He saw the Statue of Liberty being forced to drink from a cup of God's wrath. Next, a black skull came across Alaska and Canada and blew a vapory mist over the United States. Millions choked and died. At the same time, rockets burst out of the ocean and descended on the land in what appeared to be nuclear explosions.[69] September 11, 2001 may be a warning of the chemical and/or biological and nuclear warfare yet to come upon the world should the signs of the times keep maturing.

There is no way to authenticate this vision; however, it is interesting that as the evangelist stares aghast at the devastation he hears beautiful singing and music. He looks up into the heavens and sees a huge mountain which he understood to be the mountain of God. Here, in a great cleft in the mountain, the saints of God are singing and dancing, protected by the hand of God. Jesus Christ is the rock cut out of this mountain as foretold in the dream given to king Nebuchadnezzar regarding the future world kingdoms to come.[70] This vision also parallels the resurrection of the Bride of Christ to their heavenly rooms, described in Isaiah 26:19–21, while the wrath of God falls on the evil, self-seeking, rebellious nations of Earth.

WHAT A DIFFERENCE!
Satan demands worship and enforces it with death. God desires free will worship and rewards it with eternal life!

4—The World Government

Not only did Israel become a nation in 1948, but seeds for world government and world religion were sown. In 1948, Belgium, Luxembourg and the Netherlands signed the Benelux agreement, a customs and tariff arrangement that stimulated free trade. Its success spawned the linking of the countries of Europe into the modern European Economic Community (EEC) and its currency, the Eurodollar. It will be, or be part of, a military and economic might whose ten leaders will give their authority and power to a charismatic dictator. He will *"force everyone, small and great, rich and poor, free and slave, to receive a mark on his right hand or on his forehead, so that no one could buy or sell unless he had the mark."*[71] In the aftermath of terrorism, it seems so innocent to have an identifying number. Even the U.N. is suggesting that all citizens of the world should be numbered to stop the movement of terrorists, while the medical industry is promoting a thin microchip to be inserted just under the skin. In the end, the free world is handcuffed and manipulated into a police-big-brother state. True freedom can only come through a spiritual change of the heart and individual accountability.

5—The World Religion

The foundation for the World Council of Churches (WCC) was laid in Amsterdam, Holland in August/September 1948. Since then, the WCC has tried to bring all religions under its umbrella, replacing the gospel of salvation with a message of spiritual socialism. The WCC, in its present state, is trying to bring peace and goodness into the world through religious unity without the gospel message of the transforming power of the Holy Spirit. Its founding members are held together by power structures of rules, regulations and sanctimonious rituals. (World aid to the needy is very much a power base for political manipulation.) In its final degenerate state, demonic spirits will energize the religious systems with all sorts of false wonders and miracles. The world dictator will use it as a power base to gain world domination.[72] He will acclaim himself to be God in the rebuilt temple in Jerusalem and try to kill all those who will not worship him.

6—World Events

World events and political power alignments are shifting rapidly. It is often argued we interpret events as "signs of the times" according to our wishful thinking. Such was the case in the change to 1000 AD and the Y2K madness of 2000 AD. Christendom is done a disfavor by this type of imaginative clock setting. Those who try to connect the movement of history with a 6,000-year cycle of human history might not be wrong, but they should be aware this cycle has nothing to do with the modern calendar.

World events are fashioned by individual motives. Governments that are infested with bribery and corruption will collapse in rebellion and turmoil. So-called social welfare rights without reciprocal work efforts will corrode even the wealthiest of nations. Corporations that defraud their shareholders and wealthy individuals that accumulate without equity redistribution will erode their base of profitability and bring economic calamity.

Peace and stability create the illusion of wealth. Escalating interest rates are a shortcut to poverty. Attitudes of "my rights"—I want and I will take—end up in bloodshed and war. Greed, vanity and pride, the instruments of political and religious power, choke freedom. Bitterness, death and destruction are the fruits of graft, cheating, lying, stealing and deception.

A religion without forgiveness is like drinking a cup of sweetened poison. Secularism is now blatantly consuming the wine of cosmic consciousness. These principles are rapidly shaping the future because peace is trapped like a gentle dove in a thorn bush.

> **COMPOUNDING UNCERTAINTIES**
>
> Stock markets deteriorate in times of uncertainty. The world is fearful of terrorism, of racial strife, of disease epidemics, of declining resources, of the population explosion, of the world's ability to feed its people, of economic disparity and surging interest rates.

The population of the world has passed the count of 6 billion people. Powerful individuals, corporations and governments dictate the flow of capital and wealth creation. However, local fiefdoms, drug trade, racial tensions and religious struggles embroil a country into a have-not status. The country of Afghanistan is a microcosm of the world in chaos. Under a fanatical brand of Islamic rules, ancient statues of Buddha were destroyed. There was no religious tolerance. Christian aid workers were to be tried and likely would have been executed.

The Taliban dictated their brand of holiness, even killing their own brothers. Women, subservient to the dominant male ego, are cloaked to hide their femininity and have no political stature. Moderates fear this type of Islamic idealism since it is a whimsical theocratic power not a democratic one. Afghanistan has been known for its destructive opium trade where local fiefdoms control their territories by the power of the gun. Morality comes from the heart, not from the gun. Only the power of the gospel of Jesus Christ can transform the attitudes of the heart. This is what Satan and his Legions of Doom do not want to see happen. He keeps his icy grip on rebellious humanity through hate, strife, economic uncertainties and deceptive spiritualism.

7—Paranormal Spiritualism

There has always been a fascination with spiritualism of all kinds. The desire for spiritual self-esteem and paranormal powers has evolved from seeking the power "within," to flirting with spirit identities by channeling and visualization. There has been a steady shift by society to the acceptance of UFOs and the mysterious crop circles. The manner in which the UFO sightings, reported abductions and channeled communications occur is more like a complex game than a true "scientific" contact as would be conducted by mankind. The unwillingness to believe this alien manifestation could be harmful is overridden by the illusion any superior alien identity must be good. The world is now psychologically prepared for its third encounter with the alien as foretold by Jesus that, at His return, it would be *"as it was in the days of Noah"* (Luke 17:26).

8—Israel Amongst the Nations

World News: "Jewish settlements shelled; Israel hits back with missiles." "Ayatollahs cast hungry eyes on Palestinian power vacuum."

LONDON—Iran has substantially increased its financial support for Hamas, the Palestinian terrorist group, in the hope that it will succeed in establishing an Islamic regime in the West Bank and Gaza. ...Suicide bombings in Jerusalem and Haifa has led Iran's hardline ayatollahs to conclude that there is now a realistic possibility that Arafat's regime could be replaced by a Teheran-style theocracy.[73]

Hard line Islam is a theocracy whose agenda is to annihilate Israel and subject the infidel to the iron rule of their particular brand of Islamic philosophy. If the John Walker Lindhs of America and David Hicks of Australia are any indication of the product of Islam, the Western world is in serious trouble.[74] Ted Byfield writes:

The first reality is that we are now engaged in a religious war. The world's militant Islamists, an estimated 150 million strong, have declared war on us—thus inextricably combining the secular and the religious.

Historically, militant Islam's greatest fear has not been the military strength of the Western world, but our spiritual strength: the power of the Christian gospel. That's why any Muslim who converts to Christianity is subject to the death penalty and why in countries with Islamic governments, anyone who preaches Christ commits a capital offence. They dare not loose the Christian faith.

Thus our other, and vital, defense is to rid ourselves of the idiotic present-day attitudes which lead to such nonsense as the prime ministerial order that prohibits Christian prayers at the Swissair memorial, while allowing Muslim and Jewish ones. Or Billy Graham's decision not to call his latest mission "a crusade." Or the decision of some jackass English bishop who rebuked a congregation for praying for the conversion of Muslims because that would be "divisive." (Hasn't he heard that within 10 years, unless something changes, more people in Britain will be attending mosques than Anglican churches?) Or public school prohibitions on the singing of Christmas carols. Or decisions like that of the Saskatchewan Human Rights Commission prohibiting Bible quotations in a newspaper ad because gays may feel offended.

That is, we should stop crippling ourselves. It is on the spiritual level that this war will ultimately be won or lost. The whole secular thrust of our government and higher educational establishment has been to abandon the spiritual field to the enemy. This is wrong and foolish, and may soon become disastrous. We must stop it.[75]

Israel will become the crisis point in the world. God has said: *"I am going to make Jerusalem a cup that sends all the surrounding peoples reeling. Judah will be besieged as well as Jerusalem. On that day, when all the nations of the earth are gathered against her, I will make Jerusalem an immovable rock for all the nations. All who try to move it will injure themselves."*[76] Demonically driven anti-Semitism lies just beneath the surface of forbearance. At a private dinner party in London, the French ambassador to London is reported to have referred to Israel as "that shitty little country Israel."[77] He, of course, says he really said "little Israel" in the sense it is geographically small.

The warmongering madness of the world seems like it will never end. Instead of visions of utopia, civilization seems to be entangled in a web of earthquakes, famine, killer plagues, diseases and international strife. From the viewpoint of man-made history, as "evolution's gods," we would like the Middle East conflict to just go away or at least be able to institute a enforceable solution for peace and prosperity. This can happen if such a premise is true. However, it is not. What the world of naturalists does not understand is that it is not a human solution, it is a cosmic conflict that has dire consequences for Satan and his Legions of Doom. Israel must be destroyed, the Jews annihilated and Christianity eliminated or Satan and his Legions of Doom will be confined to the Lake of Fire forever. This is the path of history.

Secular society has been seduced and psychologically manipulated by these malevolent forces. What will happen next? How and when will it happen?

Notes:

[1] 1 Thessalonians 5:2, 4

[2] Strieber, Whitley, "The Reason For the Secrecy Redux," Feb. 18, 2002 <unknowncountry.com/journal/?id=88>

[3] Waller, Douglas, "The Vision Thing," *TIME*, December 11, 1995, p. 35

[4] Crawford, Ian, "Where Are They," *Scientific American*, July 2000, p. 38

[5] Acts 4:12

[6] <msnhomepages.talkcity.com/spiritst/s8int/phile1.html>

[7] <auralee.com/japan.htm>

[8] Jeffrey, Grant R., *Heaven: The Mystery of Angels*, Frontier Research Publishing Inc. 1996, p. 196

[9] Hunter, Frances and Charles, "Angels on Assignment," as told by Roland Buck, Hunter Books, 1979, p. 39 (Note: This book is criticized by some Christians. Either Pastor Buck was deceived or it is true—the quote is to show large angels.)

[10] Genesis 6:4 (Amplified Bible, Zondervan)

[11] Deuteronomy 2:10, 3:11

[12] <msnhomepages.talkcity.com/spiritst/s8int/phileatomic.html>

[13] <members.tripod.com/wlsaylor/nuclear_warefare.htm>

[14] <ee.fit.edu/users/lpinto/sections/ancientvisitors/archive/Indian_tech.shtml>

[15] <msnhomepages.talkcity.com/spiritst/s8int/phileatomic.html>

[16] <spacedaily.com/news/geenhouse-01c.html>

[17] <thule.org/tiahuanaco.html>

[18] <earthfiles.com/earth303.htm>

[19] <biblemysteries.com/library/blacksea>

[20] biblemysteries, Ibid

[21] Jacobs, Russell and Wilson, *Physics and Geology*, McGraw-Hill, 1959, pp. 305–309

[22] Patten, Wesley Donald, *Catastrophism and the Old Testament*, Pacific Median Publishing Company, 1988, p. 272

[23] Isaiah 14:26–27

[24] Acts 2:19–21

[25] Missler, Chuck, *The Magog Invasion*, Western Front, Ltd., 1995, pp.130-132.

[26] Genesis 9:25

[27] Ezekiel 37:21–22

[28] Ezekiel 4:3–6

[29] Leviticus 26:18

[30] Jeffrey, Grant R., *Armageddon Appointment With Destiny*, Frontier Research Publications, 1988, p. 40

[31] Matthew 24:7

[32] Luke 21:24

[33] Jeffrey, Ibid. p. 184

[34] Daniel 4:19–27

[35] Ezekiel 36:34

[36] Ezekiel 37:19

[37] <www.us-israel.org/jsource/history/palname.html>

[38] Joel 1:6–7; Hosea 9:10

[39] Matthew 21:18–19

[40] Luke 19:41–44

[41] Luke 21:29–33

[42] Acts 2:41

[43] Good, Joseph, *Rosh HaShanah and the Messianic Kingdom to Come*, Trinity Broadcasting Network, Inc. p. 74

[44] Ibid. p. 75

[45] Walvoord, Dr. John, *Daniel: The Key to Prophetic Revelation*, Moody Press 1971, p. 240

[46] Jeffrey, Ibid. p. 28 and Daniel 9:25

[47] Jeremiah 25:12

[48] Rusk, Professor Roger, *The Other End of the World*, Plantation House Inc., Knoxville, Ten., 1988, p. 112, 248

[49] Daniel 5:1–31

[50] Jeremiah 25:12

[51] Leviticus 25:10

[52] Leviticus 27:25

[53] Joshua 7:21

[54] Rusk, Ibid. p. 113–114

[55] Malamat, Abraham, "Let My People Go," *Biblical Archaeology Review*, January/Feburary 1998, Vol. 24, p. 62

[56] Sellier, Charles and Brian Russell, *Ancient Secrets of the Bible*, Dell Publishing, 1994, p. 319

[57] "David's Jerusalem: Fiction or Reality," *Biblical Archaeology Review*, July/August 1998, Vol. 24, No. 4, pp. 25–45

[58] "Questioning Masada," *Biblical Archaeology Review*, November/December 1998, p. 30

[59] <www.geocities.com/engvaj/scrolls.html>

[60] 1 Thessalonians 5:2–3

[61] Matthew 5:17

[62] 1 Corinthians 15:6

[63] Joel 2:20

[64] Behe, Michael J., Professor of Biochemistry at Lehigh University, *Darwin's Black Box*, A Touchstone Book, Simon & Schuster, 1996, pp. 24 and 252

[65] Zechariah 5:6–11

[66] Zechariah 14:12

[67] Ezekiel 38:22, 39:6

68 Drosnin, Michael, *The Bible Code*, Simon & Schuster, 1997, pp. 177, 179

69 Taylor, Dr. Charles R., *World War III and the Destiny of America*, Today in Bible Prophecy Inc., pp. 85–96

70 Daniel 2:45

71 Revelation 13:16–17

72 Revelation 17:1–18

73 *Times Colonist*, Victoria, B.C., World, Sunday, December 9, 2001

74 <BC News.com>, December 14 and 22, 2001

75 Byfield, Ted, "The Report," *Westview*, November 19, 2001

76 Zechariah 12:2–3

77 <BBC NEWS.com>, "'Anti-Semitic' French envoy under fire," Thursday, December 20, 2001

Sound the Shofar

he news is true; there is great excitement and preparation taking place in heaven! It is reported the Bridegroom may be coming soon with a great trumpet shout of the shofar!

"Awake you sleepers from your sleep, and you slumberers arise from your slumber—examine you deeds, repent and remember your Creator. Those of you who forget the truth in the vanities of the times and dwell all year in vanity and emptiness, look into your souls, improve your ways and actions, let each of you forsake his evil path and his thoughts, which are not good." [1]

There are years when nothing seems to go right—this is one of them. There is no money in the bank account, but at least I'm not seriously ill like a good friend of mine. The story is told of a couple about to lose their house after Christmas due to the collapse of their business. They decorated a spindly cedar tree with small pieces of dangling paper, and on each piece they noted a blessing they had received over the year. Later they remarked that this had been one of their most special Christmases.[2] Guess I'll go up stairs and start cutting paper. Maybe I'll make snowflakes and stars, or a reindeer or two.

When you and I started this adventure together, I commented that I wanted this book to be an encouragement to you. There is nothing worse then reading a book of lifeless theory. I like those written by the "been there and done that" type of author. Not to bore you with details, but I have always desired to be "of the something more" in my Christian walk—maybe a sergeant or a five-star general in God's army. In 1989, while driving across Ontario to Red Lake, a friend and I were discussing this subject. The date is marked in my Bible—October 17, 1989—beside the verses that God gave to me—Jeremiah 33:2-3: *"This is what the LORD says, he who made the earth, the LORD who formed it and established it—the LORD is his name: 'Call out to me and I will answer you and tell you great and unsearchable things you do not know.'"* I called out!

Well, I guess if you want to be a five-star general in God's army, you are going to get shot at, big time. Within two years, my business had collapsed, and we lost our home. Three years later, on a business trip to Europe and an Arabic country, several situations occurred that gave evidence to the reality of demonic forces and how they can influence people. In two weeks, everything I had built and stood for was smashed. Remarkable coincidence, isn't it?

Years ago, a business acquaintance ran into perceived difficulties. He despondently went and hung himself in his garage. In the early 1980s, another friend and I were the jolly two that made things happen at social functions. Unfortunately, he got caught in the high-interest rates back then and lost everything. It was sad to see his happy, quick-witted personality shrivel and be replaced by a despondent spirit of bitterness. Their example to me was—it is how you handle life's unruly challenges that becomes encouragement or discouragement to others. Praise God for the support of my family and friends. People see how you handle difficulties and quickly ascertain whether or not you truly believe that "God is good and His love endures forever."

This is what the Prince of Darkness wants us to believe: that money, esteem and worldly accomplishments are the value of your self-worth. Don't fall into this self-pity trap of despair. Yes, you may be handicapped, have health problems, have lost loved ones, have no job, have had your professional or general reputation blackened, and nothing may seem to be going right. Make the decision to trust in God's grace, mercy and provision. Create your little golden cube. Things of this world seem to be so important, but they are only temporal; seek that which is eternal. Be a celestial citizen; show the hope, strength and courage only God can give. As you let God make a difference in you life, you will make a difference in someone else's such that your Lord and redeemer, Jesus Christ, will be glorified, and your rewards will be great in the kingdom to come.

The unwanted down time and financial struggles have given me the opportunity to study, reflect and to write *Schism of the Cosmos* and this book, *Of the Something More*. They are my faith and intellectual struggles with the existence, provisions and purposes of God. The foundation of my faith had to come from intellectual reasoning not a blind leap in the dark. You may have heard of the saying, "Faith is the action taken to sit on a chair." Yes, but let's back up a step or two. How do I know if the image of the chair that I am seeing is real? Is it painted on a canvas or made of paper, or is it a holographic projection?

FAITH IN ACTION

Action is taken to determine if it is rationally possible and reasonable to sit on the perceived image. One walks over and determines if it is an article situated in three-dimensional space. It is hard and heavy. It does not wiggle. It seems to have the necessary physical attributes to hold my weight. Oh, one thing more; is there a string attached which can be pulled just as I sit down? No? Okay—sit down. Wait, there is just one more hesitation. Even though all my logic says, "sit down," my heart, for all its unknown reasons, says, "don't." So… which wins out—logical intellectual reasoning or illogical rationalizations? Faith is buttressed by intellectual logical reasoning, and I sit down. Yes, the chair is comfortable. From the foundation of a logical intellectual belief that Jesus is who He claimed to be, when the surreal blackness of despair and hopelessness invades your life, you have the basis to fortify your faith and dispel the mist of insecurity.

I have to admit after all this study—and I do not mean this in a sacrilegious way—if we were God and wanted the fellowship of eternal, independent, God-like, sentient beings, we would have to undertake the same plan He is unfolding in the Bible. Our space-time world, which is of order and design, is the test environment in which there have been supernatural revelations of the Bible and of the God-man, Jesus Christ. Satan and his Legions of Doom are a defeated sideshow that God has allowed to exist such that there is a counterpoint to permit free will, spiritual decision-making in this free will environment. The struggle is of the intellectual logical reasoning against the illogical rationalities of the self-taking will. There is no other way to become a Christ-like, celestial citizen than through the new spiritual birth into the Bride of Christ.

LITERAL INTERPRETATION OF SCRIPTURE

Not only was the shofar sounded for festivals and coronations, it sounded to warn of danger and to muster the troops for battles. It is likely the shofar will sound to call the Bride of Christ to her heavenly dwelling. Scholars have differing ideas as to when the Bride of Christ will be taken to heaven, and when the tribulation, or time of Jacob's trouble, begins on Earth. The author has taken the literal approach rather than the allegorical; otherwise, even salvation can be allegorized to be meaningless. Sufficient to say, a number of religious systems in Christendom allegorize the literal 1,000-year rule of the Messiah on Earth, described in Revelation 20, into a spiritual concept (though not all their individual members do).

The reason for this is embedded in ecumenical history. The merging of Church and state by the Emperor Constantine in 312 AD submerged the revelations of God under a wave of political influence. No Roman emperor would be favorable to the thought that his base of power would be overthrown by the return of Jesus Christ. Even the great theologian Augustine, a little later in that era, succumbed to this persuasion and went so far

> **THE SHOFAR**
>
> The shofar is the ceremonial instrument of Judaism. Wherever the Scriptures read "trumpet," they almost certainly refer to a shofar. Shofroth are made from the horns of kosher animals (except cattle), usually sheep or the African antelope called the kudu. Other animals whose horns can be made into a shofar include goats and other antelope such as the oryx.[3]

as to allegorize the return of Christ, the battle of Armageddon and the period of the millennium. There are many people today who call themselves Christians who have no biblical concept of the "end times" and have never read and studied the Bible.

BE PREPARED!

Jesus warned that His return would come suddenly, like a thief in the night. *"So you also must be ready, because the Son of Man will come at an hour when you do not expect him."* [4] He also made it clear: *"At that time the sign of the Son of Man will appear in the sky, and all the nations of the earth will mourn. They will see the Son of Man coming on the clouds of the sky, with power and great glory."*[5]

These two statements are incompatible and are similar to the confusion prevailing in Judaism concerning the suffering Messiah of Isaiah 40 to 53 and the glorious Messiah of Isaiah 63 to 66. The suffering Messiah would be rejected, die for the sins of the world and be resurrected by God. The glorious Messiah would bring peace and reign triumphantly. From the passage of time we know these two events are separated by almost 2,000 years—or more.

For the Bride of Christ to return with Him, arrayed in white royal apparel of the robes of righteousness described in Revelation 19, her joyous calling home and the receiving of her crowns and rewards have to have taken place at some unknown interval previously.

> **MY SPECULATION**
>
> Something unsual will be seen in space along with startling unexplained flashes of light; and on Earth, there will be a steady increase in earthquakes and atmospheric rumbling booms.

The translation of the Church to Heaven likely takes place before, close to or at the beginning of the last prophetic week of Daniel when profound evil rules the world. There are those who reason that, since the Church has always been persecuted, it, too, will face the wrath of God on rebellious planet Earth. The wrath of God is not about a potential World War III but a judgment on rebellious God-cursing mankind and rebel angels who will have been driven and confined to planet Earth.

God's revelation to the apostle John is that one third of the Earth will be burnt up, one third of the oceans will be destroyed,[6]fresh water will be polluted and anywhere from two thirds to three quarters of Earth's human population will be killed. This amounts to approximately 4 billion people; this is not persecution, it is annihilation. It is no wonder God's warning of this time to come is so urgent and intense. These warnings seem surreal. In fact, as you look around, everything seems so natural, just like it has always been, just normal every-day events—and then comes September 11, 2001.

The nightmare forces are already at work. Just as witchcraft invaded Germany leading to World War II, demonic forces are invading so-called "enlightened" Western civilization. Witches and warlocks are hosted on TV shows. Groups are meeting to use "ancient meditation" to contact angels and to try and open up mysterious vortexes to contact the alien. Humanity has lost its way in the darkness of morphing evolution. The logical reasoning of God, creation and His provision of salvation are discarded by illogical rationalities of self-serving spiritual mysticism. Satan and his Legions of Doom are happy to provide all sorts of mystical wonders to deceive those who vainly desire to be "as gods."

> **ENCOURAGE ONE ANOTHER**
>
> We know *"God did not appoint us to suffer wrath but to receive salvation through our Lord Jesus Christ. ...Therefore encourage one another and build each other up."*[7] Jesus encouraged His believers: *"I will also keep you from the hour of trial that is going to come upon the whole world to test those who live on the earth."*[8]

At the same time, the nations of the world are becoming a boiling caldron of political, religious and racial tensions. Astronomers are seeing closely approaching asteroids that would fulfill the predictions of Revelation 8 were they to smash into the oceans, causing devastating loss of human life. A temporary solution for peace will be found for the Middle East crisis, but it will not last.

The removal of Arafat and his Tunisian, Mafia-style terrorist organization in the Palestine territories may bring moderate leaders to the negotiation table. An international group of peacekeepers headed by the United States or the EEC could provide a stable situation for hostilities to slowly abate if both sides are willing to try. If trade and commerce were allowed to increase dramatically between Israelis and Palestinians, prosperity, hope and an illusion of peace would follow. Proposals to build a Jewish temple around the small cupola away from the Dome of the Rock may take place.

Yet the demise of the kingdom of Babylon in one night seems to foretell that God-denying civilizations will be weighed in the spiritual balances and found insufficient. At that time, explained Jesus, suddenly, just as on the day when Lot left Sodom, when *"people were eating and drinking, buying and selling, planting and building... fire and sulfur rained down from heaven and destroyed them all."* [9] Instantly, chaos and terror will reign. This devastation will prepare the world for a dynamic world leader. How could it happen?

The powerful world government and religious system will not come into place *"until the rebellion occurs and the man of lawlessness is revealed, the man doomed to destruction."* [10] The phrase "rebellion occurs" (or "falling away") is a possible translation of the Greek word *apostasia*, which can also mean "departure." Joseph Good comments:

> Kenneth Wuest, a noted Greek scholar, states in his word studies an interesting point that has much to do with the catching away of the living believers. He states that the phrase "falling away" is a mistranslation of the Greek word apostasia and should rather be translated departure.
>
> "The root verb aphistemi is found fifteen times in the New Testament. It is translated 'depart' eleven times." Although it is often found translated in similar meanings, "the predominant meaning of this verb in the New Testament... is that of the act of a person departing from another person or from a place... Lidell and Scott in their classical lexicon give as the second meaning of apostasia, 'a departure, a disappearance.' Dr. E. Schuyler English, to whom the author is deeply indebted for calling his attention to the word 'departure' as the correct ren-

dering of apostasia in this context, is authority for the fact that…the Greek word (means) 'a departure.'" [11]

Thus, the Scripture could very well read, "Don't let anyone deceive you in any way, for that day will not come until the 'departure' occurs and the man of lawlessness is revealed, the man doomed to destruction." This translation then correctly reflects Paul's opening words: *"Concerning the coming of our Lord Jesus Christ and our being gathered to him, we ask you, brothers, not to become easily unsettled."* [12] The words that day mean the time of great tribulation and the day of God's wrath.[13] Paul describes this sudden departure of believers: *"For the Lord himself will come down from heaven, with a loud command, with the voice of the archangel and with the trumpet call of God, and the dead in Christ will rise first. After that, we who are still alive and are left will be caught up together with them in the clouds to meet the Lord in the air. And so we will be with the Lord forever. Therefore encourage each other with these words."* [14]

When the Holy Spirit and God's ambassadors[15] are gone, *"then the lawless one will be revealed…. The coming of the lawless one will be in accordance with the work of Satan displayed in all kinds of counterfeit miracles, signs and wonders, and every sort of evil that deceives those who are perishing. They perish because they refused to love the truth and so be saved. For this reason God sends them a powerful delusion so that they will believe the lie and so that all will be condemned who have not believed the truth but have delighted in wickedness."* [16]

THE WORK OF THE HOLY SPIRIT

The person of the Holy Spirit of God has sealed and indwells each believer[17]. When the Bride of Christ is called home, the Holy Spirit also leaves. Afterwards, His administration on earth becomes similar to the Old Testament days when He works as an "outer" God-consciousness agent rather than an indwelling, sustaining Spirit.

The major question is, what sort of lie and powerful delusion would so enrapture the world with all sorts of counterfeit miracles, signs and wonders? It would appear, based on the signs of our times, many people do not care what the philosophy of the origin of life is as long as it is not God the creator. The problems of terrestrial evolution, because of the tremendous interest in the paranormal, could quite readily be replaced with a belief of friendly extraterrestrial genetic evolutionary management, particularly if contact is made with advanced aliens who then perform all sorts of miraculous wonders and manipulate delusions of cosmic consciousness.[18] Liberal Christians who remain, and those of other world religions, would certainly have no scriptural foundation to refute this astounding spiritual evolutionary advancement.

Powerful governments will quickly succumb to their control. The prophet Daniel was given a vision of the end time. He describes this new world leader. *"He will attack the mightiest fortresses with the help of a foreign god and will greatly honor those who acknowledge him. He will make them rulers over many people and will distribute the land at a price."* [19] *"The whole world was astonished and followed the beast* [the world ruler]. *Men worshiped the dragon* [Satan] *because he had given authority to the beast, and they also worshiped the beast and asked, 'Who is like the beast? Who can make war against him?'"* [20]

HOW MIGHT ALL THIS BEGIN?

The United States is the dominant world power. Fortu-

THE END TIMES

Jesus, in Matthew 24, tells us what will take place during this period. He states: *"Nation will rise against nation, and kingdom against kingdom. There will be famines and earthquakes in various places. All these are the beginning of birth pains."*[21] The Messianic-millennial kingdom will be born out of this world of chaos.

nately, the USA and coalition partners are trying to maintain order in a world of irrational terrorism instead of embarking on a campaign of world domination. These nations, though not "Christian," practice Judeo-Christian principles. It is likely they will be able to defeat blatant terrorism and maintain some semblance of world peace including leading a multinational group of peacekeepers to observe the Israelis and Palestinians. However, Dr. Taylor proposes that America is the mystery land described in Isaiah 18. Chapter 18 describes a nation that once followed God more passionately. It is pruned at its prime, "before the harvest." Dr. Taylor writes:

> "For before the Harvest, when the bud is perfect and the sour grape ripening…"—at a time when the country under consideration is in the time of its greatest production, when it potential for good is "ripening"—then is the time when the judgment of severe pruning is proclaimed against it.
>
> In accordance with this prophecy, therefore, the judgment of this nation could come at any moment, for the prophesied status of "this nation" fits America today.[22]

How much more does the power of America fit today than it did in the early 1970s when this was written!

The prophet Ezekiel is told what will happen in Israel in latter days.[23] Russia and a consortium of what are now Muslim countries around the Black and Caspian Seas will suddenly attack Israel. Muslim Arab countries described as Persia—likely Syria, Iran and Iraq—are also aligned with Russia since Isaiah describes the defeat of the Assyrian (Iraq) on the mountains of Israel,[24] and Damascus (in Syria) becomes a city of ruins.[25] Troops from Cush, which is Africa, and Libya, the ancient land of Phut,[26] are also part of this invading force. Is this the ultimate Jihad? Interestingly enough, Egypt and Ethiopia are not mentioned. Ezekiel declares God's words: *This is what will happen in that day: When Gog* [the leader of Russia] *attacks the land of Israel, my hot anger will be aroused, declares the Sovereign LORD. In my zeal and fiery wrath I declare that at that time there shall be a great earthquake in the land of Israel. The fish of the sea, the birds of the air, the beasts of the field, every creature that moves along the ground, and all the people on the face of the earth will tremble at my presence. The mountains will be overturned, the cliffs will crumble and every wall will fall to the ground. I will summon my sword against Gog on all my mountains, declares the Sovereign LORD. Every man's sword will be against his brother. I will execute judgment upon him with plague and bloodshed; I will pour down torrents of rain, hailstones and burning sulfur on him and his troops and on the many nations with him. And so I will show my greatness and my holiness, and I will make myself known in the sight of many nations. Then they will know that I am the LORD."* [27]

Egypt and Ethiopia have both played a part in Israel's history. God says of Egypt: *"When they cry out to the LORD because of their oppressors, he will send them a savior and defender, and he will rescue them. So the LORD will make himself known to the Egyptians, and in that day they will acknowledge the LORD."* [28] Ethiopia was possibly the home of the Queen of Sheba who visited King Solomon. [29] Grant Jeffrey makes a case for the true Ark of the Covenant being hidden in that land. [30] In addition, just after the resurrection of Jesus, the *"Ethiopian eunuch, an important official in charge of all the treasury of Candace, queen of the Ethiopians"* [31] accepted Jesus Christ as his Lord and Savior and was baptized by Philip, a disciple of Jesus. In the last days, it is likely Egypt, as king of the South, will attack the world despot who sets up his military headquarters in Israel. [32]

A CATACLYSMIC MODEL

How then, shall the King come? From the signs of the times and biblical prophecy, a tentative earthquake model is suggested. Other scholars believe nothing supernatural will happen, and everything will slowly come about. This might be so, except the prophetic signs and wonders still have to be accounted for. The earthquakes now occurring around the world are nothing compared to what will come. Any geophysicist or geologist can tell you of the large earthquake fault zones that circumference the world. This model proposes that several massive earthquakes, exceeding all known earthquakes, will precipitate the "end of days." *I will shake the heavens and the earth. I will overturn royal thrones and shatter the power of foreign kingdoms,"* [33] states the Lord. When "Gigantous" happens, Earth's thin crust will heave on the molten magma underneath causing major crustal adjustments around the world.

Based on the unsuspected fall of ancient Babylon in one night, in this tentative cataclysmic model, the world could be unexpectedly destabilized in a single day. The energy to precipitate "Gigantous" may very well come from a near miss of a large asteroid which in itself would cause world panic. Global destruction may well be initiated, with simultaneous catastrophic earthquakes, possibly commencing beneath the western mountain ranges of North and South America, as the oceanic floor of the Pacific Ocean is jammed under them. Massive after-jolts will shift the trans-Atlantic and Pacific Ocean ridges and radiate across all continents causing massive earthquakes along the Asia-Pacific rim.

A PAPER BAG

The thickness of the Earth's crust has been compared to a paper bag filled with water, the paper being the thickness of the crust.

Suddenly, the shofar may sound and the Bride of Christ be called home to her crowns and rewards. Also missing would be children under the age of accountability. Just as people watched replay after replay of the surreal destruction of the Twin Towers in New York, so would they see similar devastation in many cities of the world. Mountains would collapse, temporarily plugging river systems. Huge hydroelectric dams may very well break causing catastrophic floods that cannot be imagined. International power grids would be knocked out.

It is postulated this gigantic earthquake would take several days to roll around the world. Russia may not be as quickly affected. It is then, with the Statue of Liberty down on her knees, Gog and her Muslim consortium would devise an evil scheme[34] and come against Israel as a massive wave of air and ground infantry. The nations surrounding Israel have continued to re-stockpile Russian armaments over the years since Israel captured the hidden supplies in the invasion of Lebanon in 1982. Nuclear ICBMs may drop onto America; the return fire would decimate Russia. It is God who defends Israel. Likely, a storm of trailing mini-asteroids would strike the Middle East, causing fire and brimstone, precipitating unnatural hurricanes with monsoon rain and hailstones. As "Gigantous" reachs Palestine, major topographic changes would take place along the Dead Sea valley. The power of the radical Muslim world would be broken. Iran, Syria and Iraq would be immobilized.

At the same time, the great lie will begin to unfold. It would take time for communication to be re-established. Missing people may be attributed to the earthquake damage, but many people would realize the truth. UFO starships may appear. The helpful aliens may say that the massive earthquakes released quantum energy allowing them to penetrate our space-time dimension just in time to save us from further devastation. Since the world's wealth would be in ruins, it might be proposed Babylon be rebuilt as the oil capital of the

DEATH AND DESTRUCTION

Jesus made this statement: *"For then there will be great distress, unequaled from the beginning of the world until now—and never to be equaled again. If these days had not been cut short, no one would survive, but for the sake of the elect those days will be shortened."*[35]

world. Many Jews might immigrate to Israel bringing untold wealth. The Dome of the Rock would likely have been obliterated by the catastrophic earthquake. The Jewish temple will be rebuilt on the ancient temple site of King David. Now the two conflicting cities of the ages would face each other—Jerusalem backed by God's heavenly city of Zion, and Babylon by Satan's ethereal city of darkness.

This will be the time of the despot antichrist, the one-world government and one-world religion. Signs and wonders will be prominent. Deluded humanity will be convinced they have evolved global consciousness and supernatural powers. The Jews will finally recognize this charismatic world leader as a fraud when he attempts to set himself up as God in the newly built temple. It will be an unprecedented time of destruction, murder and terror.

Citizens of Planet Earth,

You still have the opportunity to become celestial citizens—the Bride of Christ. WARNING: TIME MAY BE SHORT! Realize that this is not about evolutionary history; it is about the conclusion of a great and terrible cosmic war. *"In that day the LORD will punish the powers in the heavens above and the kings on the earth below. They will be herded together like prisoners bound in a dungeon; they will be shut up in prison and punished after many days."* [36] Earth is that dungeon for the cosmic rebels. To maintain his freedom, Satan will have to either annihilate the Jews and new Christians or, as a last resort, eliminate all humanity.

Rest assured, by aligning your will with that of the Great King, you will be "of the something more." The battle for the wills of men between the Angels of Glory and the Legions of Doom rages around us. This war is not won with guns and violence but through the intercession of the Holy Spirit in the mind and will of each individual heart—"that God is good and His love endures forever." It is only when we view our lives from the perspective that Jesus is the focal point of history, we can we make sense of the twisted arts and sciences, the spiritual delusions, the injustices, the turbulence and turmoil in life's situations and know that there is a future for the **whole Heaven** of the cosmos.

King Jesus assures you: *"I have told you these things, so that in me you may have peace. In this world you will have trouble. But take heart! I have overcome the world."* 37 *"Behold, I will create new heavens and a new earth. The former things will not be remembered, nor will they come to mind."* 38 *"He who testifies to these things says, 'Yes, I am coming soon.' Amen. Come Lord Jesus."* 39

Respectfully,
An Ambassador for King Jesus to Planet Earth,

NOTES:

[1] Good, Joseph, (Rambam; Hilchot Teshuvah, Chapter 3) Rosh HaShanan and the Messianic Kingdom to Come Inc. Hatikva Ministries 1989 p. 36

[2] Yoder, Joanie E., "The Blessing Tree," Our Daily Bread, RBC Ministries, December 20, 2001

[3] <kirschccc.com/shofar.htm>

[4] Matthew 24:44

[5] Matthew 24:30

[6] Revelation 8:6–13

[7] 1 Thessalonians 5:9 and 11

[8] Revelation 3:10

[9] Luke 17:28–29

[10] 2 Thessalonians 2:3

[11] Good, Ibid. p. 63

[12] 2 Thessalonians 2:1

[13] Isaiah 13:9–13

[14] 1 Thessalonians 4:16–18

[15] 2 Corinthians 5:20

[16] 2 Thessalonians 2:8–12

[17] Ephesians 1:13–14

[18] Matthew 24:24

[19] Daniel 11:39

[20] Revelation 13:3–4

[21] Matthew 24:7

[22] Taylor, Dr. Charles, *World War III and the Destiny of America*, Today in Bible Prophecy Inc. 1971, p. 71

[23] Ezekiel 38 and 39

[24] Isaiah 14:25

[25] Isaiah 17:1

[26] Missler Chuck, *The Magog Invasion*, Western Front Publishing,

1995, chapter 7, p. 107 following

27 Ezekiel 38:18–23

28 Isaiah 19:20–21

29 1 Kings 10:1–13

30 Jeffrey, Grant, *Armageddon Appointment with Destiny*, Frontier Research Publications, 1988, p. 113

31 Acts 8:27

32 Daniel 12:40–45

33 Haggai 2:21–22

34 Ezekiel 38:10–11

35 Matthew 24:21–22

36 Isaiah 24:21–22

37 John 16:33

38 Isaiah 65:17

39 Revelation 22:20

INDEX

abductees, 20, 120, 135, 140, 146

Abraham, 34, 84, 86, 87, 148, 171, 213, 220, 221, 227, 262, 229, 234, 262

Africa, 112, 113, 254, 262, 301

Ages of Ages, 10, 23, 220, 223, 234

Alien evolution, 15

Allah, 224, 226, 227, 229

Ambassadors, 158, 159, 299

angels, 14, 30, 31, 56, 57, 58, 59, 60, 62, 119, 136, 137, 139, 144, 150, 168, 189, 216, 256, 297

Angels of Glory, 60, 67, 161, 164, 166, 208, 243, 305

anthropocentric, 131, 134

anthropoids, 136

anthropomorphic, 9

Armageddon, 68, 88, 262, 276, 279, 295

asteroids, 297, 303

Atlantis, 223, 258, 260, 277

Babylon, 220, 263, 268, 269, 270, 271, 273, 298, 303, 304

baptism, 159

Beast, 195, 225, 227

Behe, 27, 277

Belshazzar, 270, 271

Big Bang, 15

biologically engineered, 16

Black Sea, 260

born again, 30, 33, 36, 38, 41, 152

Bride of Christ, 150, 175, 183, 184, 187, 197, 198, 200, 206, 208, 222, 233, 267, 275, 276, 280, 294, 299, 303, 305

Brooke, 39

Calvary, 79, 160, 174, 214, 215, 220, 229, 233

Canaanites, 87

Cave Art, 103

CDs, 97

Cherubim, 33, 70, 138, 145, 220

clone, 43, 121, 135

Cloning, 42, 45

Colson, 195

cosmic consciousness, 14, 20, 51, 55, 282, 300

cosmos, 9, 10, 14, 15, 23, 30, 35, 41, 55, 56, 58, 61, 63, 70, 72, 75, 76, 78, 79, 80, 83, 86, 91, 103, 105, 111, 122, 134, 136, 141, 147, 156, 158, 166, 189, 214, 234, 261, 305

Creationists, 16

crop circles, 120, 121, 122, 146, 253, 283

Crowns for the Bride, 236

Darwin, 27, 108, 109, 110, 130, 277

Davidic covenant, 221, 223, 230, 233, 234

demonic, 37, 38, 166, 255, 281, 285, 297

demons, 30, 31, 58, 60, 72, 166

dinosaurs, 255

divorce, 173

DNA, 9, 27, 28, 43, 117, 122, 133

Dome Of The Rock, 304

Drosnin, 279

Earthly administration, 171, 219, 223, 230

Egypt, 67, 121, 221, 230, 274, 301
Entropy, 55
ethereal beings, 14, 20, 30
Fruit of the Spirit, 36
Gabriel, 224, 232, 233, 262
Garden of Eden, 29, 35, 93, 110, 135, 137, 138, 141, 142, 143, 145, 185, 219
Gaverluk, 17
genome, 27, 42, 43, 45, 81, 110, 115, 132
Giants, 255
gigantous, 303, 304
Gilgamesh, 18, 259
Global Consciousness, 162, 191, 305
God consciencousness, 21, 135, 140
golden cube, 199, 293
gradualism, 109, 115
Hades, 58, 213, 226, 275
heavenlies, 54
heavenly administration, 169, 170, 172, 214
heavens, 17, 20, 31, 54, 56, 57, 67, 72, 79, 84, 88, 132, 137, 143, 146, 148, 150, 214, 219, 227, 238, 245, 252, 261, 277, 280, 303, 305
Hell, 10, 41, 58 , 82
Hindu, 61, 144, 165, 257
Hiroshima, 273
hominid, 112, 113, 114
hominoid lines, 128
Hope, 36, 80, 264
humanism, 9, 255
Hunt, 86
irreducible complexity, 277
Ishmael, 219, 221, 223, 227, 228, 229
Israel, 18, 56, 67, 72, 83, 84, 86, 87, 88, 147, 164, 169, 171, 174, 221, 222, 223, 227, 230, 232, 233, 234, 252, 262, 263, 264, 265, 267, 268, 269, 271, 274, 276, 280, 283, 285, 301, 304
Jeffrey, 256, 262, 263, 302
Jerusalem, 68, 71, 82, 86, 88, 170, 174, 216, 220, 222, 227, 232, 234, 262, 264, 265, 267, 268, 271, 274, 278, 281, 284, 304
Job, 37, 54, 80, 240, 244
Josephus, 69, 70, 71
Laetoli footprints, 112
Lake of Fire, 58, 285
laparoscopy, 25
Larkin, 33, 170
Lazarus, 34, 58
Legions of Doom, 9, 10, 14, 36, 37, 40, 50, 59, 60, 63, 67, 101, 119, 143, 146, 148, 150, 159, 160, 161, 164, 166, 174, 177, 189, 208, 243, 253, 255, 261, 283, 285, 297, 305
local evolution, 15
Lubenow, 113
Lucifer, 14, 20, 22, 29, 79, 137, 138, 219
macroevolution, 15, 116
Mars, 16, 17, 18, 20, 58 , 137, 146, 260, 277
Mecca, 224
Messiah, 86, 228, 230, 236, 261, 262, 267, 295
Michael (Archangel), 31, 56, 71
microevolution, 116
Millennial, 169, 230, 234, 236, 275, 295
miracles, 51, 56, 61, 90, 91, 93, 146, 262, 281, 299, 300
Monogamy, 172
moral guilt, 21, 22
Moses, 18, 22, 33, 84, 140, 147, 186, 219, 221, 227, 229, 234, 275
Mother Earth, 50, 111, 112
NDE, 34, 40, 41, 42, 59, 111, 137, 218
Neanderthal, 116

Nephilim, 18, 136
neurological inputs, 32
Noachian flood, 17, 146, 256
noosphere group, 162, 191
OBE, 40, 41, 111, 137, 218
Omega Point, 42, 58
Other Man Syndrome, 194
Other Woman Syndrome, 194
Palestine, 85, 86, 264, 266, 297
panspermia, 15, 214, 252
paradigm, 14, 255
Paradise, 34, 59 , 213, 227, 228
Passover, 69, 70, 71, 158, 275
Patten, 18, 263
Pentecost, 69, 70, 71, 158, 164, 267, 275
Petah Tikva, 264
Pharisees, 31, 90, 173
Phillips, 66, 76
philosophy of naturalism, 177, 214, 254
Professor Mayer, 108, 110, 115, 130
psychics, 251, 253
psychological guilt, 21
punctuated evolution, 109
quantum mechanics, 44
Radiometric age dating, 114
Raelians, 45, 121
rapture, 36, 71, 215, 276
Rawlings, 41, 59
Reformation, 108
Reptilians, 144
retribution, 81, 82, 84, 88, 93, 238
RNA, 28, 43, 44
rock music, 97, 101, 102
rules and regulations, 21, 71, 90, 135, 183, 184, 185, 187, 225, 227, 229, 243, 265
Schaeffer, 43, 150, 161
Schroeder, 44

Sci-Fi, 146, 220
Seiss, 234
serpent, 19, 29, 138, 140, 141, 142, 143, 144
Shekinah Glory, 33, 70, 159
Shem, 262
shofar!, 291, 303
signs of the times, 276
sons of God, 18, 22, 57, 58, 77, 145, 148, 218, 220, 244, 256
soul, 32, 34, 35, 42, 43, 44, 45, 64, 102, 119, 147, 152, 189, 191, 194, 203, 205
Soulish body, 34, 42
Spaceships, 216
starry host, 56
Swindoll, 186
synthesis, 9
Tabernacle, 33, 70
Taliban, 225, 282
Tasteless Saints, 241
Tiahuanaco, 259
Times of the Gentiles, 264
Titus, 69, 266
Torments, 34, 58
Typhon, 19
UFO, 20, 45, 55, 72, 120, 122, 140, 145, 166, 252, 253, 283, 304
Velikovsky, 18, 109, 263
Vimanas, 258
Walvoord, 30, 31, 36, 175
White Throne Judgment, 58
whole heaven, 214, 215, 219, 235, 245, 306
Wollemi Pine, 257
Yeshua, 22, 267

Schism Of The Cosmos

Also by Glen White, *Schism Of The Cosmos*, is an easy-read, 600-page adventure of encouragement that explores the space-time interaction of Heaven and Earth.

As we speed into the 21st century, humanity, Earth's sentient guardians, is aware of itself as never before. We question whether we are alone in the cosmos. Is Earth just a lonely little planet adrift in the vastness of space? Are we created beings with purpose and meaning to our lives, or merely statistical accidents of evolution?

The monotheistic God of the Bible declares that by design He created mankind and all that exists. Proponents of evolution present a logical case that evolution by natural selection *is* design, but neither evolution nor creation is proven; belief in either requires faith. Moreover, both philosophies are being attacked by the idea that an "alien" did it.

Creation, whether by God or alien demands accountability to an intelligence greater than ourselves. However, if we are a product of spontaneous local evolution, with a lucky combination of unique body design and sentiency, we can be "as gods." In *Schism Of The Cosmos* we examine who God says that He is and seek arguments for His existence, other than by "creative design." We examine the validity of the Bible, from Genesis to Revelation, as a supernatural message to mankind, which reveals that Earth is under the domination of ethereal forces—the Legions of Doom—in rebellion against the Great Assembly in the Heavens.

Schism Of The Cosmos takes a unique approach to this war in the universe by detailing it from God's viewpoint, looking down on Earth from Heaven. Logic and imagery from Bible stories present the Bible in its entirety as an extraterrestrial message warning of ethereal deception of rebel angels and demons battling against the Angels of Glory to affect the destiny of our world.

Find out about the secret Bible code that validates Jesus as the son of God, and the recent discovery which shows how the historical dates of the seven churches, described in the letter to the seven churches in the book of Revelation, point to the end times.

The author has brought his years of training and knowledge as a geophysicist to the study of God's message to the prophets about what will happen to Earth. We find that there will be dramatic adjustments to the geography in the Middle East, and that when the veil between Heaven and Earth is lifted there will be major environmental changes, which will bring utopia to mankind.

If you enjoyed the message in *Of The Something More,* you will be moved by the gripping story of how God intervenes from Heaven to effect a rescue of Adam's race from the powerful supernatural forces of evil, which are usurping control of our planet. You will be fascinated by seldom discussed passages of Scripture that indicate we will attain eternal life and a civilization of technological complexity and incredible beauty.

Order Form

To order *Of the Something More,* by Glen White, please use the order form below (please print):

Name: _____

Address: _____

City: _____ State / Prov: _____

Zip / Postal Code: _____ Telephone: _____

_____ copies @ $24.95Cdn./$19.95US: $_____

Shipping:

Canada ($5.00 first book – $1.25 each add. book) $_____

US ($3.00 first book – $1.00 each add. book) $_____

Canada add 7% GST $_____

Total amount enclosed: $_____

Payable by Check or Postal Money Order

(Please make checks payable to Kargen Books.
Allow time for checks to clear.)

Send to: *Kargen Books*
P.O. Box 1754
Vernon, BC V1T 8C3 Canada
www.kargenbooks.com
1-877-4-THE MORE